INVEN
THE PASSION

INVENTING THE PASSION

How the Death of Jesus Was Remembered

Arthur J. Dewey

POLEBRIDGE PRESS
Salem, Oregon

*To the countless innocents who
have suffered and are suffering*

Polebridge Press is the publishing arm of the Westar Institute, a
non-profit, public-benefit research and educational organization.
To learn more, visit westarinstitute.org.

Cover and interior design by Robaire Ream

Library of Congress Cataloging-in-Publication Data
Names: Dewey, Arthur J., author.
Title: Inventing the passion : how the death of Jesus was remembered / by
    Arthur J. Dewey.
Description: Salem, Oregon : Polebridge Press, [2017] | Includes
    bibliographical references and index.
Identifiers: LCCN 2017027292 | ISBN 9781598151763 (alk. paper)
Subjects: LCSH: Jesus Christ--Passion--History of doctrines. | Passion
    narratives (Gospels)--Criticism, interpretation, etc. | Jesus
    Christ--Resurrection--History of doctrines. | Jesus Christ--Historicity.
Classification: LCC BT431.3 .D49 2017 | DDC 232.96--dc23
LC record available at https://lccn.loc.gov/2017027292

Contents

Acknowledgments

This book began in the summer of 1987. As Sister Ruth Graf and I constructed our course *Healing Deadly Memories*, designed to deal with the issue of anti-Semitism and the New Testament, Ruth's relentless questions and enduring encouragement led me to consider the problematic passages of the passion narratives. We both knew that handling this scriptural material was hardly a neutral affair. I am ever in her debt. Even then I was drawing insight from George Nickelsburg's magisterial work *Resurrection, Immortality, and Eternal Life in Intertestamental Judaism*. George provided the significant historical matrix of social upheaval out of which such narratives arose.

Later in the fall of 1987 I began to teach an undergraduate course entitled *The Death of Jesus*. This has continued to the present day. Throughout these years my students' honest reactions, emotions, and leading questions have forced me to become ever more aware of my assumptions. For some time, I taped these lectures. Bob Cotter, who later rose to direct Technological Services at Xavier University, proved invaluable by providing the equipment, patience and know-how.

I would also thank one of my oldest intellectual colleagues and fellow translator Ron Cameron for challenging me to respond to John Dominic Crossan's initial analysis and interpretation of the fragment Gospel of Peter; a text that held the interest of very few scholars. I began to look at the passion tradition from a distinctly different angle. My response to Dom Crossan's analysis resulted in two articles, the second of which was edited by Ron. I would also express my warmest regards to Dom Crossan who has been my finest interlocutor on the Gospel of Peter. We may disagree on some niceties but we both conclude that this gospel has been greatly neglected and misunderstood. I cherish the memory of our debates at the Jesus Seminar. I would also note my appreciation for the work and discussions (especially our informal ones) with Burton Mack. His sage insights have been immensely challenging and invaluable.

A major breakthrough in my research came in London 2003. Glenna Jackson graciously invited me to speak at a section of the International Society of Biblical Literature as she confidently expected that I would come up with a paper for the event. It was my good fortune to visit bookstores at Oxford that summer with a dear colleague John La Rocca. There I fell into a trance reading Mary Carruther's *The Craft of Thought*. Oddly enough, a week later when circling the copy of Trajan's Column at the Victoria and Albert Museum, I began connecting the dots between memory *locus* and the imaginative structure of the Tale of the Suffering Innocent One. It was at that Cambridge meeting where I first presented my take on how the death of Jesus was remembered. I received significant feedback and encouragement there to continue.

Tom Thatcher edited three different articles wherein I had the opportunity to explore this work of social memory. I value his constant collegial support and fine editorial sense. I am also grateful to Karl Galinsky, who invited me to speak at a section of Memory and the First Century at the annual meeting of the Society of Biblical Literature in 2010. His encouragement and critical conversation before and after the event were much appreciated. I would also thank L. Michael White for his nuanced response and helpful suggestions to my presentation. Andries van Aarde more recently invited me to submit my consideration of the invention of the passion material for the University of Pretoria's *Theological Studies*. It was an honor to be part of that Journal's anniversary volume. It was even more a delight to work again with an esteemed colleague. I cannot forget the sensitive reading of my work by Werner Kelber, a scholar and colleague who has made so many scholars so much better by his creative challenging, comments and collaboration. Werner's appreciation of what I have been attempting has kept me going.

I would also express my gratitude to Canon Joanna Leiserson who invited me, in 2013, to give the Lenten Lectures at Christ Church Cathedral in Cincinnati. These lectures on the death of Jesus gave me the opportunity to test my work with a diverse, interested and challenging audience. With the publication of this book I finally finish the task of my research leave granted by Xavier University in the fall of 2014. Two books intervened before I could get to the final version of this book.

This book cannot go to press without acknowledging those who spent significant time poring over the manuscript. First, I thank once again Ken Overberg, S.J., a dear friend and co-conspirator for over three decades. His incredible eye for detail and his instinct for what matters were ever at the ready. He has read this book in every single incarnation. I would also thank Brandon Scott, who has soldiered on with me in a variety of ways at Westar. Brandon read the manuscript so deeply that he would anticipate what I would say and *even what I should have said*! I cannot thank him enough for his candid remarks, encouragement, and creative advice. I also add my gratitude to Cassandra Farrin who waded deep into this text and provided much needed critique, understanding and advice. Lastly, Barbara Hampson has once again taken my text in hand and has lent a steady and compassionate eye to each page. Larry Alexander must be thanked; he originally saw the merit in this project for Polebridge. Once more I am indebted to Robaire Ream for his extraordinary cover and overall design. Finally, I thank Char Matejovsky, who was there for my first publication so many years ago and continues to deliver a volume of quality and grace.

Sigla

Used in Translation

< > Pointed brackets indicate a subject, object, or other element implied by the original language and supplied by the translator.

[ ] Square brackets indicate words which have been restored from a lacuna or emended from a scribal error.

[...] A lacuna or gap in the manuscript that cannot be satisfactorily restored.

( ) Parentheses are used in the usual sense, to indicate parenthetical remarks and narrative asides in the original text.

Abbreviations

1, 2 Cor	1, 2 Corinthians
Dan	Daniel
Deut	Deuteronomy
Did	Didache
Exod	Exodus
Gal	Galatians
Gen	Genesis
Isa	Isaiah
Jn	John
Lk	Luke
1, 2 Macc	1, 2 Maccabees
Mk	Mark
Matt, Mt	Matthew
Num	Numbers
Pet	Gospel of Peter
Phil	Philippians
POxy	Papyrus Oxyrhynchus
Prov	Proverbs
Ps	Psalms
Q	Sayings Gospel
Rom	Romans
1, 2 Sam	1, 2 Samuel
1 Thess	1 Thessalonians
Thom	Thomas
WisSol	Wisdom of Solomon
Zech	Zechariah
RSV	Revised Standard Version
SV	Scholar's Version

Introduction

The haunting tradition of the death of Jesus originates out of a raw and fragile trauma. The Roman executioners employed their most vicious means to eradicate a peasant artisan.[a] Crucifixion meant not simply death; it deleted victims from society's memory (see cameo on "Crucifixion," pp. 17–20). The wave of trauma was meant to wash all away. That Jesus was remembered at all speaks to those unknown followers choosing to resist the dissolving protocols of the Empire. How they remembered the death of Jesus is the subject of this book.

From the Alexamenos Graffito in Rome to the *Ten Punching Bags* of Andy Warhol and Jean-Michel Basquiat,[1] from early gospel confabulations to *Jesus Christ Superstar*, from the grotesque death scenes mirroring the Black Death of the late Middle Ages to the gnarled crucifixes carved in contemporary Latin American base communities, for nearly two millennia the death of Jesus of Nazareth has conspicuously concentrated the Christian imagination. Yet, as Werner Kelber astutely observes:

> No event in Christian origins is less likely to be transmitted in its factual rawness, and no experience is more in need of mnemonic frames and mediating patterns, than Jesus' death. (Kelber, *The Works of Memory*, 293)

Each succeeding generation has added layer upon layer to the traditions of the unsettling death of Jesus. Ironically these subsequent layers may actually cover up the horror of the original

---

a. The reason for the Roman execution is not totally clear. While many scholars presume that Jesus' words and actions provoked the Roman action and that the *titiulus (King of the Jews)* indicates the Roman assessment of his revolutionary program, there might not have been such a necessary cause and effect. What can be said is that the Romans did crucify Jesus. That is the historical fact. Why they did is another matter. Moreover, the brunt of this book addresses the very nature of the evidence of his death. We cannot presume that this evidence was intended to provide documentary proof that we moderns obsess over. Few ever contemplate that Jesus' death was incidental or even accidental. To a Roman official the words, acts and reputation of a Jewish peasant were at best a nuisance. From the imperial perspective a peasant's execution was hardly memorable; it was a signal, however, of Roman rule and invincibility. See cameo on "Another Jesus," pp. 29–30.

event. Moreover, contemporary Bible readers often assume that the ways in which they recall situations mirror how the ancients remembered. Such an assumption passes over the texture of the evidence and, with it, some significant clues to the ways in which the early followers of Jesus remembered his death. Thus, this study tries to be alert to the traumatic effect Jesus' death had on his followers and to recognize the need to be attentive to the very texture of the resulting memories of the earliest communities.

Since the eighteenth century the historical imagination has introduced a novel perspective on the death of Jesus. The imaginative categories of time and space furnished a distinctive point of view.[b] Scholars gradually realized that their interpretive horizon differs greatly from that which underlies the writings they examine.[c] They must be attentive not just to a different historical situation but even more to the ways in which the ancients communicated meaning. Critical scholars have removed the death of Jesus from ecclesial wraps and have attempted to place the question of Jesus' fate within a public forum where a variety of critical eyes can consider the evidence. Their endeavor, however, has not stopped many in the churches from dismissing such enterprise. The death of Jesus, embedded in primordial images and emotional overlays, speaks volumes to many churchgoers. Unfortunately, such uncritical acceptance of the "traditional" story of the death of Jesus often has had tragic ramifications. Many churchgoers have been pressed into guilt complexes unwittingly. Most horribly, the very telling

---

b. From the amateur observations of the Enlightenment's gentlemen "naturalists" to the more detailed examination of material layers of evidence, the science of Geology came into its own in the nineteenth century. A radically different theory of the formation of the earth emerged to account for the distinctive layers of sediment as well as for the various locations of puzzling fossils. In the early nineteenth century scientists measured the earth in biblical years (four thousand to six thousand years old); by the publication of the *Origin of Species* they spoke in terms of millions of years. The re-imagination of the temporal dimension greatly ramified scholarship on every level.

c. In brief, when Luther or Aquinas, for example, read the New Testament, neither had the sense that the reader's present differed greatly from that conveyed by the text. There might be some question over the meaning of a word but the solution was not found by referring to a different temporal context. To use a graphic example, consider how mediaeval and Renaissance artists simply put their own clothing and ornamentation into their paintings of a first century subject. No one thought that anachronistic.

of the death story of Jesus has become the occasion (since the late second century) for generating anti-Semitism in the West.[d] Salvation by the blood of the Lamb has had its price, a very human price.

Quite recently the public debate over the question of the historical Jesus has resumed the Enlightenment's agenda. The Jesus Seminar has gone on record, publishing their attempts to detect the historicity of the death of Jesus.[2] Yet what is clear from the present debate is that many, both scholars and believers, still share a common presupposition of the tradition of the death of Jesus. *They assume that the tradition delivers a report of what actually happened.*[e] Such a position is found not only among most conservative scholars. While admitting that the gospel evidence is more complicated than what a literalist would allow, even many liberal scholars assume that one can *plausibly suppose* that some history lies behind the later communities' constructions. This position is both metaphysical and religious. It not only supports the claim to historical fact but also, albeit covertly, is underpinned by religious conviction.

Yet many general readers of the Bible understand the traditions of the death of Jesus in an ahistorical fashion. The overarching narrative (from Genesis to Armageddon) defines the conditions of imagining. The readers have no sense of the consequences of living within the historical imagination. There is little or no regard for the ways in which the stories of the death of Jesus were fabricated and remembered. The readers show little awareness that a distinct cultural background is in play in what appears to be a common foreground. Certainly there is no concern to detect the groping developments that emerged from the various Jesus traditions.

This ahistorical understanding is coupled with an ahistorical self-understanding. Many Bible readers do not realize how

---

d. Such anti-Semitism becomes dramatically clear when one considers how the numerous passion plays, performed prior to Easter each year, have a decidedly emotional effect, especially upon young children, unable to filter the turbulent experience (see J. Carroll, *Constantine's Sword*).

e. This assumption is based on what I have called "the Markan default." Even when scholars consider the relationship among the gospels, they assume that the narrative of the earliest canonical gospel reflects historical events. As we shall see below, that assumption is quite problematic. See cameo on "Temple Incident," pp. 94–97.

complicated they are. They do not suspect that they are actually engaged in interpreting the fate of Jesus, effectively extending and transmuting the present moving tradition. Rather, they overlook their own role in interpreting the gospels, which they assume are fixed scripts. Their task becomes one of simple, neutral transmission. Such an assumption allows readers to evade the obvious: the historical responsibility of those who convey and are concerned about the tradition. They try to avoid at all costs the realization that such storytelling of Jesus' death cannot prevent their own demise. Many live vicariously through the "blood of Jesus," allowing the hero to die for them. They use this passion tradition to serve as a firewall to the obscene incursions of history and human mortality.[3]

But in this ahistorical understanding lies something even more insidious. Uncritical reading permits the maintenance of past and present power already in play. It gives no consideration to ones who define the terms of the discourse or to what the discourse permits to be heard. Do we want to admit that within the very texture of the text there might be embedded a *servile consciousness*? Given the long-standing biblical tradition, we are reluctant to question how the passion story has reached us. Under what conditions was it then and is it now transmitted? Can we freely interrogate it? Could we detect whether an uncritical reading of the story unwittingly echoes the power play that liquidated Jesus? Do we abrogate responsibility as readers by accepting the texts as innocent reports of what had happened?[4]

This book proposes to re-read the traditions of the death of Jesus by asking how the various Jesus communities remembered the death of Jesus. The arguments and conclusions of the Jesus Seminar will be taken seriously in the discussion.[f] The Seminar has resisted the usual reading of the passion narratives as factual reports by maintaining that the burden of proof rests upon those who claim authenticity for the words and deeds of Jesus. But the Jesus Seminar did not depart significantly from the mainline biblical scholarship on the death of Jesus. In fact, the Seminar replicated many of the results of redaction criticism in concluding that the narratives of the death of Jesus reflected

---

f. For a detailed review of the Seminar's findings, see Appendix A.

the concerns of the later gospel community.[g] Ever vigilant against a "congenial Jesus," the Seminar was alert to the later constructions of the different communities. My colleagues in the Seminar nevertheless tended to work upon an unspoken assumption, namely that the Markan passion narrative reflected some historical basis. Ironically, when the specific passages of the Markan passion narrative were considered individually, very little survived as historical.[5] My own research into the Gospel of Peter had led me to discover how ancient memory worked. This provided me with the critical tools to see how narrative material was woven. I saw the possibility of how the death traditions were constructed and transmitted. This led me to see that our modern assumptions actually prevented a critical understanding of what the ancient evidence was attempting to express.

A simpler way of saying this is that research into the death of Jesus is not a simple reflection of one's desires. In fact, a critical reading of the death traditions of Jesus can help us view the death of Jesus in human terms other than our own thereby gaining an appreciation of the unsung human efforts that went into such constructive remembering.

As we shall see, a historical reconsideration of the traditions of the death of Jesus dislocates any hard and facile understanding of Jesus' fate. Rather than serving as reliable reports, the passion narratives express the creative registers of each historical community. What can be gleaned from the earliest layers of the traditions will surprise the conventional appraisal of the death of Jesus. Not all followers of Jesus were preoccupied with his death. At least twenty years went by before we have any indication that there was a need to construct an overarching narrative to Jesus' fate. Even then, it was still not a universal concern in the developing traditions. We shall further see that the death story of Jesus is eventually constructed along the

---

g. Where the Jesus Seminar dramatically differed from many contemporary scholars was in asking whether specific passages in the passion narratives were historical. Many scholars work upon the argument of plausibility: If the passage appears plausible, given certain historical and cultural understandings, then it is likely. What is usually overlooked is that plausibility is not probability. For more on this see cameos on "A Case of True Fiction?" pp. 87–88 and "The Temple Incident—Fact or Fiction," pp. 94–97.

mythic lines of a well-known Jewish narrative frame and that this construction arises out of a concern for the destiny of those in the later communities rather than simply for the fate of Jesus.

Today we cannot presume that the death story of Jesus has any automatic currency for the global community. So many death narratives haunt our world. Indeed, such a presumption would come from a neo-colonial employment of the tradition and is tone deaf to the innumerable cries of suffering. In fact, the experience of many pastors and theologians points to the folly of such a position. They have found that the use of the story of Jesus' death in an exclusivist fashion prevents an understanding of the story tradition within a liberating perspective.

Instead of such presumption the post-modern interpreter must risk the chance that there is no meaning whatsoever. It might well be that the hope of setting the tradition free will come only by patiently listening again to those unknown voices of the first century and by recognizing that their very human attempts may echo the hopes of untold millions around the globe.

Coda*
The Blasphemy of Art

Some years ago, far outside the gated community of theological discourse, a remarkable religious display went on international tour. Madonna, the pop diva and recent Kabbalah devotee, cut a triumphant swath around the globe and with it drew condemnations from every religious authority in her wake.

The Church of England worried aloud why such a talented person would need to offend so many people, while Vatican spokesmen vented their spleen on such blasphemy. Even Danes and Russians agreed on someone to censure. Wherever Madonna went, from Los Angeles to London, from Rome to Düesseldorf, from Horsens to Moscow, religious leaders tried to pre-empt her arrival. But to no avail. Predictably, she played everywhere to sold-out venues.

*Throughout this book the reader will find six reflections entitled "coda." They present other perspectives on the material under investigation. Each one suggests that the matter of the Suffering Innocent One is not far from our shared experience.

What was the breach of religious decorum in her international *Confessions* tour? At one point in her show, Madonna re-emerged on a mammoth disco crucifix wearing a crown of thorns to perform the song "Live to Tell." Suspended on the giant cross encrusted with Swarovski crystals, she devoted her song to African victims of AIDS. It could have been more provocative but Madonna had no "wardrobe malfunction." A salmon blouse, with her blond hair down, black jeans and boots, cut a demure figure.

This was actually a tame image. Years ago, Edwina Sandys sent her four-foot bronze statue of "Christa," a bare-breasted, wide-hipped woman, on a decades-long tour around the world. St. John's Cathedral in New York was only one among many locales that took a great amount of heat for displaying it.

Then there are the haunting words of Billie Holiday:

Black bodies swinging in the southern trees
fruit hanging from poplar trees
Pastoral scene of the gallant south
The bulging eyes and the twisted mouth.
("Strange Fruit," Lewis Allan)

Until she died in 1959, she continued to bring the tremulous reality of the crucified to the shadows of a segregated society.

Artists have understood—long before and better than theologians—that the crucified one has entered into the global domain. The memory of the death of Jesus has long since leaked out of the ecclesial ghettoes.

Artists have intuited that crucifixion was a primary metaphor—not to be written about since it was so degrading. It signified the dominating power of the Empire; an unspoken threat to those who would dare to rise up.

Throughout history artists have not settled for a factoid memory of the death of Jesus. The history of Western Art attests to the creative remembering of the death of Jesus. This did not simply mean populating the death scene with friends and patrons. The varied tradition suggests that, just like the earlier gospel writers, artists continued to inflect the death of Jesus in meaningful directions. We can see this already, for example, in a thirteenth-century corpus that sags under the weight of torture, or in Grünewald's stark figure that sums up much of his plagued and war-torn world.

More recently, the *Ten Punching Bags* by Andy Warhol and Jean-Michel Basquiat carries on this tradition by delivering a telling exposé of the death-dealing effects surrounding the Jesus tradition.

Artists in their own ways continue to let us in on that dirty little secret of domination through controlled violence. And then they note the twist to the tale. The lost one, the zero, becomes a point of identification and solidarity. Something human is detected in the very midst of the forces of domination and dissolution. The voice considered silenced gains new strength and new legs.

Even the awkward appearance of Madonna plays upon this creative remembering. But other artists and images prove to be more poignant. Remembering the dominating downbeat behind the death of Jesus can continue to expose the violence in a situation. It also can detect hints of humanity where none would be found. It can become a tool, an imaginative vehicle for reframing the human condition.

Consider what most of us have quickly consigned to oblivion: the cruciform, hooded figure standing helpless in the prison of Abu Graib. Why is this not an image of veneration? Tasteless? Unpleasant? Does it not bring us back to the breaking point of power?

1

How Little There Is

The Lack of Material Evidence

Let us begin our investigation with a most puzzling observation. Despite what appears to be a longstanding preoccupation with the death of Jesus throughout the centuries, *no iconographic evidence featuring the death of Jesus is found until the fifth century.* In his thoroughgoing study, *Ante Pacem,* Graydon Snyder[1] has noted that, while images of Jesus as a healer and teacher can be found, we have no images of the death of Jesus from the first four centuries. Such an observation is rather jarring, since, by the beginning of the second century, significant narratives of the death of Jesus are circulating in the tradition. Why do images of Jesus as wise teacher and healer emerge in the iconographic evidence? Are they telltale hints of where the popular tradition was going? Did they speak more forcefully to various communities than the death narratives? Or, was there a general reluctance to embody the crucifixion concretely due to its traumatic effect and associations?

There are two possible exceptions to Snyder's findings.[2] The first is the lampooning Alexamenos graffito dated to the late second–early third century. The graffito shows a man standing in front of a donkey-headed victim on a T-shaped cross. The Greek text scrawls "Alexamenos worships his god." This mocking carving may well represent either an anti-Jewish[a] or an anti-Jesus slur. The second is a carved gemstone amulet from Syria (third century CE). The bloodstone intaglio shows a crucified Jesus, tied to a T-shaped cross. The Greek text invokes: "Son,

---

a. A lingering slur upon the cult of Israel was that the Jews did not permit non-Jews to approach the Holy of Holies because they actually worshipped an ass.

9

Father, Jesus Anointed." It would have been used as a magical protection for the wearer. Indeed, both exceptions actually sustain Snyder's assertion of the dearth of iconographic evidence for the death of Jesus. The first runs sharply against the developing Jesus traditions, as it denigrates the crucified victim. In a certain perverse fashion it echoes the shameful intent of the executioners as it continues the social stigmatization they originally intended. The amulet, on the other hand, reduces the crucified figure and his name to an apotropaic ("turning away") instrument, magically warding off evil. Neither piece plays into the developing narrative material of the death of Jesus. Instead they provide tantalizing slivers of popular prejudice and fears. Thus, it would seem that the oral and literary traditions were the sole avenues through which the memory of the death of Jesus was transmitted.

Second, a fundamental social reality cannot be neglected. We can find little mention, let alone description, of crucifixion in ancient literature. Crucifixion was reserved for slaves and rebels; it was hardly considered worthy of taking up space on a costly scroll. There are, however, indirect hints of what this entailed, such as in the Gemma Augustea. In this brooch we find the divine Augustus sitting on Zeus's throne, flanked in glory by the Goddess Roma, while at the bottom left, a captured Dacian is about to be shamed and possibly executed and exhibited upon a trophy pole. This fine piece of jewelry gives a clear indication of how the power relationships within the First Century World were maintained and enforced through humiliation and torture. Cicero (106–43 BCE) breaks the literary silence on crucifixion by declaring that death by crucifixion should not be considered, let alone remembered:

> The very name of 'the cross' should be absent not only from
> the body of Roman citizens but even from thought, eyes,
> and ears. For of all these things not only the occurrence and
> endurance but even the [legal] possibility, expectation, and
> finally the mention itself is unworthy of a Roman citizen
> and a free person. (Cicero, "The speech in defense of Gaius
> Rabirius")

Cicero, in fact, speaks to the social atmosphere surrounding the act of crucifixion. While the Romans did not invent crucifixion, they were adept in applying it. It served as a legal and social weapon to strike fear into those they ruled. It was reserved for slaves and rebels, all those who lifted a sandal against the imperial regime. The intent was to wipe a person out, physically and socially. The victim was not simply executed, but rendered a "nobody." Finally, as lime, poured over the remains, dissolved whatever was left of the body, the victim was deleted forever from any social connection and recollection.

The Non-Christian Material

Given the general reluctance to speak of crucifixion due to the inevitable social shame, it is not surprising that little mention of Jesus' crucifixion can be found in any extant non-Christian material. The only Roman citation comes from the early second century, as Tacitus (56–120 CE), writing on the rule of Tiberius, touches on the death of Jesus in his typically dark fashion:

> God's Anointed, the founder of the name [of the sect], during the rule of Tiberius was put to death by the procurator Pontius Pilate. Restrained for the moment, the deadly superstition broke out again, not only throughout Judea, the origin of the evil, but also through the city in which everything nasty and naughty flows and grows. (Tacitus, *Annals* 15.44, 112–113 CE, my translation)

From this brief passage we can note that Jesus suffered a Roman execution. Second, Tacitus knows of Jesus through his title ("God's Anointed"). Third, the execution occurred during the rule of Pontius Pilate. This would place his death between 26 and 36 CE Lastly, the movement around Jesus continued after his death. Despite these points it should be noted that there is no description of the event. At best we can see that Tacitus regards the "sect" as a "deadly superstition" and therefore worthy of social liquidation.

A passage found in the Jewish historian Josephus (37–100 CE) appears to tell us more about the death of Jesus. The text from Josephus is quite highly debated among scholars. This passage is the only one that mentions the crucified Jesus. Some critics have regarded the entire passage to be a later Christian interpolation. However, most scholars find the material in italics below to be from Josephus with the rest a later Christian elaboration. It is significant that the passages considered to be authentic share some agreement with the passage from Tacitus. Jesus was executed under Pilate and had a following that did not dissipate after his demise. But Josephus provides some additional notes. Jesus was a "wise man" and a "performer of extraordinary deeds," who had followers from among the Jews and Greeks. Further, he was "indicted by the first men" of the Jews. In effect, Josephus includes the Jewish leadership in the liquidation of Jesus. The lingering question for the historian is whether there is any substance to Josephus' additions. Jesus' reputation as a wise man and wonder worker may have come from legend; but does the indictment of Jewish leaders come from anything more substantial? Usually scholars assume this is the case since the description comports with the gospels' narrative. But this assumption overlooks a tendency of Josephus to critique Jewish leaders. He criticizes the leadership of the Jews during the rebellion against Rome as being divisive and blind to God's signs of warning. Could this critique of misguided leadership by Josephus underpin his remarks on the death of Jesus? Or, did he have some "inside information," given his previous status among the Jewish elite? We shall never know for certain. But we can say that even this minimalist description is a far cry from the extant gospel narratives.

> *Around this time there was a wise man Jesus,* if one could call him a man. For *he was a performer of extraordinary deeds,* a teacher of people who take pleasure in the truth. *He won over many Judeans and many from the Greek world.* He was the "Anointed." *Although Pilate, on the indictment of the first men among us, condemned him to the cross, those who loved him from the first did not stop.* For he appeared alive again to them on the third day as the sacred prophets had spoken of these and many other wonders about him. *Even now the clan of the Anointed One, named after him, has not declined.* (Josephus, *Antiquities* 18.63–64, 93–94 CE, my translation)

One other piece of evidence remains from the Jewish tradition. It is from the Babylonian Talmud and dated to the sixth century CE:

> On the eve of the Passover Yeshu was hanged. For forty days before the execution took place, a herald went forth and cried, "He is going forth to be stoned because he has practiced sorcery and enticed Israel to go astray. Let anyone who can say anything in his defense, come and plead on his behalf." But since nothing was brought in his defense he was hanged on the eve of the Passover.

This late Jewish text comes from what was already a long-standing debate between Christian and Jews. What we have in this passage is a midrash, that is, a weaving of scriptural passages that compose a scene responding to Christian claims about Jesus. Jesus is seen as a false prophet. The basis of this charge can be found in Torah:

> Deut 13 If a prophet arises among you, or a dreamer of dreams, and gives you a sign or wonder, [2]and the sign or wonder which he tells you comes to pass, and if he says, "Let us go after other gods," which you have not known, "and let us serve them," you shall not listen to the words of that prophet ... [9]but you shall kill him ... [10]You shall stone him to death with stones, because he sought to draw you away from the Lord your God. (RSV)

> Deut 21 [22]And if a man has committed a crime punishable by death and he is put to death, and you hang him on a tree. (RSV)

What we have here is one side of a rather nasty long-standing debate over the honor and worth of the one upon which Christians pin their hopes. The Jewish response already works with the standard Christian narrative about Jesus. The "herald going forth" is no longer John the Baptizer but a man announcing Jesus' fate "before the Passover." His shameful death has been revised according to Deuteronomic requirements. Since Jews in the sixth century understood Jesus as a false prophet, he would have been seen as subject to the penalties for such. His lack of defenders (noted in the Christian narratives) supports the charge of being a false prophet. Interestingly, the prescribed death by stoning was altered due to the fact that Jesus was indeed crucified. Another line from Deuteronomy 21:22, however, saved the interpretive day. Already in the first century Paul was aware of such an interpretive possibility:

> Gal 3 [13]God's Anointed freed us from the curse of subjection to the law, by becoming a curse for us, since it is written, "Anyone who is crucified is accursed." (SV)

Thus, we really gain nothing from this late fragment. It tells us more about the sixth century Jewish-Christian antipathy than anything in the first century. The Jewish response in fact presupposed the long-standing Christian storyline. But it rearranged that narrative along the lines of the traditional accusation of a false prophet, thereby reinforcing the Jewish characterization of Jesus in order to deny any validity to the opposing Christian claims. Moreover, while it might be thought that this passage points to the Jewish execution of Jesus, one must be careful. Notice that it says twice "He was hanged." No agent is actually mentioned. The passage was interested not in the "facts of the case" but in reinforcing the later Jewish condemnation of a false religious leader.

One Final Fragment from Non-Canonical Material

The only other fragments of non-gospel evidence come from an early Roman creedal formula (late second century–early third century CE) and in the *Apostolic Tradition* of Hippolytus (215 CE). The creedal formula simply declares that Jesus was

> crucified under Pontius Pilate and buried

while Hippolytus inserts

> and died

after *"Pontius Pilate"* in noting what has been handed on. Hippolytus was attempting to correct any interpretation of the death of Jesus that held that the death of Jesus was only an apparent death. He wanted to assert that Jesus truly died. Once again the brevity of the sources denies any claim of an extended death narrative. Certainly there was no intention to provide one. But it is dangerous to assume how much those who used these formulae knew of the death of Jesus. All we can derive from this material is that Jesus died under Roman auspices.

Concluding Observations

If we only had the evidence brought forward so far, if we did not have the gospel narratives in front of us, little would need to be said about the death of Jesus.[3] Until the beginning of the fifth century only a mocking graffito and a magical charm admit to a crucified one. Jesus had been portrayed as a teacher and healer long before that—but nothing spoke of his death. These pieces of evidence actually point to the shadow side of crucifixion. Nothing is elaborated; all that exists is a shocking image.

Tacitus and Josephus tell us that Jesus died at the hands of the Romans. Depending on how much we can trust Josephus' remark there may have been some collusion by the Jewish leaders. Yet neither tells us anything more about the stark brutality of his death. The later Jewish denunciation of a false prophet in the Babylonian Talmud gives us nothing useful in historical terms. Finally, the two extra-canonical fragments simply reinforce the Roman execution of Jesus.

Extended familiarity with the gospel narratives lead Christians to expect more. Because Jesus is significant to them, they presume that the ancient world would have been interested in the death of Jesus. That assumption is rather anachronistic. To those outside the circles of the fledgling Jesus movement, the death of a peasant artisan was hardly significant. Indeed, the social stigma attached to crucifixion would have predisposed any who heard of the event to discard it immediately. As we shall see, there may even be evidence that some of the early followers of Jesus were also reluctant to speak of his execution. That some nevertheless faced the shame and social stigma of Jesus' death may well represent a radical refusal to give in to the expectations of an imperial world.

Coda
Without Sanctuary

For over fifteen years I have opened my course on "The Death of Jesus" with a series of images, ranging from a second- or third-century graffito to the latest cultural interpretations of the crucified Jesus. But some images are not sketched or painted. They come from the disturbing volume *Without Sanctuary* by James Allen.

In 2000 James Allen published a collection of photos, mostly postcards, of lynchings that occurred throughout the United States. Allen discovered them as he went "picking" at flea markets. He eventually gathered a collection of these postcards and turned his findings into a startling exhibition that was seen in a number of American cities. A website (http://withoutsanctuary.org) provides the substance of the introductory remarks and a complete presentation of the photos. Allen discovered meaning in what was now neglected and "secondhand." Even more disturbing than the tortured victim were the crowds encompassing the scene. Children and teenagers stood among the approving adults, often with smiles on their faces. These postcards exposed an ignominious American heritage. Allen himself admitted that these postcards challenged him:

> These photographs provoke a strong sense of denial in me, and a desire to freeze my emotions. In time I realized that my fear of the other is fear of myself. Then these portraits, torn from other family albums, became portraits of my own family and of myself. And the faces of the living and the faces of the dead recur in me and in my daily life... With each encounter I can't help thinking of these photos, and the march of time, and of the cold steel trigger in the human heart. (Allen, 205)

I begin my class with these photos precisely because they are the best introduction to the death traditions about Jesus. They are raw, terrible in aspect, and designed with sinister intent. When juxtaposed with Christian narratives of the death of Jesus, these postcards short-circuit attempts by those familiar with the Christian passion tradition to keep the death of Jesus at a safe distance—from the degrading reality of public execution. They keep the focus on the harsh reality of a tortured death scene. They refuse to deny the power dynamics embedded in the scene. Moreover, the viewer of these postcards cannot but be stunned by the evident cruelty as well as by the insouciant presence of the crowds. These photos are not neutral items, nor are they simple "facts" but were designed to send messages. Their publication was designed to send a message. They were in fact "trophies," distributed among the organizers of the lynching. For them each postcard was a victory declaration. But there was another message. For African Americans and other minorities these postcards served as warnings not to get "uppity." In fact, one student of mine, David West (later to become an All American basketball player and NBA star) volunteered to make a presentation on the book. When I asked why he was so eager, he said that his grandfather knew of these postcards for most of his life and wanted his grandson to know "what was really going on." Both David and his grandfather recognized that these images were hardly neutral. They celebrated "winners" determined to maintain their domination over fellow Americans.

Crucifixion

The punishment of crucifixion probably originated in Mesopotamia. It was practiced by Assyrians, Persians, Phoenicians, Carthaginians, Greeks, Jews, and Romans. It may have developed from the Assyrian procedure of impaling. The Persians and Carthaginians imposed it on high officials, commanders, and rebels. The Romans, through their experience in the Punic Wars, quite likely took the practice from the Carthaginians. For the most part, the Romans carried out this form of execution on lower classes (slaves, violent criminals, unruly elements), non-citizens, and traitors. Serving as a political and military punishment, allegedly an effective deterrent, crucifixion was a very public display. (The largest mass execution occurred at the end of Spartacus revolt (73–71 BCE) when six thousand gladiators and slaves died a slow death, crucified along the Appian Highway to Rome.) Costing relatively little, crucifixion produced a significant public effect. Order throughout the empire was maintained as the general population saw a criminal receiving a just punishment. There was neither a desire nor the power to abolish it. To give up this form of execution might undermine the authority of the state and jeopardize the hard-won peace of the Roman empire.

Crucifixion had a history within the land of Israel. The Hasmonean King Alexander Jannaeus (103–76 BCE) carried out a mass execution of hundreds of his people (Josephus, *Antiquities* 13.14.2/380; *War* 1.4.6/97). Shimon ben Shetach executed eighty witches (probably Sadducees) near Ashkelon after the death of Alexander Jannaeus (Josephus, *Antiquities* 13.410ff.). With the coming of Herod this practice did not continue. But upon the revolt after the death of Herod the Romans crucified two thousand Jews (Josephus, *War* 2.5.2 /75). From then on, crucifixion was carried out as a Roman form of punishment in this occupied territory. From that time to the Jewish War, Josephus reports only two crucifixions in Palestine (*War* 2.5.2/75): Jesus (*Antiquities* 18.3.3/64) and the sons of Judas the Galilean during the great famine when Tiberius Alexander was prefect (42–48 CE). Gessius Florus applied it to Jews who were Roman citizens of lower rank and provincials in 66. He had them scourged and nailed to crosses (Josephus, *War* 2.14.9/308). Vespasian crucified one rebel at Jotapata (Josephus, *War* 3.7.33/321). Titus crucified a Jew as a warning, (Joseph, *War* 5.6.5/289). Then, in the last months of the siege of Jerusalem, mass executions occurred daily (Josephus, *War* 5.11.1/450–51).

The public display of a crucified one represented the utmost humiliation. In the ancient honor/shame society such an end would signal a human being reduced to nothingness. It was not only the worst of Roman punishments (*summum supplicium* — extreme penalty) to be meted out, but also drove all to forget the one liquidated (*damnatio memoriae*). In his defense of Rabirius, Cicero speaks to the social horror of crucifixion. It should not even be mentioned.

> But the executioner, the veiling of the head and the very word "cross" should be far removed not only from the person of a Roman citizen but from his thoughts, his eyes and his ears. For it is not only the actual occurrence of these things or the endurance of them, but the liability to them, the expectation, indeed the very mention of them, that is unworthy of a Roman citizen and a free man. (Cicero, *Pro Rabirio*, 16)

Thus, it is not surprising that there is little mention or description of crucifixions in ancient literature or inscriptions. Moreover, victims were often not buried. They became food for wild beasts and birds of prey. The lack of a burial for so many spoke volumes to the ancient world. That final human dignity was usually denied.

Roman crucifixion consisted usually of three parts: scourging, carrying of cross, nailing and lifting. Often a sign (*titulus*), inscribed with black letters, indicating the nature of crime, was carried before the condemned. A cross consisted of an upright beam planted in fixed position and a crossbar (*patibulum*) movable and carried by the condemned. The naked criminal would bear the crossbar to the place of execution. There the hands or wrists were nailed to the crossbar, which was lifted and secured either on the top of a T-shaped cross or in a mortise of a dagger-shaped cross. The victim's feet were then nailed to the upright beam. There were "low crosses," ten to eighteen inches above ground, and "high crosses," three feet above ground. Beasts easily devoured those on the low cross.

Death was usually not quick. Victims might last several days. Medical studies along with reports from German practices in World War I and Nazi executions in deportation camps suggest that death occurred through asphyxiation.[a] Seneca, in defending the act of suicide over a long, slow death, presents a unique glimpse of crucifixion:

> Can anyone be found who would prefer wasting away in pain dying limb by limb, or letting out his life drop by drop, rather than expiring once for all? Can any man be found willing to be fastened to the accursed tree, long sickly, already deformed, swelling with ugly weals on shoulders and chest, and drawing the breath of life amid long-drawn-out agony? He would have many excuses for dying even before mounting the cross. (Seneca, *Dialogue* 3.2.2 [*De ira* 1])

When the crucified were buried it was usually in mass graves. There is, however, a finding in 1968 of a buried young man with broken legs and a right heal pierced by a four and one half inches long nail that suggests that some executed victims could be claimed and buried privately.

Crucifixion continued as a public punishment until it was abolished by Constantine in the fourth century.

As Martin Hengel observes, crucifixion was an "utterly offensive affair." It was "obscene" in the original sense of the word.[b] It brought the pornography of violence into the public realm. "Crucifixion was a punishment in which the caprice and sadism of the executioners were given full rein."[c] The primitive lust for revenge and the sadistic cruelty of rulers and crowds found a focus and a target. All this was compounded under the iron rule of law and the maintenance of order. Some ancient philosophers would use crucifixion as a metaphor to enable the wise man to approach suffering and death with a sense of serenity and calm, as the soul sheds its mortal limits. Ancient romance writers sometimes employed the element of crucifixion to excite readers as protagonists were threatened

---

a. Rousseau and Arav, *Jesus and His World*, 75.
b. Hengel, *Crucifixion*, 22.
c. Hengel, *Crucifixion*, 25.

but eventually freed from such a fate, thereby delivering a happy ending. But the reality of crucifixion could not be easily dismissed. Every slave knew that this could be his or her fate. Anyone who thought of raising a sandal or a weapon against authority could anticipate a tortured outcome. The total loss of honor, the dissolution of one's social ties, and the damning of one's memory pulverized the condemned one. Crucifixion enacted the ultimate obscenity: it pushed—with every lost breath—the condemned into oblivion.

2

Facing Death
Did the Historical Jesus Anticipate His Fate?

The Passion Predictions

Before we move into an investigation of the primary literary evidence for the death of Jesus, it would be advisable to ask at this point whether the historical Jesus said anything about his future death. The canonical gospel narratives tell of Jesus' anticipating his death. In fact, from the earliest of the canonical gospels on, we hear Jesus actually predicting his death three times.

> Mark 8 [31]He started teaching them that the Human One was destined to endure much, and be rejected by the elders and the chief priests and the scholars, and be killed, and after three days rise.

> Mark 9 [30]They left there and started going through Galilee, and he did not want anyone to know. [31]You see, he was instructing his disciples and telling them, "The Human One will be turned over to his enemies, and they will kill him. And three days after he is killed he will rise."

> Mark 10 [33]"Listen, we're going up to Jerusalem, and the Human One will be turned over to the chief priests and the scholars, and they will sentence him to death, and turn him over to foreigners, [34]and they will make fun of him, and spit on him, and flog him, and kill <him>. But after three days he will rise."[1]

It would seem at face value that he did so. But are these the words of the historical Jesus? The three predictions in Mark actually summarize the Markan story about Jesus. In this gospel, written shortly after the fall of Jerusalem (70 CE) for a community thinking that they were about to witness the "end time" and the return of "the Human One," the passion predictions prove to be key elements in what has been called the "heart of the Gospel of Mark."[2] From Mark 8:22 to the end of chapter 10, the writer has crafted an elegant teaching section, focusing on what discipleship means to that community. Two healing stories (8:22–26; 10:46–52) provide the frame containing the three passion predictions, followed by the disciples' misunderstanding and Jesus' correction (8:27–9:1; 9:30–50; 10:32–45). Interspersed between the teaching episodes are the Transfiguration scene (9:2–29) that leads to teaching on discipleship and a series of teaching pronouncements (10:1–31). Thus, the passion predictions serve as crucial moments in the teaching of discipleship. The followers of Jesus in the narrative serve as foils for the Markan community to draw out what discipleship entails. In short, *as evidence, the material reflects the concerns of the later Markan community*. The predictions serve critically as defining moments in the Markan narrative. They point to and underpin the later Markan passion narrative. They provide a *post factum* explanation to the developing community for the execution of Jesus. For this reason many scholars consider them not to be from the historical Jesus but are a Markan construction.

Nevertheless, despite this compelling argument, what if we were to detach these predictions from the surrounding material? Can we then argue that they go back to the historical Jesus? Actually this two-step formulation of dying and rising reflects the earlier tradition found in Paul's first letter to the Corinthian community (1 Cor 15:3–4):

> [3]I passed on to you as of paramount importance what I also had received:
> that the Anointed died to free us from the seductive power of corruption
> according to the scriptures,
> [4]and that he was buried, and that he was raised "on the third day"
> according to the scriptures.

Here Paul is writing of a tradition that he himself heard ("I passed on to you … what I also had received"). He then points out that the "Anointed died" and "was raised on 'the third day.'" Such assertions were understood as happening "according to the scriptures." Already an interpretative tradition, invoking the use of the Hebrew Scriptures, was in play for Paul to witness. The Markan passion predictions hearken back to this formulation that predates Paul. The writer of Mark then tailored the predictions to fit nicely into his ongoing narrative. In sum, the passion predictions do point to an earlier layer of material. But they do not go all the way back to the historical Jesus. They reflect the post mortem concerns of the developing Jesus communities.

The Words of
the Historical Jesus

What then did the historical Jesus say about death? Is there any evidence that he anticipated his fate? From 1985 to 1991 a large gathering of scholars, called the Jesus Seminar, met to consider all the words attributed to Jesus in the first three centuries. They began with an initial inventory of the data. No saying was considered out of bounds. Nor was a saying found in the New Testament canon privileged over a non-canonical saying (such as in the Gospel of Thomas). The scholars, who came to be called Fellows, divided up into working groups to research each saying and make the strongest case for authenticity. After each working group deliberated, their recommendations were returned to the entire Seminar in plenary session to debate the sayings and vote on them. The Seminar sorted through about fifteen hundred versions of approximately five hundred sayings ascribed to Jesus. A compendium of about ninety authentic sayings and parables was determined.

In publishing its sometimes provocative findings (*The Five Gospels*, 1993), the Jesus Seminar concluded that Jesus was an itinerant wordsmith who invited his audience into his experimental vision of the Empire of God. But the question of death was another matter. The usual sayings that would furnish Jesus' anticipation of death were not included in the database. We have seen the reasons why the Passion Predictions (Mark 8:31; 9:30–32; 10:32–34) are not from the historical Jesus. Likewise the monumental Farewell Address of the Last Supper in John was also seen as a later construction. The Lukan journey to Jerusalem that anticipated Jesus' fate (Luke 9:51, 19:28) was found to be a later construction by the gospel writer.[3] Moreover, the Seminar found that subsequent writers placed the seismic remarks of Mark 13 and the various other scripts of imminent doom on Jesus' lips. The historical Jesus was not an apocalyptic seer.[4] In sum, the very verses most readers of scripture would use to claim that Jesus anticipated his tragic fate can be better understood as coming from the later gospel writers.

Turning to those ninety sayings judged authentic by the Seminar,[a] we find the following sayings directly or indirectly touching upon the subject of death.

Q/Luke 9 [58]Jesus said to him, "Foxes have dens, and birds of the sky have nests, but the Human One has nowhere to rest his head." [P][b]

Q/Luke 9 [59]Another said to him, "Master, first, let me go and bury my father." [60]Jesus said to him, "Follow me, and leave it to the dead to bury their own dead; but you go out and announce the Empire of God." [P]

Q/Matt 6 [11]"Provide us with the bread we need for the day!" [P]

Q/Luke 12 [6]"What do five sparrows cost? Five bucks? Yet not one of them is overlooked by God. [7]In fact, even the hairs of your head have all been counted. Don't be so timid: You're worth more than a flock of sparrows." [P]

Luke 12 [16]There was a rich man whose fields produced a bumper crop. [17]"What do I do now?" he asked himself, "since I don't have any place to store my crops. [18]I know!" he said, "I'll tear down my barns and build larger ones so I can store all my grain and my goods. [19]Then I'll say to myself, `You have plenty put away for years to come. Take it easy; eat, drink, and enjoy yourself.'" [20]But God said to him, "You fool!

---

a. For a collection of all the sayings of the historical Jesus as determined by the Jesus Seminar, see Funk and Dewey, *The Gospel of Jesus*.

b. The letters P and G refer to the votes of the Jesus Seminar. A P (pink) vote meant that the saying quite possibly came from Jesus, while a G (grey) vote meant that there was something could be from Jesus but the Seminar could not be exactly certain. In this case of G, it meant a vote that was often evenly divided between authentic and inauthentic.

This very night your life will be demanded back from you. All this stuff you've collected—whose will it be now?" [P]

Q/Luke 12 ²²He said to his disciples, "That's why I'm telling you: Don't fret about life, what you're going to eat—or about your body, what you're going to wear. ²³Remember, there is more to living than food and clothing. ²⁴Think about the crows: they don't plant or harvest, they don't have storerooms or barns. Yet God feeds them. You're worth a lot more than the birds! ²⁵Can any of you add an hour to life by fretting about it? ²⁶So if you can't do a little thing like that, why worry about the rest? ²⁷Think about how the lilies grow: they don't toil and they never spin. But let me tell you, even Solomon at the height of his glory was never decked out like one of them. ²⁸If God dresses up the grass in the field, which is here today and is tossed into an oven tomorrow, how much more will <God take care of> you, with your meager trust." [P]

Q/Luke 14 ²⁶"If any of you comes to me and does not hate your own father and mother and wife and children and brothers and sisters—yes, even your own life—you're no disciple of mine." [P]

Q/Luke 17 ³³Jesus said, "Whoever tries to hang on to life will lose it, but whoever loses life will preserve it." [P]

Q/Luke 12 ³³"Sell your belongings, and donate to charity; make yourselves purses that don't wear out, with inexhaustible wealth in heaven, where no burglar can get to it and no moth can destroy it. ³⁴As you know, what you treasure is your heart's true measure." [G]

Thomas 42 Jesus said, "Get going!" [G]

What is most interesting about this remarkable assortment is how vital and fresh the sayings sound. No anguish or self-conscious martyrdom appears. In short, *Jesus did not apparently anticipate his death in tragic or sacrificial terms*. The language of the sacrificial martyr comes from the post mortem tradition. Some might attribute this vigorous language to a youthful enthusiasm or idealism, yet the story of the rich man (Luke 12:16–20) cautions against this consideration. This wisdom tale indicates that death was part of Jesus' world. But evidently neither death nor its customs held him at bay (Q 9:59–60). He lived out of a fundamental trust in Reality (Q 12:22–28). This sense of trust allowed him to see the critical choices that living entailed (Q 14:26; Q 17:33). In the very midst of human contingency (Q 9:58) and need (Q Matt 6:11) stood the opportunity of experiencing God's Empire (Q 9:59–60). We do not see some heroic pose, anticipating a traumatic conclusion. Nor do we see some overarching narrative that attempts to make sense of his impending death.

Now some scholars (even among the Seminar participants) argue that Jesus *must have known* the political score.[5] He would have known that what he said and did would eventually meet political resistance. Yet such speculation is precisely that. It is built upon the argument of plausibility. I would contend that it is used to support a position assumed rather than proven. The words of the historical Jesus noted here would appear to give a lie to their "political realism." The peasant wordsmith may have had other things in mind. I contend Jesus envisioned a Reality much more immediate (and with greater social consequences) than the ordinary politico.[6] It would not be surprising for the Romans to sniff something amiss. Moreover, Pilate did not need certain evidence to liquidate a perceived threat, albeit a fly on the Roman elbow. The "carelessness" of Jesus for his fate may well be a consequence of his trusting vision of God's effective presence. We also cannot dismiss outright another version of Jesus' end: his death may well have caught everyone off guard, including Jesus.

From our investigation so far we can begin to see that:

- the evidence for an extensive portrayal of the death of Jesus does not seem to exist
- iconographic evidence in the first four centuries has not been found
- material outside of the New Testament provides only the slimmest information
- the passion predictions in the canonical gospels are secondary at best
- the sayings of the historical Jesus leave us with no sense that he sought out a martyr's death
- we already have had indications that an understanding of Jesus dying as a martyr enters in the post mortem tradition

It is time to turn to the earliest gospel evidence to see when and why this understanding enters the ongoing tradition.

A Test Case
Jesus' Anguished Prayer (Mark 14:32–42)

[32]And they go to a place named Gethsemane, and he says to his disciples, "Sit down here while I pray." [33]And he takes Peter and James and John along with him, and he grew apprehensive and full of anguish. [34]He says to them, "I'm so sad I could die. You stay here and be alert." [35]And he would move on a little, lay face down on the ground, and pray that he might avoid the crisis, if possible. [36]And he was saying, "Abba (Father), all things are possible for you. Take this cup away from me. But it's your will that matters, not mine." [37]And he returns and finds them sleeping, and says to Peter, "Simon, couldn't you stay awake for one hour? [38]Be alert and pray that you won't be put to the test. The spirit is willing, but the flesh is weak." [39]And once again he went away and prayed, saying the same thing. [40]And once again he came and found them sleeping, since their eyes had grown very heavy, and they didn't know what to say to him. [41]And he comes a third time and says to them, "You may as well sleep on now and get your rest. It's all over! The time has come! Look, the Human One is being turned over to sinners. Get up, let's go! See for yourselves! Here comes the one who is going to turn me in." (SV)

Perhaps one of the most moving passages in the death narrative of Jesus centers on his final anguished prayer in the garden. Bible readers, understandably, are touched by this scene. The question of its authenticity, nevertheless, must be raised. How certain are we that Jesus actually prayed what Mark presents? First of all, the probable source of this material is Mark. Matthew and Luke take over this scene with their own modifications (Matt 26:36–46; Luke 22:39–46). There are even later echoes of the scene also in the texts of John 12:27; 18:11 and Hebrews 5:7. Thus, the question of authenticity rests with the primary source, Mark.

When we focus on the Markan material, two important observations must be made. First, the scene very much plays within the overall portrayal of Jesus as a martyr. Already in Mark 14:24 the Markan Jesus says that his blood "has been poured out for many." The past tense of the verb ("poured out") indicates that the language has been taken from an earlier liturgical formula,[7] now taken up into the Markan narrative.

The gospel reinterprets the death of Jesus along the lines of the heroism of a Jewish martyr.[c] As a martyr Jesus would have been portrayed anticipating his fate. Being a faithful Jew would have entailed the possibility of expressing such anticipation in prayer.

It is precisely the contents of Jesus' prayer that directly touches on the matter of the scene's authenticity. A close reading of the passage leads us to see that there are no witnesses to what Jesus prayed! The three closest to Jesus are all asleep. Indeed this is affirmed in triplicate. How then can the writer give us Jesus' anguished prayer? The writer actually fills in the blank! The first clue is found in Mark 14:38 where Mark alludes to the Lord's prayer ("pray that you won't be put to the test"/ cf. Luke 11:4; Matt 6:13).[8] The proverb ("The spirit is willing, but the flesh is weak") in Mark 14:38b is hardly distinctive and could have been a commonplace saying that helps build the scene. The invocation "Abba (Father)" echoes not simply the Lord's prayer (Luke 11:2–4; Matt 6:9–13) but the experience of the early Jesus communities:

> Gal 4 [6]Now because you are adopted, God sent into your hearts the same filial attitude toward God that was in Jesus, that can call God, "Abba! Father!"

In fact, the translation of Abba found in Galations 4:6 is found also in the Markan narrative. Thus, what appears at first blush to be a historical account is actually a construction by the writer of Mark. Mark creates this scene in keeping with his portrayal of Jesus as a martyr who dies for "the many." This heroic characterization is filled in with the experience of the early communities. The prayerful expression of the Jesus communities is placed on the lips of the Markan Jesus. The writer of the first gospel has constructed a scene for his audience to be inspired by as they themselves face an uncertain future. The community of Mark considered themselves to be the last generation due to the recent destruction of the Temple in Jerusalem. Living out of the seismic shock of the Jewish War the community looked to

---

c. The term martyr does not refer to the later Christian usage. Rather, it expresses the conviction of Jewish writers, as was the case also with Greek and Roman writers, that these individuals heroically met their fate for a cause or for their people. Socrates, for example, died for the Truth, for the sake of Philosophy.

the death of Jesus as a cypher of their own fate. The story was told not to deliver documentary evidence but to bolster the community's conviction and hope.

Another Jesus

An argument often made is that the actions and words of Jesus must have precipitated an inevitable Roman reaction. While this is plausible, given the political reality in Israel at the time, it was not inevitable. If Jesus was provocative in speech and action, so the argument goes, the Roman option would have been to suppress this danger with dispatch. Certainly Pilate's reputation suggested this. Yet, we forget that Jesus lived in relatively peaceful times. We can point to a much more embroiled period, shortly before the Jewish rebellion. Here we discover evidence in Josephus' writings of another person named Jesus, who could not have been more provocative towards Rome. But this Jesus was flogged, not executed, despite being an impossible pest from his incessant clamor. It is only by accident that the outcries of this Jesus were silenced (probably to the relief of Jews and Romans!).

> [300] But, what is still more terrible, there was one Jesus, the son of Ananus, a common man and a husbandman, who, four years before the war began, and at a time when the city was in very great peace and prosperity, came to that feast whereon it is our custom for everyone to make tabernacles to God in the temple, [301] began suddenly to cry aloud, "A voice from the east, a voice from the west, a voice from the four winds, a voice against Jerusalem and the holy house, a voice against the bridegroom and the bride, and a voice against this whole people!" (Jer 7:34) This was his cry, as he went about by day and by night, in all the lanes of the city.

> [302] However, certain of the most eminent among the populace had great indignation at this dire cry of his, and took up the man, and gave him a great number of severe stripes; yet he did not either say anything for himself, or anything peculiar to those who chastised him, but still went on with the same words which he cried before.

[303] Hereupon our rulers supposing, as the case proved to be, that this was a sort of divine fury in the man, brought him to the Roman procurator; [304] where he was whipped till his bones were laid bare; yet he did not make any supplication for himself, nor shed any tears, but turning his voice to the most lamentable tone possible, at every stroke of the whip his answer was, "Woe, woe to Jerusalem!" [305] And when Albinus (for he was then our procurator) asked him, "Who he was? and from where he came? and why he uttered such words?" he made no manner of reply to what he said, but still did not stop his melancholy dirge, till Albinus took him to be a madman, and dismissed him.

[306] Now, during all the time that passed before the war began, this man did not go near anyone of the citizens, nor was seen by them while he said so; but he every day uttered these lamentable words, as if it were his premeditated vow, "Woe, woe to Jerusalem!" [307] Nor did he give ill words to any of those who beat him every day, nor good words to those who gave him food; but this was his reply to all men, and indeed no other than a melancholy presage of what was to come. [308] This cry of his was the loudest at the festivals; and he continued this dirge for seven years and five months, without growing hoarse, or being tired therewith, until the very time that he saw his presage in earnest fulfilled in our siege, when it ceased; [309] for as he was going around upon the wall, he cried out with his utmost force, "Woe, woe to the city again, and to the people, and to the holy house!" And just as he added at the last, "Woe, woe to myself also!" there came a stone out of one of the engines, and smote him, and killed him immediately; and as he was uttering the very same presages he gave up the ghost. (Josephus, *Jewish War* 6.300–309)

30

3

Evidence from
the Sayings Gospels

The historical Jesus left a fragmentary legacy, the earliest elements of which would have been remembered sayings and deeds, and patterned clusters of sayings and actions. Fortunately some of the oral tradition survived in written manuscripts. We now turn to three instances where the sayings of Jesus coalesced eventually into manuscripts.

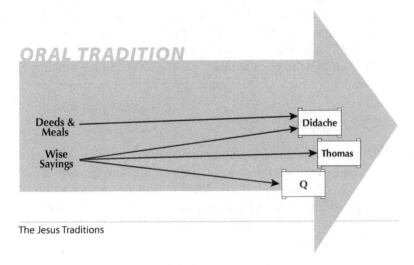

The Jesus Traditions

The Sayings Gospel (Q) and the Death of Jesus

In the view of a great many scholars, Matthew and Luke knew and used a written collection of the sayings of Jesus in composing their own gospels. If this hypothesis is correct, that source may well have been the very first written gospel.[1] This material can be found by noticing the material common to Matthew and Luke but not in Mark. Scholars have called this material (much in word-for-word agreement) Q from a German word meaning "source" (Quelle); it is now usually referred to as the Q Gospel or, more recently, the Sayings Gospel.[a]

The format of the Sayings Gospel was hardly unusual in the ancient world. Sayings of the sages (*ta logia ton siphon*) were collected throughout the Hellenistic world. The Sayings Gospel is like or similar to other collections of wise sayings in antiquity. Although it did not survive as a separate document, this collection of Jesus' sayings became an important part of Matthew and Luke.

When we read through the Sayings Gospel we have to take into account what isn't there: the Sayings Gospel does not have a passion narrative. The death of Jesus[2] was known, but it was not seen as salvific in any way. Instead, the death of Jesus became absorbed into the tradition of prophets' deaths (see Luke 11:49–51; 13:34). Nothing beyond this alludes to his death:

> Q 11 [49]That's why Wisdom has said, "I will send them prophets and sages, and some of them they are always going to kill and persecute." [50]So, this generation will have to answer for the blood of all the prophets that has been shed since the world was founded, [51]from the blood of Abel to the blood of Zechariah, who perished between the altar and the sanctuary. Yes, I'm telling you, this generation will have to answer for it.

> Q 13 [34]Jerusalem, Jerusalem, you murder the prophets and stone those sent to you!

The Sayings Gospel understands Jesus as a prophet and man of wisdom, who dies a martyr's death. The Q Jesus delivers words of challenging wisdom. In the transmission of its subsequent redactions of the wise sayings of Jesus, the Sayings Gospel characterizes Jesus (and John the Baptizer) as one of the children of Wisdom.[3]

> Q 7 [33]Just remember, John appeared on the scene, eating no bread and drinking no wine, and you say, "He's possessed." [34]The Human One appeared on the scene both eating and

---

a. A reconstructed Q may be found in Miller, *The Complete Gospels* and Dewey and Miller, *The Complete Gospel Parallels*.

drinking, and you say, "There's a glutton and a drunk, a crony of toll collectors and sinners!" [35]Indeed, Wisdom is vindicated by her children.

Jesus' death likewise partakes of the Jewish tendency to interpret meaning in larger, corporate terms, as a further instance of the many teachers and prophets killed by a faithless people (Q 11:49–50, 51b; 13:34). As part of the wisdom tradition the Sayings Gospel views Jesus as the just one, who was God's prophet, was rejected and murdered by his enemies and was taken up, assumed, and will then stand in judgment at the end (Q 17:34, 30).

The death of Jesus in the Sayings Gospel, however, is not a focal point for the community. The words of Jesus form the atmosphere of this early community. One wonders whether this emphasis carried forward the tone of the historical Jesus. If the historical Jesus was more attentive to his provocative envisioning of God's Empire than to any concern over his own death, as I have suggested above,[4] then we might see in the Sayings Gospel a continuation of his imaginative enterprise. The assimilation of Jesus under Lady Wisdom's banner may well have been an attempt by the community not only to locate this wise teacher within Israel's traditions but also to make sense of the community's rejection by their own people (Q 11:49, 51b). Jesus' death, nevertheless, does not seem to have been a major issue for the Sayings Gospel Community. Even when the community's later experience and hope (Q 11:30; 22:28) are mentioned, there is no reference to Jesus death. In fact, the only mention of "cross" comes under the topic of discipleship.[5]

Q 14 [27]Unless you carry your cross and follow after me, you cannot be my disciple. (Cf. Matt 16:24; Mark 8:34; Luke 9:23)

It is evident in this well-known saying about discipleship that it is a challenging word rather than a reference to the actual death of Jesus. The language of this saying indicates the concerns of a developing Jesus community. The emphasis is upon the follower's own fate.

Gospel of Thomas

The Gospel of Thomas is also a sayings gospel. It contains 114 sayings ascribed to Jesus. It lacks narrative connections; it does not have a passion story, or appearance stories, or birth and childhood stories. The Coptic text of Thomas was discovered at Nag Hammadi, in upper Egypt, in 1945. Three Greek fragments of Thomas had been discovered earlier, but scholars were unable to identify them as fragments of Thomas until the Coptic text was unearthed. There is about a 40 percent overlap between the Sayings Gospel and Thomas.

While the Gospel of Thomas was originally dated to about 120 CE, many scholars of that gospel now argue that it was composed around 70 CE[6] with many of the sayings (such as those from Q) coming from an earlier period.

The Gospel of Thomas' format, like that of the Sayings Gospel, precludes any construction of a biography. It is a collection of sage sayings—such as those found in Proverbs, Sirach, or the Sayings Gospel—of interest to a community that saw Jesus as a teacher of insight. His words of wisdom were essential. Biographical matters were not important, nor were particulars such as marital status or age. The community is not interested in what later readers would desire. The Gospel of Thomas thus continues in that vein of transmitting wisdom sayings. Going beyond the Sayings Gospel there is not a hint of either the death of Jesus or a fragment of a passion narrative. Real life, in contrast, can be attained through insight into the words delivered by the Living One. In fact, those who gain insight through comprehending these sayings will "not taste death."[7] Identification with Jesus the revealer brings the follower into the life and likeness of divine wisdom:

> Thom 108 Jesus said, "Whoever drinks from my mouth will become like me. I myself shall become that person and the hidden things will be revealed to him."

The Didache

While the Didache ("Teaching") was mentioned during the second to fourth centuries, the actual text only came to light in 1873 in an eleventh-century Byzantine manuscript from Constantinople. The dating of the text is usually placed in the early to mid-second century. It probably originated in a Syrian community. It may well include materials dating as early as the middle of the first century. It has some apparent connections to the Gospel of Matthew and may reflect a form of Jewish Christianity.[8] Once again a close reading discloses that there is no hint of the death of Jesus. While there are wisdom sayings that echo the Sayings Gospel,[9] there is no touching on the death of Jesus. Moreover, while there is an eschatological finish (ch. 16: "When the Lord is coming") there is still no reference to the earlier death of Jesus. In the Eucharistic prayers (9:1–5) although Jesus is described as a "servant/child" (*pais*) there is no mention of his death nor is the Eucharist a memorial of his death. Precisely in these liturgical prayers where one would think that the death of Jesus would be remembered, there is no reference to the death of Jesus. Rather, the prayers reflect a Jewish thanksgiving to the "father."

Concerning the Eucharist, Didache 9:1–4 eucharizes thus:

9 First, concerning the cup:
²We give you thanks, our Father,
for the holy vine of your servant David
which you have revealed to us through your servant Jesus.
To you is the glory forever.

³And concerning the broken loaf:
We give you thanks, our Father,
for the life and knowledge
which you revealed to us through your servant Jesus.
To you is glory forever.

⁴Just as this broken loaf was scattered
over the hills as grain
and, having been gathered together, became one;
in like fashion, may your assembly be gathered together
from the ends of the earth into your kingdom.
Because yours is the glory and the power
through the Anointed Jesus forever. …

10 ²We give you thanks, holy Father,
for your holy name,
which you tabernacle in our hearts,
and for the knowledge and faith and immortality
which you revealed to us through your servant Jesus.
To you is glory forever. (Trans. Milavec)

In fact, we see even in these Eucharistic prayers thanksgiving being given for the "life and knowledge" through the "servant Jesus." The Didache Eucharist actually underscores the wisdom tradition found in its sayings, as well as echoing the wisdom tradition in the Sayings Gospel and Thomas. One can see that these early collections of Jesus sayings reflect the continuing activity of his followers. Jesus' stories and sayings did not silence his audience; rather, the growing tradition gives evidence of their attempts to continue to transmit and share the wisdom of their experience. What is crucial for our investigation is to note that none of these three significant texts in the early Jesus tradition focus upon the death of Jesus. Only the Sayings Gospel alludes to Jesus' death as being that of a prophet, while Thomas and the Didache make no mention of Jesus' death. For many Bible readers such an observation may well be startling, for it suggests that the emphasis upon the death of Jesus found so much in other parts of the tradition (such as in Paul or the canonical gospels) was not paramount throughout all of the early Jesus movement in the first century. It then becomes necessary to ask when and why does concern for the death of Jesus enter into the tradition in a more concentrated fashion.

4

The Re-imagination of a Death

The Pauline Material

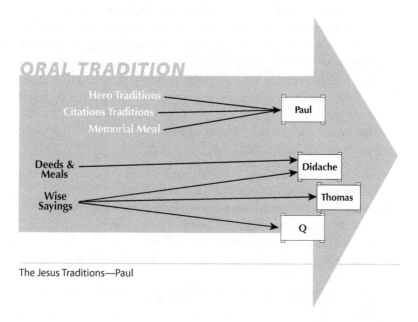

ORAL TRADITION

Hero Traditions
Citations Traditions
Memorial Meal

Paul

Deeds &
Meals

Didache

Wise
Sayings

Thomas

Q

The Jesus Traditions—Paul

Having assessed what we can learn from the fragmentary residue of the historical Jesus and from the earliest layer of the gospel material (The Sayings Gospel), we now turn to the letters of Paul. The writings of Paul[a] can be dated (approx. 48–60 CE) to

---

a. For a new translation of the Letters of Paul see Dewey, Hoover, McGaughy, and Schmidt, *The Authentic Letters of Paul.* In this chapter we are concerned with the historical Paul, not the second century construction found in the Acts of the Apostles. See below p. 189 n. 2.

about the same period as the developing Q tradition (45–72 CE). By relying on the letters most probably from the historical Paul, scholars have detected a radical Pharisaic Jew, who underwent an unexpected paradigm shift. This is not the later, second-century take on Paul from Acts, but a critically informed construction of Paul from his very words. In addition, Paul presents the earliest direct evidence about the death of Jesus.[1] Still further, there are two distinct layers within the Pauline material. In this chapter we shall consider what Paul himself has to say about the death of Jesus. Then, in the next chapter, we shall note the traditions about the death of Jesus that Paul inherited. These traditions embed creative innovations about the memory of the death of Jesus. Despite their fragmentary nature, this material displays a variety of ways in which the understanding of the death of Jesus was re-imagined. Moreover, we shall further note what were the social locations of these traditions.

We shall put this all in contrast to how Paul understands the death of Jesus. Does he simply take over the earlier traditions without modification? Or does his understanding of the death of Jesus differ from what has been handed down? How does Paul's interpretation affect the way in which the death of Jesus is remembered?

Before we turn to the particular evidence it is crucial to note that we have so far found:

- little material recalling the death of Jesus in the earliest layers, either within or without the New Testament.
- Moreover, we cannot anachronistically place later gospel passion narratives in an earlier time. The reticence about the death of Jesus should not be overlooked.
- Why is it that there is no iconic representation of Jesus' death until the fifth century?
- Why does the Sayings Gospel allude to his death as that of a prophet?

Any attempt to remember the death of Jesus would have come up against the ways in which the Roman Empire had fabricated crucifixion in the first century world. Roman authorities communicated a devastating message through the public act of crucifixion. Rome displayed its dominance, not only shocking the victim and the victim's people, but also signaling social defilement and erasure. Rome delivered a physical punishment, while attempting to effect a *damnatio memoriae* (condemnation of memory). Roman execution liquidated not simply the person but even any trace of remembrance. The social pollution of crucifixion obliterated the victim's worth and others' memory of the victim. No longer having any advantage, physical or social, the victim died in disgrace, a god-forsaken nobody. Crucifixion also traumatized all associated with the victim, anticipating any other story to be told about the victim. Roman crucifixion reduced all to social silence. It was traumatic through and through. Those who would gainsay it found themselves in a brutalized silence. The shock and awe of this imperial act must be taken into account, before one can too quickly move on to another version of the event.

Keeping in mind the cultural shock and awe of crucifixion, we may begin to understand not only Paul's harsh persecution of the early Jesus community but also the innovative move by those unknown Jesus followers who turned a catastrophic end and brutal attempt at erasure into a heroic deed.

Paul's Problem

Before Paul had his insight that the God of Israel had favored Jesus (Gal 1:12, 15), it is quite clear from his own words that he "harassed God's new community" (Gal 1:13). We can only indirectly tease out what might have been the reason for this action.[2] Here is the relevant passage:

> Gal 1 [11]Let me make it clear, friends, the message I announced does not conform to human expectations. [12]I say this because it was not transmitted to me by anyone nor did anyone teach it to me. Rather, it came to me as an insight from God about Jesus as God's Anointed. [13]Surely you've heard of my own behavior as a practicing Jew, how aggressively I harassed God's new community, trying to wipe it out. [14]I went way beyond most of my contemporaries in my observance of Judaism, and became notably zealous about my ancestral traditions. [15]However, when the One, who designated me before I was born and commissioned me to be an envoy, surprising all human expectations, chose to make his son [16]known through me with the intent that I would proclaim God's world-transforming news to the nations ...

Paul describes to his Galatian audiences his former behavior as a practicing Jew. In his estimation he went beyond most of his contemporaries in the observance of Jewish traditions. Saying that he was "notably zealous" for his ancestral traditions marks him out as a Pharisee and comports with his remarks in Philippians 3:5–6. As a Pharisee Paul's concerns over purity matters would have had their basis in his understanding of the purity and integrity of the God of Israel. But why would such an excellent Pharisee, competitive and seeking an advantage before his God, be concerned with Jesus followers? Here the solution gets murky. We do know that he was familiar with these communities (probably Syrian). But what would they be doing to cause his energetic opposition? We know that Paul was aware of a memorial meal tradition (1 Cor 11:22ff.) that might have proven difficult for Paul to countenance. Such a meal tradition (as we shall see below) would be part of the ancient formal meal format and, as such, would include not only recollection of the hero but also prayers to the god. Paul's harassment of communities of Jesus believers may have come from the fact that some early Jesus communities (Syrian) were celebrating the death of Jesus as a hero and, in so doing, were invoking the God of Israel. From Paul's perspective such an association of God with a criminal who had been shamefully executed is tantamount to blasphemy. His concern for the integrity of God may well have fueled his attempts to harass these communities. Moreover, this concern for God's integrity cannot be removed from the political reality of the death of Jesus. The fact that Jesus was executed by Rome sent the message that Rome had won. Any community associating with such a criminal would risk the wrath of Rome. Pamela Eisenbaum, summarizing numerous Pauline scholars, has pointed out:

> For his followers to carry on in his name would no doubt
> have been threatening to those who did not wish to perturb
> the Romans further, as was the case for Jewish authorities, re-
> ligious and political, and for any Jews who had an interest in
> the status quo or at least tolerated Roman rule. (Eisenbaum,
> *Paul Was Not a Christian*, 146)

As a Pharisee, Paul would have accepted or at least tolerated the present political situation. The communities' remembrance of the death of Jesus was not simply blasphemous (linking the

One, pure God with a shamed criminal) but it was politically ill-advised and dangerous. Paul's action may have sprung from a desire to avoid a direct conflict with the dominating power of Rome. Brandon Scott deepens the point by noting:

> [For Paul] Jesus could not have been the Anointed because Rome crucified him. This means that Rome won and Jesus lost, which is the whole point of crucifixion. ... In Paul's "before" logic, Jesus' crucifixion means that claims made on his behalf are false. (Scott, *The Real Paul*, 24)

Before Paul's breakthrough insight the crucifixion to him was evidence of a life relocated to the debris of history.

Paul's Breakthrough Experience

Paul characterizes what happened to him as a prophetic experience. He uses traditional prophetic language to describe what he sees as a prophetic call ("when the One who designated me before I was born and commissioned me to be an envoy"). Paul never saw himself as a "convert" as some would say today. He never stopped being a Jew (see Rom 9:3), although he has moved beyond his Pharisaic self-understanding. Instead, he takes up the vision of the Jewish prophets in their call to the nations. It could be said that what had actually changed was Paul's vision of God.[3] Somehow his vision of God's integrity was transformed by seeing what God had done for Jesus. In accepting this shamed criminal the God of Israel had taken an outrageous step. God had accepted the impure, the socially damned and disadvantaged. Rome's sentence on Jesus was not the final word. From that changed understanding of God, Paul concludes that a new chapter of God's action has begun. Paul sees his task as announcing this vision. Because God had accepted this shamed nobody, Paul could understand that his mission was to go to those nations whom the Jews, generally speaking, regarded as morally inferior peoples and thus at a distinct religious disadvantage. Paul had undergone a paradigm shift in his understanding of God and the nations. Brandon Scott has put it this way:

> For him the answer to this problem is revealed in his *apocalypsis*/insight. God has acted in his son the crucified Anointed to save the nations, and Paul has been called to announce this good news to the nations. (Scott, *The Real Paul*, 75)

But this announcement to the nations stood in stark contrast to the prevailing gospel of Rome. God's acceptance of the crucified one as the Anointed signaled a radical change. The apocalyptic vision of Paul comes from a realization that the gospel of God stands in opposition to the dominating propaganda of Rome.

> This is the true opposition that drives Paul. The Anointed as son of God is the opposite of the emperor as son of god. For Paul the gospel of God implies freedom and life; the gospel of Rome implies slavery and death. (Scott, *The Real Paul*, 75–76)

Paul's insight into what God has done to Jesus sparks his re-interpretation of his fate.

The Death of Jesus in Paul

Because of the enormous amount of research on Paul's understanding of the death of Jesus, it is actually surprising to find out that when one counts the actual number of times Paul mentions the death of Jesus the percentage is quite low. This finding may be surprising on account of the centuries of Christian theological overlay on the authentic letters of Paul. Forty-six verses refer to the death of Jesus in authentic Pauline letters (46 verses out of 1475 vv.—3.1 percent).[4] Certainly the death of Jesus was important to Paul. But we must take off our Reformation glasses to perceive what the historical Paul was about when he mentioned or referred to the death of Jesus.

From the actual material in Paul we can say the following. *Jesus actually died.* This is a given for Paul. Paul takes pains to make sure this is the point in Philippians 2:8.

> And became trustfully obedient all the way to death
> Even to death by crucifixion.

Second, *Jesus was crucified* (e.g. 1 Cor 1:23). But there is nothing beyond the mere mention of crucifixion. The only exception seems to be 1 Corinthians 2:8, where the "rulers of this age crucified" Jesus. The mythic description points to a theological intent. While it does not directly identify those responsible, Paul knows it was a Roman execution, thereby the Roman officials would be included as "rulers of this age." First Thessalonians 2:15 would link the Judeans with the death of Jesus.

> For their fellow countrymen killed Jesus.

However, this verse is quite probably part of an insertion (1 Thess 2:13–16).[5]

Paul shows no awareness of any extensive narrative about the death of Jesus. He used traditions about the death of Jesus that already had been interpreted theologically. He continued this interpretive tradition, using the earlier images—for example, Jesus' death as that of a martyr (Rom 3:24–26); Jesus' death as the decisive turning point (Phil 2:6–11). The manner of the death of Jesus took on metaphoric and symbolic significance for Paul. Thus, for example, Paul utilized the shameful death of Jesus as a way to understand the new relationship the "nations"[b] enjoy with the God of Israel. Galatians 3:13–14 is a prime example of how Paul turned the social stigma of Jesus' death into an opening for those who were shamed in the eyes of the people of Israel, namely the subhuman nations. The nations' limited and failed condition—"cursed" in the eyes of the tradition and society—had been preempted by God's choice to join the disgraced victim.

> Gal 3 [13]God's Anointed freed us from the curse of subjection to the law, by becoming a curse for us, since it is written, "Anyone who is crucified is accursed." [14]This was done so that Abraham's blessing might come to the nations by belonging to the Anointed Jesus, and so that we might receive the promise of God's presence and power through putting our unconditional trust in God.

The social stigma of crucifixion underlies much of Paul's mentioning of the death of Jesus. Paul was aware of the social implications of a crucified cult figure. In fact, he played upon this in Galatians 3:1–14, 1 Corinthians 1:18–25, and Romans 5:6–8. He turned a social and political liability into a conduit of benefit and hope. God's solidarity with this social failure, misfit, and disgraced nobody turns the tables against the entire Roman system.[6] The death of Jesus becomes an identification point for those in the empire who yearn for genuine liberation from the devastating power of the imperial pyramid.[7]

---

b. In *The Authentic Letters of Paul* "nations" is used instead of the usual "gentiles" which is actually a transliteration of the Latin *gentes*, a translation of the Greek *ethnoi*.

Coda
Laments and the Refusal to Forget

It is a truism for many that history is written by the winners. The losers are discarded, brushed quickly off the stage of human events. Visit a museum and see the busts of those who pushed their way into public remembrance. Certainly, such was the case in the ancient agoras of Greece and Rome. The poor who fell dead in the streets were often swept into a nearby river, or a mass grave. Crucifixion went beyond this casual disposal of expendables. This state execution consigned victims not simply to death but to extinction, a *damnatio memoriae*. Social horror and stigma prevented any effort to bring the crucified to mind.

Yet we see that in the Jesus traditions there were some who not only remembered the words and deeds of Jesus, but struggled with his troubling death. Some in Syria began to turn matters around. Some women may have begun to sing laments, as women did in those days; some tied scriptural verses onto his death. Still others dared to remember his death in a memorial meal. In short, within twenty years of his death, some communities began to reimagine the fate of Jesus. They began to see with new ears.

The refusal to forget executed victims the establishment intended to liquidate from public memory occurred on numerous occasions in the twentieth century. In my classes I present two haunting songs that display this stubborn refusal to forget. I have found that neither of these victims is usually known by my students. By taking up these songs we can begin to reimagine the ways in which the first century Jesus believers raised their voices against the dominating powers that would silence the innocent.

The first is a song written by Alfred Hayes in 1930 and set to music by Earl Robinson in 1936. It centers on the aftermath of the execution of Joe Hill (Joseph Hillstrom) on 19 November 1915. Hill was a Swedish-American labor-activist and prolific songwriter for the Industrial Workers of the World (a.k.a. "Wobblies"). He was condemned to death over the killing of a grocery store owner and his son. The evening of the killings Hill had been treated for a gunshot wound. News of the gunshot wound led to his arrest and condemnation. His execution was carried out despite international pleas for mercy. A 2011 biography by William Adler reveals that Hill had indeed been shot by a rival suiter of a girl both men had known. Hill's sense of decorum kept him from using this as an alibi. The sentiment against labor organizers overrode any attempt for clemency.

The song does not go into the particulars of Hill's death except to say that the "copper bosses" were instrumental in his death. Hill appears in a postmortem dream to assure the listeners he "never died" and to continue to "organize." This visionary song became a fulcrum for further labor action and resistance.

I dreamed I saw Joe Hill last night
Alfred Hayes

I dreamed I saw Joe Hill last night,
Alive as you or me
Says I, "But Joe, you're ten years dead,"
"I never died," says he
"I never died," says he

"In Salt Lake, Joe," says I to him,
Him standing by my bed,
"They framed you on a murder charge,"
Says Joe, "But I ain't dead,"
Says Joe, "But I ain't dead."

"The copper bosses killed you, Joe,
They shot you, Joe," says I.
"Takes more than guns to kill a man,"
Says Joe, "I didn't die,"
Says Joe, "I didn't die."

And standing there as big as life
And smiling with his eyes
Joe says, "What they forgot to kill
Went on to organize,
Went on to organize."

"Joe Hill ain't dead," he says to me,
"Joe Hill ain't never died.

Where working men are out on strike
Joe Hill is at their side,
Joe Hill is at their side."
"From San Diego up to Maine,

In every mine and mill,
Where workers strike and organize,"
Says he, "You'll find Joe Hill,"
Says he, "You'll find Joe Hill."

I dreamed I saw Joe Hill last night,
Alive as you or me
Says I, "But Joe, you're ten years dead,"
"I never died," says he
"I never died," says he

> youtube.com/watch?v=f_yC4ffyGiw
> youtube.com/watch?v=n8Kxq9uFDes&feature=related
> youtube.com/watch?v=_f2J4ceCikI&feature=related

The second song comes from Peter Gabriel, who delivers a stirring song about the teacher and social activist Steven Biko. Biko was famous for his espousal of the rights of Black South Africans during the period of Apartheid. He wanted those he taught to become aware of their political situation: "The most potent weapon in the hands of the oppressor is the mind of the oppressed." He simply wanted his people to be treated as fellow human beings. "When you say 'Black is beautiful' you are saying, 'Man you are okay as you are, begin to look upon yourself as a human being.'" In the fall of 1977 Biko was arrested by the South African police and died in their custody. Despite the claim that he had killed himself by beating his head against a wall, the subsequent autopsy indicated that he was murdered.

Biko
Peter Gabriel

September '77
Port Elizabeth weather fine
It was business as usual
In police room 619
Oh Biko, Biko, because Biko
Oh Biko, Biko, because Biko

Yihla Moja, Yihla Moja
—The man is dead

When I try to sleep at night
I can only dream in red
The outside world is black and white
With only one colour dead
Oh Biko, Biko, because Biko
Oh Biko, Biko, because Biko
Yihla Moja, Yihla Moja
—The man is dead

You can blow out a candle
But you can't blow out a fire
Once the flames begin to catch
The wind will blow it higher
Oh Biko, Biko, because Biko

Oh Biko, Biko, because Biko
Yihla Moja, Yihla Moja
—The man is dead

And the eyes of the world are
watching now
watching now

youtube.com/watch?v=iLg-8Jxi5aE&feature=related
youtube.com/watch?v=luVpsM3YAgw

5

Pre-Pauline Traditions

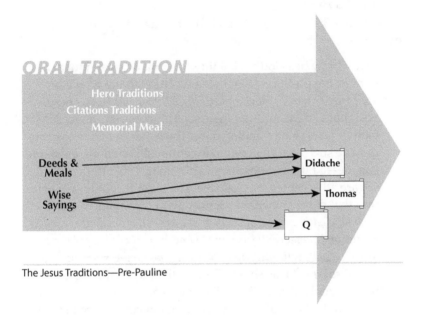

ORAL TRADITION

Hero Traditions
Citations Traditions
Memorial Meal

Deeds & Meals — Didache

Wise Sayings — Thomas

Q

The Jesus Traditions—Pre-Pauline

When we turn from the Sayings Gospel to the writings of Paul, we become acutely aware that we are in a different historical location. Paul joined a Hellenized form of the Jesus movement *that had already developed into a cult of God's Anointed.*[a] A quantum leap was made from the Jesus movements to the cult of God's Anointed. Jesus the itinerant sage had been transformed into a

---

a. The Greek word is *Christos,* often transliterated as "Christ." But that is not a translation. The Greek term refers to a Jewish title of honor and respect, rivaling the title given to Octavianus, namely, *Augustus* or the title *Caesar* to each emperor. *Christos* means that God has particularly anointed or selected the person.

divine figure whose death and resurrection the Hellenistic communities viewed as a saving event. While Bultmann's formula[1] that the proclaimer has become the proclaimed clearly summarizes this transition, it does little to assist us in determining how it occurred. The mythic language employed by the cult of God's Anointed reflects the social formation of a Hellenized Jewish-Gentile mix. The writings of Paul present us with most of the fragmentary evidence out of which the pre-Pauline situation can be constructed. In these fragments we can begin to appreciate the imaginative leap that was made to transform the catastrophe of Jesus' death into the final deed of a hero.

Death of a Hero

In Romans 3:21–26 we can pick up the use of such heroic language.

> [21]Only now has God's reliability been made clear, independent of the tradition from the law, although the whole of scripture offers evidence of it. [22]God's Reliability has now been made clear through the unconditional confidence in God of Jesus, God's anointed, for the benefit of all who come to have such confidence—no exceptions! [23]After all, everyone has messed up and obscures God's image. [24]At the same time, we are all accepted by God freely as a gift through the liberation that comes when we identify with the anointed Jesus, [25]*whom God presented publicly as the one who conciliates through his unconditional confidence in God at the cost of his life in order to show God's reliability by overlooking, by divine restraint, how we messed up.* [26]This shows God's reliability at this decisive time, namely, that God is reliable and approves the one who lives on the basis of Jesus' unconditional confidence in God. (Author's emphasis)

This passage is quite remarkable. The Greek of these verses is actually one long, convoluted sentence.[2] Modifier is piled upon modifier, phrase upon phrase. Within this twisting sentence scholars have detected an earlier tradition. The language differs from Paul's and comes from a pre-Pauline formulation (Rom 3:24–25 noted above in emphasis). This language presupposes a focus upon the death of Jesus. The sacrificial language of martyrdom underlies this material (*whom God presented publicly as the one who conciliates through his unconditional confidence in God at the cost of his life*).[b] Sam K. Williams argues that the basic image is that of a martyr proving his faithfulness to his cause by undergoing trial and death.[3] The *"unconditional confidence in God" (pistis)*[c] of Jesus in Romans 3:25 refers to the hero's endurance, while the *"conciliation"* refers to the effectiveness of the hero's death. David Seeley, in a slight contrast, would place the emphasis more upon the noble death of the martyr rather than on the sacrifice.[4] But *essentially Jesus has been cast metaphorically as one who nobly meets his death for a cause.* Pushing these insights further, Burton Mack sees the social implications for this language, arguing that Jesus' death was seen as a demonstration of Jesus' *pistis* (fidelity/loyalty/confidence) and that all who share such *pistis* were also accepted by God.[5] Jesus dies then for a new cause: for the community of God's justice. The Jewish concern for the justice of God is recast under the image of the noble one who dies for a cause. The story allows all to see how God acknowledges this event as an authentic manifestation of justice. The social experience of the Jesus people provides the basis for this interpretation of the death of Jesus. His death becomes the symbolic linchpin for a mixed association of Jews and Gentiles, enabling this community to bring forward the Jewish traditions without losing the Gentile insertion.

This transformation of the catastrophe of Jesus' crucifixion into a hero's death is not unique in the ancient world. The anonymous Jesus followers who constructed this transformation were drawing upon the cultural images and patterns of the noble death. The noble death was embedded in the cultural memory of the Greco-Roman world as a cultural pattern that gave meaning to the deaths of those who spent their lives for a cause. Roman and Greek heroes provided exemplars for that society. Indeed, the death of Socrates became a standard pattern to understand the fate of those who died for the Truth. Jews were in conversation with these cultural memes. They

---

b. To consider a martyr's death as a "sacrifice," as a means of "conciliation," is to engage in metaphorical thinking. The significance of the person's death is given in likening it to a sacrifice. A literal sacrifice is not meant.

c. The Greek *pistis* is often translated as "faith." However, readers mistakenly think that such a translation equates with propositional belief. The sense of *pistis* conveys a relational meaning. Hence, "fidelity, loyalty, and confidence" are dynamic English equivalents.

began using the pattern of the noble death to explain the tragic slaughter of innocent ones during the persecution of Antiochus Epiphanes IV (c. 215 BCE–164 BCE). We can see this already in 2 Maccabees where the execution of seven brothers, their mother, and an elderly priest are recounted. But the language of heroic death begins to sing in 4 Maccabees (probably contemporaneous with Paul).

In 4 Maccabees we have a speech honoring the martyrdom of the seven brothers, their mother and the elder Eleazar in order to exhort Jews listening to the speech to live a life of honor and even to die for a noble cause. Here are four salient passages (emphasis is mine):

> 4 Macc 16 [16]"My sons, noble is the contest to which you are called to bear witness for the nation. *Fight zealously for our ancestral law.* [17]For it would be shameful if, while an aged man endures such agonies for the sake of religion, you young men were to be terrified by tortures.
>
> [18]Remember that it is through God that you have had a share in the world and have enjoyed life, [19]and therefore you ought to endure any *suffering for the sake of God.* [20]*For his sake* also our father Abraham was zealous to sacrifice his son Isaac, the ancestor of our nation; and when Isaac saw his father's hand wielding a knife and descending upon him, he did not cower. [21]Daniel the righteous was thrown to the lions, and Hananiah, Azariah, and Mishael were hurled into the fiery furnace and endured it for the sake of God. [22]*You too must have the same faith in God* and not be grieved. [23]It is unreasonable for people who have religious knowledge not to withstand pain."

Here we see that there is a reason or cause for the martyrs' deaths. They die *for the law, for the sake of God.* Moreover, they are exhorted to have the same *faith or confidence in God* as earlier heroes.

> 4 Macc 17 [8]Indeed it would be proper to inscribe on their tomb these words as a reminder to the people of our nation: [9]"Here lie buried an aged priest and an aged woman and seven sons, because of the violence of the tyrant who wished to destroy the way of life of the Hebrews. [10]*They vindicated their nation,* looking to God and enduring torture even to death."

In this section we see that their death achieved a *vindication of their nation.*

4 Macc 17 [11]Truly *the contest in which they were engaged* was divine, [12]for on that day virtue gave the awards and tested them for their endurance. The prize was immortality in endless life. [13]Eleazar was the first contestant, the mother of the seven sons entered the competition, and the brothers contended. [14]The tyrant was the antagonist, and the world and the human race were the spectators. [15]Reverence for God was victor and gave the crown to its own athletes. [16]Who did not admire the athletes of the divine legislation? Who were not amazed?

Notice that the extended metaphor of an athletic contest now provides the significance of their suffering and death.

4 Macc 17 [17]The tyrant himself and all his council marveled at their endurance, [18]*because of which they now stand before the divine throne and live the life of eternal blessedness.* [19]*For Moses says, "All who are consecrated are under your hands."* [20]These, then, who have been *consecrated for the sake of God*, are honored, not only with this honor, but also by the fact that *because of them our enemies did not rule over our nation*, [21]the tyrant was punished, and the homeland purified—they *having become, as it were, a ransom for the sin of our nation.* [22]And *through the blood of those devout ones and their death as an atoning sacrifice, divine Providence preserved Israel that previously had been mistreated.*

In this final passage we see an example of midrash, where the quote from Deuteronomy 33:3 in verse 19 enables the imagination of the scene before the divine throne in verse 18. The writer not only recast the torture of the sons, mother, and elder as both an athletic contest and a sacrifice but envisioned the divine outcome of their glory. Further, the metaphor of sacrifice illuminates the tragedy of their death (*having become, as it were, a ransom for the sin of our nation* [v. 21b]; *through the blood of those devout ones and their death as an atoning sacrifice* [v. 22]).[6]

The language used in 4 Maccabees displays the same heroic language found in the pre-Pauline material. The martyrs fight and die for the *ancestral law, for the sake of God.* Their heroic act *vindicated their nation.* Their final act is metaphorically described as a *divine contest in which they were engaged, as it were, a ransom for the sin of our nation.* Their *bloody* deaths were seen as an *atoning sacrifice.* Those listening to this speech are exhorted to have the *same faith in God.* The tragic deaths of these Jews have been transmuted into cultural pattern of the noble one who goes in confidence towards death. The metaphors of contest and sacrifice come from the rich experience of public life.

Consider what the use of this heroic language has done to the understanding of the death of Jesus. Just as the writer of 4 Maccabees transposed the torture of Antiochus' victims by the metaphor of sacrifice for a noble cause, so too did those anonymous Jesus followers transfigure the shameful fate of Jesus. Roman crucifixion was designed to discredit and nullify a contrary life. *Roma victa!* Whoever raised a sandal against the Empire was destined to oblivion. To re-imagine the death of Jesus in terms of this heroic tradition represented a refusal to let Rome have the final word. Further, the use of the metaphor of sacrifice was quite strategic. For the act of sacrifice signaled to the ancient imagination a fundamental component in how the world works. Only the best item or animal was offered to the divine. Something of value was sacrificed in thanksgiving. In describing the fate of Jesus in sacrificial terms meant that this condemned nobody had inestimable meaning before God. They reframed the imperial liquidation of the one they had lost by discovering through their metaphorical transposition Jesus' *unconditional confidence in God at the cost of his life* (Rom 3:24). These unknown Jesus followers had used fragments of their tradition and experience to stand against the lethal force of Rome.

A Memorial Meal

Let us turn to the memorial meal celebrated by the early followers of Jesus. In addressing issues in Corinth Paul recounts the tradition of the memorial of Jesus' death.

> 1 Cor 11 [23]I received from the lord the same thing I passed on to you, that on the night when he was handed over, the lord Jesus took bread [24]and after he gave thanks he broke it and said, "This means my body broken for you. Do this to remember me." [25]And in the same way he took the wine cup after the meal and said, "This cup means the new covenant ratified by my blood. Whenever you drink this, do it to remember me." [26]So every time you eat this bread and drink this cup you are proclaiming the death of the lord until the day when he returns.

Dennis Smith[7] has demonstrated that the context for this material was that of a Greco-Roman memorial meal. The benediction over the food (v. 24) and the benediction over the wine (v. 25) indicate the two basic aspects of a formal banquet: the meal (*deipnon*) and the after-dinner drinking portion (*symposium*). Paul introduces the memorial tradition of Jesus' death with the formulaic phrase "I received from the lord the same thing I passed on to you." It is crucial to see that the bread symbolizes his body "broken for" the community, while the libation of wine conveys the "new covenant" effected through his bloody death. In each instance heroic language is invoked. Moreover, both benedictions are done "to remember" him. Verse 26 adds Paul's comment to the Corinthians that such a meal entails remembering Jesus' death. No mention is made of a resurrection. Additionally the prefatory remark "on the night when he was handed over" does not refer to any betrayal on the part of Judas; rather the passive voice indicates that the fate of Jesus was in the hands of God.[8] In other words, even from the beginning of this material, the language is mythic, not factual.

The tradition that Paul presents to the Corinthians reflects the pre-Pauline Jesus communities (probably in Syria). We already have seen that even before Paul the death of Jesus had begun to be transformed from a catastrophe into a heroic format. Both the benedictions use the heroic language that we have noted earlier in 4 Maccabees. But an added dimension appears in this passage. Heroic language is embedded in a memorial meal. The words serve to give a post mortem basis for the community of Jesus followers. The meal itself was an act of social memory and social construction. In elevating the crucifixion of Jesus to heroic status, the pre-Pauline community declares that their community emerges from and is energized by the significance of his death. It should be pointed out further that this evidence does not suggest that there was already in place a full-blown narrative about the death of Jesus. The memorial meal tells us more about the Syrian Jesus followers than it does about the last hours of Jesus' life. The language is not a historical, verbatim account of a last supper, but the commemorative tropes of the later community's transformation of the catastrophe of Jesus' death into the heroic deed of the Anointed (see cameo on "Memorial Meal and Lament," pp. 57–58).

In recognizing the social setting of this passage, Hal Taussig has pointed out that the libation of wine is fraught with political consequences. In the ancient meal tradition there would have been a libation to the emperor. That the libation was being made instead to remember someone who had been executed by the state would have signaled a remarkable stance of solidarity by this fledgling group.[9] Brigitte Kahl delineates the socio-political atmosphere surrounding such a formal meal.

> In a situation where everything is over-determined and colonized by civic religion and most of all imperial religion, nothing, not even Jewish law, Jewish identity, and the Jewish God can escape the omnipresent grip of the Roman empire and its idols. (Kahl, "Peter's Antiochene Apostasy," 31–32)

Brandon Scott, following Kahl's lead, underscores the serious implications of these memorial meals. In the face of imperial domination, the Jesus communities remembered someone damned by the state. Their meals were a response to the God who accepted the crucified. They acknowledged:

> God has called the nations from the worship of idols to the worship of the one true God in the name of the Anointed. (Scott, *The Real Paul*, 87)

A pre-Pauline Encomium

The anti-imperial stance can be seen also in Philippians 2:5–11.

> [5]I appeal to all of you to think in the same way that the Anointed Jesus did, [6]who
>
> although he was born in the image of God,
> did not regard "being like God"
> as something to use for his own advantage,
> [7]but rid himself of such vain pretension
> and accepted a servant's lot.
>
> Since he was born like all human beings
> and proved to belong to humankind,
> [8]he recognized his true status
> and became trustfully obedient all the way to death,
> even to death by crucifixion.
>
> [9]That is why God raised him higher than anyone
> and awarded him the title that is above all others,
> [10]so that on hearing the name "Jesus,"
> every knee should bend,

Memorial Meal and Lament

In the last few years New Testament scholars Ellen Aitkin, Kathleen Corley, and Angela Standhartinger have led the way in asking whether the ancient funeral practices of lament throw light upon the passion narrative tradition. Kathleen Corley has argued that some oral lamentation traditions about Jesus' death may have been transmitted by early Christian men and women. Corley contends that the cultural custom of visiting tombs on the third day after a burial, shared by women in Antiquity, gave rise to the formula "raised on the third day according to the Scriptures" (1 Cor 15:4). She, however, notes that the passion narrative of Mark does not indicate these traditions (such as antiphonal patterns or addresses to the dead). She envisions groups of poets (male and female) retelling the story of Jesus' passion and death. Dominic Crossan has argued that the gospel writers may have changed the prophetic lament into sequential written accounts.

But Standhartinger has gone beyond speculation in noticing that the memorial meal tradition in 1 Corinthians 11 echoes the performance language that can be found in various memorials to the deceased. Using ancient monuments and modern ethnic research Standhartinger points out that the memorial meal of 1 Corinthians 11 can be understood as a residue of dramatic memory, reflecting mortuary rites and laments:

> The words τοῦτο ποιεῖτε εἰς τὴν ἐμὴν ἀνάμνησιν (Do this in my memory) (1 Cor 11:24f) are well attested in various memorials to the deceased: "I (Aurelius Festus) donate and bequeath silver denarii to the village of the Rakeloi under the condition that they celebrate my memory ([ἐπὶ τῷ] τοῦτο ποιεῖν αὐτοὺς ἀνά[μ]νη[σ]ίν) (by this they remember me) within the neighborhood of Dradizane." (lectio difficilior, 5)

She argues that parallels in antiquity suggest that the presence of the deceased could constitute part of the experience of the meal. She has found in grave inscriptions and epitaphs scenes of reunion where the dead address passersby in the first person. For example:

> Alongside those which present the deceased with the words "This is the grave of ..." and those in which the bereaved

address the deceased with their own words, we have inscriptions dating back to the sixth century BCE in which the deceased speaks in the first person: "Greetings, passers-by! I, Antistates, son of Atarbus, lie here in death, having left my native land." ("Bringing Back to Life," 108)

Bread and wine shared with the deceased at funerary banquets became the connection point between the living and the dead. The meal remembering Jesus' death brings him back into their lives.

> Food and drink shared at funeral meals mediate symbolically between the realms of the living and the dead. Through their mouths and bodies, the lamenters were able to allow "the Risen One" to speak symbolic words through their voice and to perform symbolic acts through their bodies. In doing so, they would indeed have become 'actors in a divine drama.' The words "This is my body" spoken in the name of the dead and risen Jesus, might thus have originated at funerary meals in the context of dramatic retellings of Jesus' passion. (*lectio difficilior*, 15)

Standhartinger may well have hit upon the location where the narrative tradition of the death of Jesus begins to emerge and grow. There may well have been a dialectic between lament and citation traditions (see pp. 55, 62) out of which comes the passion narrative structure.

above the earth, on the earth, and under the earth,
[11]and every tongue declare: "Jesus the Anointed is lord!"
to the majestic honor of God, our great Benefactor.

Another example of a pre-Pauline "Anointed" cult is found is Philippians 2:6–11. Due to the non-Pauline language found in verses 6–11, the introductory remark of verse 5, and the concluding connection of verse 12 ("in light of this, my dear friends"), one can easily remove this material from the surrounding exhortatory remarks (vv. 5, 12–13).[10] Yet, although verses 6–11 can be isolated as pre-Pauline (vv. 10, 11 ["every knee should bend," "every tongue declare"] suggest liturgical actions) numerous debates have been launched over the source, background, structure, redaction, and meaning of the piece.

We must observe initially that this passage has long been read as reflecting what had come to be the orthodox version of the story of redemption: that the eternal Son of God descended from heaven, emptied himself of his divinity, and became incarnate in human flesh. In obedience to God's will he died on the cross to save us from our sin, was raised from the dead, and returned to his place at the right hand of God from where he will rule, world without end, his saving mission accomplished. The recent work of several scholars, taken together, has now cast this passage in a different light, that of a super-exalted affirmation of Jesus as God's Anointed without the coloration of later orthodox Christology.[11]

The poem does not give us much in the way of historical data. The debates surrounding the meaning of the poem all assume that some degree of myth-making has occurred. The poem does not give us any information regarding the actual death of Jesus, except for one point: Jesus dies through crucifixion. More recent analyses would point to a variety of backgrounds that try to locate this death within a larger sphere of meaning. Some scholars have argued that the Jewish Wisdom tradition (e.g., Prov 8–9) may well be the crucible for this material. Indeed, others have suggested more specifically that the suffering servant theme from Second Isaiah or that echoes of the vindication of the suffering righteous one (WisSol 2–5) may afford the basis for this poem.[12]

Often overlooked in searching for the imaginative realm of this poem is the propaganda surrounding the character of Alexander the Great. In Plutarch's *On the Fortune of Alexander* 1.8 (330D), Alexander is described as a conqueror quite distinct from all others. "He did not overrun Asia like a thief … nor did he consider it something to plunder. … Because he wanted to show that all things on earth were subject to one principle and one government, that all humans were one people, he conformed himself in such a way." Only Alexander's untimely death prevented this utopian vision from becoming a reality.

Three points can be made. First, there are telling linguistic similarities between the Philippian poem and Plutarch's treatment of Alexander. Second, one cannot overlook the historical background of Philippi. Originally named after the father of

Alexander the Great, the city was settled by Roman veterans of the Civil Wars and rebuilt in the splendors of Roman fashion. Third, this dream of a civilized society, brought about through the agency of a divine man, remained alive in the Roman propaganda machine.

This may well signal an important clue. The emperors exploited this lingering hope. The legendary drive of Alexander the Great, refined for the Imperial propaganda machine, may well be a foil to the image of Jesus in this poem.

Indeed, another line of analysis may actually throw light on the political dimensions of the poem. Several of the terms used in verses 6–8 echo the terminology found in the story of the creation and fall of Adam in Genesis 1 and 3 in the Greek translation of the Hebrew Bible (the Septuagint) that Paul knew and used. Adam, created in the image and likeness of God (Gen 1:26–27), succumbs to the "Serpent's seductive suggestion that, if he asserted himself, he would become equal to God" (Gen 3:5). The similarity of the language in Philippians 2:6–8 to the language in these Genesis passages points to another way of reading the poem: as contrasting the First and Second Adam—a contrast Paul explicitly draws in Romans 5:12–14, and in 1 Corinthians 15:21–23, 45–50. The structure of the passage together with its idiomatic, allusive, and celebrative (not literal) language indicate that its author did not intend to speak about the descent and ascent of a divine being, but about the exemplary earthly life of Jesus as a human being. God endorsed that exemplary life by super-exulting Jesus on high as the Second Adam, who represents the remedy for the failure of the First Adam. At the same time, this image of Jesus contrasts sharply with the one whose coins indicate one who would "be like god" as an exalted "son of God," namely the Emperor.[13] Brandon Scott is quite helpful on this point:

> The piece is not dealing with a cosmological pattern but represents a movement in status. God, as the Greek literally says, super-exults the crucified slave giving him God's own name, lord. But this very title is also an imperial title and the exaltation mocks the Roman imperial triumphs. (Scott, *The Real Paul*, 235)

In sum, Philippians 2:5–11 is another example of the pre-Pauline interpretations of the fate of Jesus. The poem extolls the one who chose to live within his humanity and to face crucifixion. His exultation contrasts sharply with the imperial propaganda machine. However, there is little concern for the actual events surrounding his death; instead a sheath of mythic meaning has been applied to his crucified death.

The Tradition of Scriptural Citation
Prophecy Historicized

> 1 Cor 15 ³I passed on to you as of paramount importance what I also had received:
>
> that the Anointed *died* to free us from the seductive power of corruption
>
> according to the scriptures,
>
> ⁴and that he was *buried*, and that he was raised "on the third day"
>
> according to the scriptures.

First Corinthians 15:3–4 furnishes another instance of the pre-Pauline traditions about the death of Jesus. Verse 3 presents a standard introductory formula of a messenger delivering what has been handed over to him (³I passed on to you as of paramount importance what I also had received). In this tradition Jewish scriptures are applied to gesture at the fate of Jesus. Besides 1 Corinthians 15:3, one can point to Mark 14:21, 49; Matthew 26:56; Luke 24:26–27; John 19:36; and Acts 2:22–36 as indications that the early communities were in the habit of using specific scriptural citations in an attempt to come to grips with the meaning of Jesus' death.[d] John Dominic Crossan's distinction becomes extremely helpful in reconstructing the historical activity. The early communities were not recalling the "facts" of the death of Jesus. They were about the business of making sense of it. It is not history remembered but prophecy historicized.

As some of Jesus' followers reflected on the events of the past, they asked themselves why these things had to happen. They became convinced that God had foreordained the events. They began looking for prophecies that would help them understand the social disgrace of the death of Jesus. The use of scriptural citations (Psalms [Pss 2:1,7; 16:8–11; 22:1, 18, 22; 69:21, 30; 110:1; 132:11] and Prophets [Amos 8:9; Isa 50:6, 7; Zech

---

d. We shall take this up again below in the section on Midrash. Pp. 68ff.

12:10]) became a shorthand way of dealing with the meaning of Jesus' death. Each citation was a creative connection by an anonymous member of the Jesus communities. The death of Jesus was so provocative that it called for a ransacking of the religious memories. In a fashion typical of first century Judaism the unknown followers returned to their basic repertoire: the Jewish Writings. We see a comparable activity at Qumran in the Hodayot (Thanksgiving Songs) and Pesharim (interpreted texts). The Psalms' staple rhythmic components furnish the themes of persecution (Pss 2:1–2; 22:1–8; 69:20–21) and vindication (Pss 2:7–8; 22:22–24; 69:30–33) for citation. However, it should be understood that there is not as yet a fully developed narrative such as we find later in Peter, Mark, Matthew, Luke, and John. An example of how much of later gospel narratives are indebted to the building blocks of scriptural citations can be found in Mark 14–15, where extensive citation, allusion, and characterization through scriptural reference abound.

We can add that this pre-Pauline material has certain features. The statements about the death of Christ (1 Cor 15:3–4a) are distinct from those about the resurrection/apparitions (1 Cor 15:5–8). Mack noted that the death statements deliver significance for the community whereas the resurrection/apparition statements refer to Jesus' fate.[14] The fragmentary pre-Pauline material already bears mythic features (1 Cor 15:3–4 presumes the entitling of Jesus as the *Anointed One* who dies "according to the writings"). Mack has shrewdly noted that, despite a multitude of scholars discerning the probable use of such scriptural citations, allusions, and themes, there is a decided reluctance on the part of many scholars to conclude that the passion narrative was a fictional composition.[15] What few have done is to see that the various scriptural citations and allusions emerging from the developing tradition were formatted into a basic narrative of the tale of the vindicated suffering one.[e]

So far we have seen a number of ways of interpreting the death of Jesus.

1. The Sayings Gospel does not make much of the death of Jesus. It has a different emphasis — words of life. This direction is maintained in the Gospel of Thomas.

---

e. See the next chapter.

2. In the pre-Pauline material we find the death of Jesus interpreted as the noble death of a martyr, who sacrifices himself for a cause.
3. In the pre-Pauline poem of Philippians 2 we can detect that the death of Jesus is interpreted in stark contrast to the imperial claims of the Emperor.
4. The citations of scripture, already in play before the composition of the narrative gospel, draw upon the themes of the vindication of a persecuted one as suggested in the Psalms and Prophets.

6

Memory and Midrash

The Locus of Memory in an Oral Culture

Before proceeding in our investigation of the death of Jesus we need to understand that the ancient world operates in an "out loud" or acoustical context. The first century was an oral society. The majority of the population was illiterate. Only 15 percent of the urban population could read, while around 5 percent were involved in the writing, reading, and production of manuscripts.[1] For anything to survive in such a culture it had to be remembered. But for something to be remembered it had to have some memorable pattern or format. This means that the worth and workings of memory are essential, for, without some scheme, some memory device, there is no survival of the meaning. The silent fragments that we have investigated so far appear to us in a printed text, but that was surely not their original context. They can be understood more accurately as memory traces whose texture may give us some clues as to how they were remembered as well as what was remembered.

The Invention of Memory

Mary Carruthers, a recognized expert on the subject of ancient memory, underscores the rhetorical reality of ancient memory in an oral society. In her two books[2] Carruthers has pointed the way to understanding ancient memory as an active craft. While appreciative of the contributions of Frances Yates to the study of memory,[3] Carruthers differs with Yates's assessment of memory. For Yates the art of memory was to repeat previously stored material. Memory has a static quality despite its fascinating, if not preposterous, constructions. Carruthers counters by arguing:

The goal of rhetorical mnemotechnical craft was not to give students a prodigious memory for all the information they might be asked to repeat in an examination, but to give an orator the means and wherewithal to invent his material, both beforehand and—crucially—on the spot. Memoria is most usefully thought of as a compositional art. (Carruthers, *The Craft of Thought*, 9)

Carruthers places the creative act of memory within the domain of ancient rhetoric, not psychology. In effect, memory for her is implicitly social, embedded in the discourse of the day. The act of memory starts with rhetorical *inventio*.[a] This means that memory is not what we moderns usually consider it to be. It is not a reiteration or a re-presentation. Instead, *it is a crafting of images as well as a construction of a place for the images to inhabit. Inventio* means both the construction of something new (the memory-store or locus) and the storage of what is remembered.[4] For Carruthers then *memoria* is a locational memory. Further, *the shape or foundation of a composition must be thought of as a place-where-one-invents*.[5]

Carruthers envisions the ancient understanding of memory as a "machine." She is not talking about some sort of artificial intelligence. Rather, she takes a cue from the ancient notion of *machina* (a device of builders). Just as a *machine* helps lift and move things, so does the "machine" of memory. What does the machine of memory build? Memory is the way in which the ancients think. Thinking is like constructing a building or a column. The act of memory is the work of invention. The person who would deliver a speech or tell a story first invents, that is, creates a structure, and provides thereby a place for the inventory of images and things about which he or she wants to speak.

There is also the matter of forgetting. Carruthers quite clearly has argued that forgetting is not erasure. Rather, forget-

---

a. The *inventio* is the starting point of the construction of an ancient speech. The author began by imagining his audience, the overall situation, the issues to be dealt with, the objections, the responses to the objections. The rhetor would set all of his construction within an overall format. Each element would have a place and sound connection with everything else. In fact, the ancient orators even had physical locations in which they imagined the various portions of their speeches. By recalling these locations, they could summon up the various parts of the speech or story. It was crucial that a *locus* or *topos* was found to contain the particular parts.

ting is essentially a displacement.[6] Within the oral competition of the ancient world, there was a struggle for acoustic space. This also included memory space, especially the location of public memories. When forgetting occurs it comes about through a displacement or trans-lation of images. A better pattern has been invented to locate and order the images.[b]

This superstructure provides memory with a place/location. Often we call this superstructure or memory location by another name: a commonplace. This term suggests a compendium where things are shared and stored. It also can mean a public memory. The Vietnam Memorial in Washington DC, is a modern example of the construction of a "commonplace" where memories can be located and where future memory construction is "authorized" by the location itself.[7] Hadrian's Column and the Arch of Titus are ancient examples of commonplaces.[8] Jewish midrash is a literary example of creating a commonplace. One can construct a midrashic tale in which to locate and re-member various scriptural lines.

Finally, in contrast to the modern assumptions about ancient memory, ancient memory was heuristic not simply mimetic. The work of memory was not to re-present, not to reduplicate but to construct, to provide a place for images. Of course this contrasts greatly with the assumptions of many modern biblical scholars who think in terms of print. They look at the passion narratives as documents, as recording (or re-presenting) what was essentially "the facts." While most would distinguish between an editorial hand and the original report or witness, they assume that the nature of the text is that of documentary. Indeed, the modern familiarity with both the photograph and the phonograph (where sight and sound are re-presented) has contributed to this sense that the evidence has a documentary nature to it.

The modern distinction between fact and fiction, between memory as reiteration and an unreal imagination, was not an ancient habit of thought. The very texture of the evidence points

---

b. This displacement effect can help us see why the Sayings Gospel (Q) has disappeared. Both Matthew and Luke have provided a better "memory space" for the sayings collection of Q. Narrative is a stronger memory space than a sayings collection, which is why Mark survives in the canon and Thomas does not. It has nothing to do with the later categories of heresy and orthodoxy.

in a different direction. We have already noted the distinction between "prophecy historicized versus history remembered." Within that opposition the scholarly battle lines have been very much formed. One side begs the question, assuming that a "kernel" of the passion narrative was there as history from the beginning, while the other side would make the case that Mark has spun an imposing fiction. Are the gospel writers delivering what happened to their listeners? Or have the writers taken earlier prophetic lines to weave a tale? Are the passion stories fact or fiction? Of course, the critical response has not always been so stark. Many scholars would have it both ways at once by concluding that there is a mixture of report and editorial revision.

The long-standing assumption that there must have been some primitive passion narrative at the very outset of the Jesus Movement becomes hard pressed when faced with the evidence in the Sayings Gospel Q as well as in Paul's letters. Rather, it would seem that the evidence for a passion narrative comes somewhat later with either an early version of the Gospel of Peter (55–65 CE)[9] or the Gospel of Mark (70+ CE).

We can move the critical conversation forward by asking a different question: Does the evidence display any clues to some sort of memory scheme? Indeed, in contemplating the use of a memory scheme, we must further wonder about the "invention" of that scheme by asking how the ancient writers crafted their material. What is the texture of the evidence at hand? Were imaginative acts providing some sort of "location" to the fate of Jesus? The Q material locates the death of Jesus within the familiar typology of the deaths of Jewish prophets (Luke 11:49–51). The pre-Pauline understanding of the death of Jesus locates the fate of Jesus within the orbit of heroic Jewish martyrs.

Carruthers' work lets us see that for the composers of the death tradition it was not simply a matter of recalling (re-presenting) the death of Jesus but rather it was a searching effort to find a location in which they could perform the craft of memory. For those who would remember, the basic task would have been to "invent" a *locus* for the death of Jesus. It was not a matter of simply relating the facts. Instead it was a matter of invention and inventory. Specifically this means that modern investigators should not look immediately for "the facts," for a simple representation of what happened. One should look, rather, for how the memory has been crafted and structured.

One can then see what has been enfolded in that memory structure. It would only be after this assessment that one could begin to determine indirectly at best what are the "facts of the case."

Returning to our earlier observations about the Sayings Gospel's version of the fate of Jesus, we noted that the writer of the Sayings Gospel placed the death of Jesus within the typological structure of the deaths of Jewish prophets (Luke 11:49–51). This does not necessarily lend itself to an extensive elaboration. Indeed, the focus of the Sayings Gospel Q lies elsewhere. The teachings and sayings of Jesus seem to carry the tradition forward.

The pre-Pauline material locates the death of Jesus within the commonplace orbit of the heroic martyrs of Hellenistic Judaism. Indeed, there is even evidence of a memorial meal celebrating the death of a hero. We have also seen that another tradition had already begun to apply verses from the Jewish tradition to provide some meaning to Jesus' fate. Paul takes over these traditions, while at the same time translating the fate of Jesus into a more imperial location. Yet for Paul the story of the vindication of Jesus does not focus upon the extended story pattern found in the later gospel traditions.

Midrash—The Scribal Composition

So far in our investigation we have seen no evidence for a full-scale narrative structure detailing the fate of Jesus. We should also note that an examination of the individual episodes that make up the extended passion narratives would give the critical reader the impression that these are not the types of stories that lend themselves to oral repetition. They make little sense as isolated anecdotes. Instead they gain their meaning only as part of a longer, connected narrative. Unlike the body of the narrative gospels, which are made up of discrete anecdotal scenes, the passion narrative appears as an extended, sequential composition from the beginning. It betrays its origins as a midrash, that is, a scribal composition prepared by those who were "searching the scriptures" for any clues about why Jesus of Nazareth met his fate. Scribes attempted through midrash "to penetrate into the spirit of the text, to examine the text from all sides, to derive interpretations not immediately obvious, to illustrate the future by appealing to the past."[10]

Midrash can be best described as a weaving of scriptural verse or verses into a narrative composition. The Jewish scribal tradition found a way of incorporating the depths of human experiences in an ever-developing religious story; a way of thinking mythically about dimensions of reality for which ordinary language was no longer appropriate. It was the Jewish way of saying that everything to be venerated in the present must somehow be connected with the sacred past by reworking an ancient theme in a new context. Midrash arose from the conviction that in the ever-developing Jewish tradition there were no closed chapters, no claim to some frozen infallibility. Jewish writers thought mythically as they plumbed dimensions of reality for which the usual language of time and space were inadequate. Midrash provided a means of collecting interpretations of the sacred writings and a method of renewing the sacred tradition. Tradition thus continued to grow as the enduring expression of the dead to which the living would add their chapter. The momentum and meaning of midrash fueled this growth.

Midrash can be differentiated into two ways of interpreting Torah: the midrash on Law (Halakah) and the midrash on events (Haggadah).[11] Halakah refers to the stories woven to interpret Jewish Law, while Haggadah relates experience to the sacred events of the tradition.[c]

Once we grasp that the function of midrash was to deliver meaning by weaving scriptural traditions, we gain a way into understanding the evidence of the passion materials. The first question should not be, did it happen? but, what caused midrashic activity? What generated further midrashic tradition? What happened in that life situation or historical moment that encouraged the tradition of midrash to embrace and interpret it? We are not leaving the historical realm but are trying to locate the historical situation out of which the midrash arises. The text is not a simple representation of the facts but an imaginative effort to construct meaning for a historical community.

Carruther's understanding of ancient memory technique combined with the Jewish tradition of midrash better positions us to consider the evidence of the passion materials. What little was mentioned of the death of Jesus in the earliest layers of

---

c. The passion narratives would fall under the definition of Haggadah.

70 Inventing the Passion

the material evidence had a surrounding frame. The Q Gospel made allusions to the death traditions of the prophets. The pre-Pauline material from Syrian communities draws on the contemporary heroic traditions. It would not be surprising then to discover that the more extensive narrative material also comes out of a meaningful frame. The work of Carruthers prepares us for the authorship of material that has an interpretive frame or locus. The midrashic tradition allows us to see that these narratives are constructed from the Jewish scriptural tradition. It would be inappropriate to ask immediately of the evidence, did it happen? For that would re-suppose a modern assumption of representational reporting. Rather, our task is to seek out indications of structure and composition. Do we see, for instance, scriptural citations used to ignite a scene? Can we detect an overall structure that puts earlier or isolated pieces into a more coherent frame? Only after answering these questions can we begin to ask what were the historical concerns that called for such a construction.

Finding the Imaginative Place
The Contribution of George Nickelsburg

Before turning to the passion materials of the gospels, George Nickelsburg's groundbreaking volume *Resurrection, Immortality and Eternal Life in Intertestamental Judaism* must be acknowledged. He presented a detailed analysis of intertestamental texts from Daniel to the Qumran Scrolls. In coming to grips with this wide-ranging material Nickelsburg wisely recognized the texture of the evidence, for the very format of the material provided essential clues to the meaning and intent of the writing. Nickelsburg noted the various components to each text as well as the overarching structure that provided the narrative spine to this material. In chapters 2 and 3 of his book he examined the traditions that led to the composition of this overarching structure: *The Tale of the Persecution and Vindication of the Innocent One.*[d] While the components of the story format

---

d. In this book we shall refer to the Tale of the Persecution and Vindication of the Innocent One as the "Tale of the Suffering Innocent One." This is not done to reduce the meaning of the memory location and structure; rather, it simplifies our repeated references to it.

were anticipated in the story of Joseph and his brothers (Gen 37ff.), a wisdom tradition was evidently developing about the fate of a wise figure. In the Book of Esther (late second or early first century BCE), the story of Susanna, and the episodes in Daniel 3 and 6 (second century BCE), Nickelsburg detected a didactic wisdom. Moreover, the texts of Wisdom of Solomon 2, 4–5 (150 BCE–70 CE), 2 Maccabees 7 (mid to second century BCE), and 3 Maccabees (end of first century BCE) (with some influence from Isaiah 52–53) represent the full manifestations of the tale's architecture.

The overarching story pattern detected by Nickelsburg can be summarized as follows:

> The actions and claims of a just person provoke his opponents to conspire against him. This leads to an accusation, trial, condemnation, and ordeal. In some instances this results in his shameful death. The hero of the story reacts characteristically, expressing his innocence, frustration, or trust in prayer, while there are also various reactions to his fate by characters in the tale. Either at the brink of death or in death itself the innocent one is rescued and vindicated. This vindication entails the exaltation and acclamation of the hero as well as the reaction and punishment of his opponents.

Nickelsburg actually characterized the various components of this tale.

a **Reason** given for the situation
a **Conspiracy** is formed against the Innocent One
an **Accusation**
a **Trial**
Helpers who are in sympathy with the Innocent One
the innocent makes a **Choice**
which occasions the **Condemnation** and **Ordeal**
a **Protest**
an expression of **Trust** by the innocent
Reaction by others occurs
a **Rescue**
an **Exaltation**
followed by more **Reactions**, and **Acclamation**
Vindication of the innocent
Punishment and **Confession** by those who opposed the
    Innocent One[12]

This story pattern arose in response to the issues of persecution suffered under Antiochus Epiphanes IV (d. 164 BCE), the Seleucid monarch, who oppressed Jews for maintaining their customs and traditions in the face of his attempts to bring the benefits of Hellenization to Israel. Because pious Jews, in keeping their covenantal responsibilities, were persecuted and executed without any apparent relief from God, enormous theological questions emerged. Where was God for those who were faithful to his covenant, to the traditions of Israel? How could God be called just if the faithful went to their death unaided? The tale of the Suffering Innocent One took these questions seriously and sought to provide a response. Working out of the words of Isaiah 52–53 (the suffering servant) the scribes constructed a creative narrative form, written out of the conviction that the God of Israel ultimately vindicates the faithful ones.

Critical for our investigation is this: The format of the tale of the Suffering Innocent One easily reminds us of the gospel passion narratives. Many would say that this brief description sums up what we usually call the death story of Jesus. Yet, this overarching composition came into existence approximately two centuries before the death of Jesus. The story pattern came into existence to make sense of the slaughter of Jews during the persecution of Antiochus Epiphanes IV. A constructed story dealt with the harsh reality of torture and death. Fellow Jews were attempting to discover meaning in desperate conditions. The composition of this story provides an imaginative space (*locus/topos*) for a response to this persecution. Moreover, the lines from Isaiah 52–53 became the basis for scribes to weave a creative response. They wove a midrash and the fundamental pattern of this story offers subsequent tellers of the story a framework in which to respond to similar situations. As Carruthers notes, the compositional framework "authorizes" further story-telling.[13] Finally, we must not overlook the fact that this basic story pattern is a *fiction*, which arises from historical concerns and crises. The scribal response was to construct a story that affirmed a vision of trust in the God of Israel who delivers the innocent—particularly in the face of harsh circumstances.

Two Examples of
New Testament Midrash

Peter's speech in Acts

Peter's speech to the people in Jerusalem on the feast of Pentecost is the first of many speeches constructed by the author of Luke-Acts.[a] In the narrative of Acts the speech seeks to provoke repentance from Peter's audience. The scriptural verses from Psalms 16, 132, and 110 provide the basis for the speech's superstructure and envisioning of the post-mortem condition of Jesus, as a midrashic construction of these verses.

Acts 2:22–36

[22]My fellow Israelites, listen to what I have to say.
There was Jesus the Nazorean, a man whom God brought to your attention by performing powerful mighty deeds, wonders and signs through him in your very midst. Of these things you are well aware.
[23]You have killed Jesus, nailed up by wicked hands, He was betrayed—but this was in accordance with God's prior knowledge and fixed plan! [24]**God cut loose Hades' dreadful cords** and brought Jesus back to life, **because death could not maintain its grip on him.**
[25]With reference to Jesus, David says: "I foresee that the Lord was always with me; because he is at my right side I shall not be perturbed. [26]Therefore my heart has been happy and my tongue full of joy. Indeed my flesh will live in hope, [27]**for you will not let my soul languish in Hades, nor will you allow your sacred one to experience decay**. [28]You have shown me the paths of life; your presence will fill me with gladness." [Ps 16:8–11]
[29]Brothers and sisters, if I may be candid with you about the patriarch David, he is dead and buried. His tomb remains in our midst today. [30]Since, then, he was a prophet and knew that God had solemnly "vowed to him" that "one of his descendants would sit upon his throne," [Ps 132:11] [31]David spoke with foreknowledge **about the resurrection of the**

---

a. See Smith and Tyson, *Acts and Christian Beginnings*, 38–46. The midrash is actually a *pesiqta*, that is, a sermon or exhortation written to bring themes of past into the present.

Messiah when he said, "He was neither left to languish in Hades, nor did his flesh face destruction."

[32]Accordingly, God brought this Jesus back to life. To that fact we can testify. [33]Therefore, after he **had been exalted to God's right hand** and had received from the father the promised Holy Spirit, he poured it out in your sight and hearing. [34]David did not ascend into the heavens, but he does say, "The Lord says to my Lord, '**Take a seat at my right** [35]until I make your enemies a resting place for your feet.'" [Ps 110:1] [36]The entire nation of Israel must recognize beyond any doubt that God has made him both sovereign and Messiah, this Jesus whom you crucified.

The opening remarks about "Jesus the Nazorean" reflect and sum up the activity of Jesus that informs the point of view of the Gospel of Luke. Peter then turns to his audience and accuses them of killing Jesus. Although the phrase "wicked hands" may well refer to the Romans,[b] the onus of guilt is placed upon the Jewish people, a theme very much a construction of the writer. Even the betrayal is mentioned but, as in 1 Corinthians 11:23, it is a matter of divine will (v.23). Verse 24 has been constructed out of Psalm 16:8–11. Significantly the personal pronouns in the actual psalm have been changed from second person singular to third person singular to accommodate the reference switch from David to Jesus. The very terms of the psalm bring Jesus back to life. The speaker makes it clear that David is not the primary reference in the psalms cited (vv. 29–31). Jesus' enthronement is constructed out of Psalms 132 and 110.

This passage exemplifies how a speech can be woven out of scriptural material. It provides little information regarding the actual death story of Jesus. In fact, it has already undergone a theological makeover. Although the Romans executed Jesus, the blame is laid upon the listening audience of Jews. A vision of enthronement and sovereignty emerges from this creative collage. Modern readers would tend to reduce this construction

---

b. The death of Jesus was the result of Roman crucifixion. One cannot avoid considering the supercessionism inherent in the Acts narrative. Sadly, this theological fiction has become a tragic fundament in the history of Jewish-Christian relations.

as a "mythic" or fictional fabrication. What would be lost in this reductive characterization is the creative weaving of scripture into vision. Precisely through this construction the ancient writer communicated meaning. That it was a second-century invention of the author of Acts is a further matter of investigation and outside the scope of this study.

Mark 13 "The Little Apocalypse"

The thirteenth chapter of Mark presents a remarkable midrashic composition of an apocalyptic exhortation. The situation is set upon the Mount of Olives with the disciples asking Jesus, "When will these things happen?" The passage provides a series of three apocalyptic scenarios followed by three exhortations to the Markan community. The first scenario (vv. 5–8) tells of wars, the rumors of wars, earthquakes, and famines. This is followed by an exhortation to endure in the face of possible persecution, trials, and ordeals (vv. 9–13). The second scenario (vv. 14–20) speaks of the "devastating desecration" (taken from Daniel 9:27) as well as the trauma of "those days." We can see that the language of verse 24 utilizes Joel 2:10 and Isaiah 13:10; verse 25 that of Isaiah 34:4; v. 26 Dan 7:13; v. 27 uses Deut 30:3–4; Zech 2:10. Advice follows (vv. 21–23), urging the listeners not to be taken in by phony prophets and messiahs. A third vision (vv. 24–27) of the coming of the Human One is followed by the example of the "fig tree" (vv. 28–32) and a final exhortation to the Markan community to stay alert (vv. 33–37). The entire chapter displays the texture of a skillful composition. With a setting established, three exhortations to the Markan community are joined to apocalyptic visions. The writer of Mark used various apocalyptic images that speak to the experience and concerns of the late first-century community. The entire scenario provides encouragement to those who see themselves as the final generation.

7

The Markan Passion Narrative

We now turn to the question of the earliest passion narrative within the canonical New Testament. In each of the four canonical gospels there is a passion narrative. But upon examination of the extended passion narratives, the individual episodes are not the types of stories that lend themselves to oral repetition: they make little sense as isolated anecdotes; rather, they gain meaning only as part of a longer, connected narrative. The passion narrative was not made up of discrete anecdotal "scenes" strung together, but was an extended, sequential composition from the beginning. It betrays its origins as a scribal composition prepared for those who were "searching the scriptures" for clues about why Jesus was crucified. All five surviving versions of the passion narrative (including the non-canonical Peter) exhibit a single, relatively coherent narrative. This suggests that all of those versions are derived from one source, which may be one of the five surviving accounts, or a hypothetical source no longer extant. In either case we are dependent on a single source for all our data.[1] Here are the basic structural agreements:

Structure of the Passion Narrative

Conspiracy against Jesus	Mark 14:1–2; Matt 26:1–5; Luke 22:1–2
The Anointing	Mark 14:3–9; Matt 26:6–13; Luke 7:36–39; John 12:1–8
Judas' Betrayal	Mark 14:10–11, 43–52; Matt 26:14–16; 26:47–56; Luke 22:3–6; 22:47–53
Last Supper	Mark 14:12–26; Matt 26:17–30; Luke 22:7–23, 39; John 13:1–18:1

Peter's Denial	Mark 14:27–31; Matt 26:31–35; Luke 22:31–34
Gethsemane	Mark 14:32–42; Matt 26:36–46; Luke 22:39–46; John 18:1; 12:27; 18:11b
Arrest	Mark 14:43–52; Matt 26:47–56; Luke 22:47–53; John 18:1–11
Trial before Council	Mark 14:53–72; Matt 26: 57–75; 27:1; Luke 22:54–62; John 18:12–13, 15a, 18, 25–27
Trial before Pilate	Mark 15:1–15; Matt 27:2–26; Luke 23:1–25; John 18:28–40; Pet 2:5; 11:4
Mocking and Crucifixion	Mark 15:16–41; Matt 27:27–56; Luke 23:26–49; John 19:1–37; Pet 3:1–5:6; 8:1b
Burial	Mark 15:42–47; Matt 27:57–61; Luke 23:50–56; John 19:38–42; Pet 2:1–2; 6:3a, 4

We begin with the Gospel of Mark because a majority of New Testament scholars regard this gospel as being the first gospel among the canonical gospels. Matthew, Luke, and John depend upon Mark for their basic narrative backbone.[a]

Many scholars have observed that the Gospel of Mark consisted of a passion narrative with an elaborate preface of stories and sayings.[2] Indeed, most have assumed some "kernel" of history underlies the passion material. Rudolf Bultmann advanced the argument by proposing that the proclamation (*kerygma*) of Christ's death and resurrection was the earliest account of the passion. The development from the meager proclamation to the full-blown passion narrative was assumed as a straight-line development. Much research following Bultmann attempted to fill in this trajectory.[3] However, an irony lingers in the claim that the proclamation constituted the initial historical level. As we have seen, the kerygmatic proclamation was not a historical description but from the outset a mythic formulation. To speak of the death of "Christ," that is, "God's Anointed one" as well

---

a. In the illustration we can see that Matthew and Luke are dependent on Mark. Many scholars now think that John also knows Mark. It may be that an earlier of version of John called the Signs Gospel is dependent on Mark or that the later version of John is more directly dependent on Mark. In any event, one can see that Mark becomes the basis for the subsequent narratives.

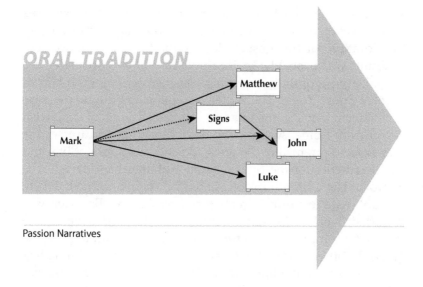

ORAL TRADITION

Mark → Matthew

Mark → Signs

Mark → John

Mark → Luke

Passion Narratives

as to say that Jesus has been "raised" moves out of the realm of history. For both the title given to Jesus and the description of his fate reflect subsequent interpretation of the post-mortem period.[4] Upon examination scholars clearly assumed that there was some basic historical report from the outset. Ironically, even if the proclamation of Jesus' death contains a "kernel" of a historical report, that kernel would only be that he was crucified. There is no information beyond that, nothing suggesting the extended narrative of Mark. More importantly, what scholarship did not address was *how* the ancient imagination dealt with matters of meaning and consequence. The ancients did not intend to provide historical proof for the theological arguments of later generations. As we shall see, by paying attention to the texture of the text, we discern how and what these passion narratives were communicating.[b]

First, some basic observations about the Gospel of Mark. The Gospel of Mark comes most probably from a "post-war" setting.[5] Written in the seismic aftermath of the First Jewish

---

b. The most obvious uncritical reading of the passion material is that of assuming an eye-witness account. However, that position has been long ago discredited. It assumes that the gospels were simply historical reports and overlooks the clues to a much more nuanced reading of the evidence, yet a reading more attune to the way in which the ancients imagined and constructed meaning.

War (66–72 CE) this gospel addresses a community who see themselves as the last generation before the final end of things.[6] The location for this gospel, despite the traditional placement in Rome, was probably Antioch in Syria.[7] This gospel attempts to make sense of the aftermath of the disastrous Jewish War of revolt against Rome. The writer is at pains to critique the false messianism that accompanied and triggered much of the Jewish revolt from Rome. At the same time, this gospel addresses the distress and anguish of the Jews, the enormous loss of life, and the destruction of the central symbol of ancient Judaism—the Temple. The community of Mark saw their imminent future fraught with genuine threat. Just as John the Baptizer was "handed over" (1:14) and as Jesus was "handed over," (9:31) so too the community saw themselves facing a similar prospect (13:9). In other words, the Gospel of Mark was no simple historical report on the life of Jesus. Rather, the story of Jesus was told to make sense of the lives of a community working out of the catastrophic fall of Jerusalem (70 CE).[8]

Josephus indicates the trauma of the final days of the battle for Jerusalem. He focuses upon those in Jerusalem who would flee the devastating siege and the internecine warfare among the various Jewish factions (*Jewish War* 5, 449–451):

> 449 The severity of the famine made them bold in going out; so nothing remained but that, when they were concealed from the robbers, they should be taken by the enemy; and when they were going to be taken, they were forced to defend themselves for fear of being punished: as after they had fought, they thought it too late to make any supplications for mercy: so they were first whipped, and then tormented with all sorts of tortures before they died, and were then crucified before the wall of the city.

> 450 This miserable procedure made Titus greatly to pity them, while they caught every day five hundred Jews; nay, some days they caught more; yet it did not appear to be safe for him to let those who were taken by force go their way; and to set a guard over so many he saw would be to make such as guarded them useless to him. The main reason why he did not forbid that cruelty was this, that he hoped the Jews might, perhaps, yield at that sight, out of fear lest they might themselves afterward be liable to the same cruel treatment.

451 So the soldiers, out of the wrath and hatred they bore the Jews, nailed those they caught, one after one way, and another after another, to the crosses, by way of jest; when their number was so great, that room was lacking for the crosses, and crosses lacking for the bodies.

Crucified victims surrounded the fated city. Crucifixion and the fall of the Temple preceded the Markan construction. Those traumatic echoes would reverberate throughout the region. Such were the imaginative acoustics for the composition of Mark.

If we then reread the passion narrative in Mark with such historical soundings in mind, we can consider how these Jesus followers would begin to make sense of these upheavals. The apocalyptic chapter of Mark 13 makes complete sense when read from this experience of disaster. Such a midrashic collage of warning and encouragement would be an expected response to the situation.

But why did the narrative of the suffering and death of Jesus become part of this response? Again, we are not assuming that the gospel was written to give later generations the facts of Jesus' life. We are trying to detect how the texture of the evidence gives us a clue to the way in which meaning was created by the Markan author.

Thus, as others have noticed, the writer very much treats his material in midrashic fashion. There are scriptural antecedents to the narrative, especially to the Psalms:

14:18	Betrayal by friends	Ps 41:9
14:34	Sadness and anguish	Pss 42:6, 11; 43:5
15:24	Clothes divided	Ps 22:18
15:29	Taunts of passersby	Pss 22:7; 109:25
15:34	Abandonment declared	Ps 22:1
15:36	Sour wine to drink	Ps 69:21

Beyond references there are thematic allusions reflecting the language of the Psalms:

14:1	Conspiracy to kill	Pss 31:4; 35:4; 38:12; 71:10
14:56–57, 59	False witnesses	Pss 27:1; 35:11; 109:2
14:61; 15:5	Silence before accusers	Pss 38:14–16; 39:9
15:20, 29	Mocking	Pss 22:7; 31:11; 35:19–25; 69:20; 109:25

Lastly, the overarching motif of persecution by enemies instantiated throughout the passion narrative echoes the tradition found in:

Ps 22:7, 12–13, 16–18
Ps 27:2–3
Ps 31:8, 11–13, 15
Ps 34:17, 20–22
Ps 35
Ps 38:12, 19

In sum, the writer of Mark clearly was drawing on the sources of his tradition. However, these various citations of the Psalms are not isolated elements in the continuing narrative. The Markan narrative has gone beyond the citation tradition, noted earlier in the pre-Pauline material. What we find in Mark is a connected narrative. The use of Jewish scripture would indicate that the writer engages in midrash. Particular lines from the sacred writings are used to construct a narrative. The question for us is: does this narrative display a particular arrangement? What did the author intend by structuring the material in this way? What clues can be detected?

Both George Nickelsburg and Burton Mack have argued that the overall format of the Markan passion material draws upon the Tale of the Suffering Innocent One. Mack has added a few more parts to this structure that help fill out the composition.[9] The Markan narrative containing the elemental components of Nickelsburg's description of the Tale of the Persecution and Vindication of the Innocent One, can be summarized:

> The actions and claims of a righteous person provoke his opponents to conspire against him. This leads to an accusation, trial, condemnation, and ordeal. In some instances this results in his shameful death. The hero of the story reacts characteristically, expressing his innocence, frustration, or trust in prayer, while there are also various reactions to his fate by characters in the tale. Either at the brink of death or in death itself the Innocent One is rescued and vindicated. This vindication entails the exaltation and acclamation of the hero as well as the reaction and punishment of his opponents.

The formal components of the Markan passion narrative[10] can be thus outlined (all passages taken from SV):

Provocation 11:15–17; 12:12

11 ¹⁵They come to Jerusalem. And he went into the temple and began throwing the vendors and the customers out of the temple area, and he knocked over the currency exchange tables, along with the chairs of the dove merchants, ¹⁶and he wouldn't even let anyone carry a container through the temple area. ¹⁷Then he started teaching and saying to them, "Don't the scriptures say,

My house shall be designated a house of prayer for all peoples? But you have turned it into 'a hideout for bandits'!"

12 ¹²They kept looking for some opportunity to seize him, but they were afraid of the crowd because they understood that he had aimed the parable at them. So they left him there and went away.

Conspiracy 11:18; 12:12–13; 14:1–2; 14:10–11

11 ¹⁸And the chief priests and the scholars heard this and kept looking for a way to destroy him. (You see, they were afraid of him because the whole crowd was astonished at his teaching.)

12 ¹²They kept looking for some opportunity to seize him, but they were afraid of the crowd because they understood that he had aimed the parable at them. So they left him there and went away. ¹³And they send some of the Pharisees and the Herodians to him to trap him with a riddle.

14 Now it was two days until Passover and the festival of Unleavened Bread. And the chief priests and the scholars were looking for some way to seize him by trickery and kill him. ²For they kept saying, "Not during the festival, otherwise the people will riot."

¹⁰And Judas Iscariot, one of the Twelve, went off to the chief priests to turn him over to them. ¹¹When they heard, they were delighted, and promised to pay him in silver. And he started looking for a good opportunity to turn him in.

Decision 14:6–8; 14:35–36; 14:41–42

14 ⁶Then Jesus said, "Let her alone! Why are you giving her a hard time? She has done a good deed for me. ⁷Remember,

the poor will always be around, and whenever you want you can do good for them, but I won't always be around. [8]She did what she could; she has planned ahead by anointing my body for burial."

[35]And he would move on a little, lay facedown on the ground, and pray that he might avoid the crisis, if possible. [36]And he was saying, "Abba (Father), all things are possible for you. Take this cup away from me. But it's your will that matters, not mine."

[41]And he comes a third time and says to them, "You may as well sleep on now and get your rest. It's all over! The time has come! Look, the Human One is being turned over to sinners. [42]Get up, let's go! See for yourselves! Here comes the one who is going to turn me in."

Trust 14:35–36

14 [35]And he would move on a little, lay facedown on the ground, and pray that he might avoid the crisis, if possible. [36]And he was saying, "Abba (Father), all things are possible for you. Take this cup away from me. But it's your will that matters, not mine."

Obedience 14:3–9; 14:35–36

14 [3]When he was in Bethany at the house of Simon the leper, he was just reclining there, and a woman came in carrying an alabaster jar of aromatic ointment made from pure and expensive nard. She broke the jar and poured <the ointment> on his head.

[4]Now some were annoyed <and thought> to themselves, "What good does it do to waste this ointment? [5]She could have sold the ointment for more than three hundred denarii and given <the money> to the poor." And they were angry with her.

[6]Then Jesus said, "Let her alone! Why are you giving her a hard time? She has done a good deed for me. [7]Remember, the poor will always be around, and whenever you want you can do good for them, but I won't always be around. [8]She did what she could; she has planned ahead by anointing my body

for burial. ⁹Let me tell you, wherever the good news is announced in all the world, the story of what she's done will be told in her memory."

³⁵And he would move on a little, lay facedown on the ground, and pray that he might avoid the crisis, if possible. ³⁶And he was saying, "Abba (Father), all things are possible for you. Take this cup away from me. But it's your will that matters, not mine."

Accusation 14:57–61; 15:2–3

14 ⁵⁷And some people stood up and testified falsely against him, ⁵⁸"We have heard him saying, 'I'll destroy this temple made with hands and in three days I'll build another, not made with hands!'" ⁵⁹Yet even then their stories did not agree.

⁶⁰And the chief priest got up and questioned Jesus, "Don't you have anything to say? Why do these people testify against you?"

⁶¹But he was silent and refused to answer.

Once again the chief priest questioned him and says to him, "Are you the Anointed One, the son of the Blessed One?"

15 ²And Pilate questioned him: "You are 'the King of the Judeans'?"

And in response he says to him, "If you say so."

³And the chief priests started a long list of accusations against him. ⁴Again Pilate tried questioning him: "Don't you have some answer to give? Look at the long list of charges they bring against you!"

Trial 14:53–64; 15:1–15

14 ⁵³And they brought Jesus before the chief priest, and all the chief priests and elders and scholars assemble.

⁵⁴Peter followed him at a distance until he was inside the courtyard of the chief priest, and was sitting with the attendants and keeping warm by the fire.

⁵⁵The chief priests and the whole Council were looking for evidence against Jesus in order to issue a death sentence, but they couldn't find any. ⁵⁶Although many gave false evidence against him, their stories didn't agree. ⁵⁷And some people stood up and testified falsely against him, ⁵⁸"We have heard him saying, 'I'll destroy this temple made with hands and in three days I'll build another, not made with hands!'" ⁵⁹Yet even then their stories did not agree.

⁶⁰And the chief priest got up and questioned Jesus, "Don't you have anything to say? Why do these people testify against you?"

⁶¹But he was silent and refused to answer.

Once again the chief priest questioned him and says to him, "Are you the Anointed One, the son of the Blessed One?"

⁶²Jesus replied, "I am! And you will see the Human One sitting at the right hand of Power and coming with the clouds of the sky!"

⁶³Then the chief priest tore his vestments and says, "Why do we still need witnesses? ⁶⁴You have heard the blasphemy! What do you think?" And they all concurred in the death penalty.

15 And right away, at daybreak, the chief priests, after consulting with the elders and scholars and the whole Council, bound Jesus and led him away and turned him over to Pilate. ²And Pilate questioned him: "You are 'the King of the Judeans'?"

And in response he says to him, "If you say so."

³And the chief priests started a long list of accusations against him. ⁴Again Pilate tried questioning him: "Don't you have some answer to give? Look at the long list of charges they bring against you!"

⁵But Jesus still did not respond, so Pilate was astonished.

⁶At each festival it was the custom for <the Roman governor> to set one prisoner free for them, whichever one they requested. ⁷And one called Barabbas was being held with the

insurgents who had committed murder during the insurrection. [8]And when the crowd arrived, they began to demand that he do what he usually did for them.

[9]And in response Pilate said to them, "Do you want me to set 'the King of the Judeans' free for you?" ([10]You see, he realized that the chief priests had turned him over out of envy.)

[11]But the chief priests incited the crowd to get Barabbas set free for them instead.

[12]But in response Pilate again said to them, "What do you want me to do with the man you call 'the King of the Judeans'?"

[13]And they in turn shouted, "Crucify him!"

[14]Pilate kept saying to them, "Why? What has he done wrong?"

But they shouted all the louder, "Crucify him!" [15]And because Pilate was always looking to satisfy the crowd, he set Barabbas free for them, had Jesus flogged, and then turned him over to be crucified.

A Case of True Fiction?

Mark 15 [6]At each festival it was the custom for <the Roman governor> to set one prisoner free for them, whichever one they requested. [7]And one called Barabbas was being held with the insurgents who had committed murder during the insurrection. [8]And when the crowd arrived, they began to demand that he do what he usually did for them. [9]And in response Pilate said to them, "Do you want me to set 'the King of the Judeans' free for you?" ([10]You see, he realized that the chief priests had turned him over out of envy.) [11]But the chief priests incited the crowd to get Barabbas set free for them instead. [12]But in response Pilate again said to them, "What do you want me to do with the man you call 'the King of the Judeans'?" [13]And they in turn shouted, "Crucify him!" [14]Pilate kept saying to them, "Why? What has he done wrong?" But they shouted all the louder, "Crucify him!"[15] And because Pilate was always looking to satisfy the crowd, he set Barabbas free for them, had Jesus flogged, and then turned him over to be crucified.

This dramatic scene from the Markan narrative has a riveting effect. The choice is both stark and tragic. Most readers assume this scene is historical. However, a number of concerns call that assumption into question. Is there any evidence for this "custom"? Moreover, would Pilate, the Roman governor, indulge the crowds in that fashion? First, we do not have any evidence for such a situation. Leaving the prisoners' fate up to the crowd would have been seen as an admission of weakness. Second, Pilate had established himself as notorious in Israel. His modus operandi was hardly deferential to Jews. On the other hand, if we consider this to be one of the components of the Tale of the Suffering Innocent One we see that Nickelsburg includes "helpers" of the innocent victim within the story pattern. Pilate functions as a helper, attempting to mitigate Jesus' fate. Moreover, the story presents a lingering dramatic irony. The insurgent is named Barabbas, which means in Aramaic "son of the Father." The character Pilate sarcastically describes Jesus as "King of the Judeans." From the perspective of the Markan community neither Pilate nor the crowd can detect Jesus' true identity. The chief priests persuaded the crowd to choose unwisely. Thus, the actions of the crowd and Pilate fit the demands of the dramatic scenario. This scene propels the narrative along to the final fate of Jesus. The scene is not historical but a fiction designed to further intensify the narrative action.

Yet, there is a great deal of historical truth in this fiction. It does not rest in the "fact" that this scene happened but on the social-political reality that the scene suggests. Pilate asks a Jewish audience to decide the fate of two of their own countrymen. The decision is hardly free; rather it exposes the occupied status of Israel in the first century. The Roman sets the terms of the decision. And the decision was to determine which of the people of an occupied country was to die, which was to live. This question is analogous to that of the mother in *Sophie's Choice*. It is not a free choice but a declaration of who truly rules. Thus, the scene with Pilate can be characterized as a "true fiction," for it betrays the harsh reality of an occupied nation.

Condemnation 14:64; 15:15

14 ⁶⁴"You have heard the blasphemy! What do you think?"
And they all concurred in the death penalty.

15 ¹⁵And because Pilate was always looking to satisfy the
crowd, he set Barabbas free for them, had Jesus flogged, and
then turned him over to be crucified.

Protest

Such a note is eliminated by the writer when accusation is
true.

Prayer 14:35–36; 15:34

14 ³⁵And he would move on a little, lay facedown on the
ground, and pray that he might avoid the crisis, if possible.
³⁶And he was saying, "Abba (Father), all things are possible
for you. Take this cup away from me. But it's your will that
matters, not mine."

15 ³⁴And at three o'clock in the afternoon Jesus shouted at the
top of his voice, "Eloi, Eloi, lema sabachthani" (which means
"My God, my God, why have you abandoned me?").

Assistance 15:9–14; 15:21

15 ⁹And in response Pilate said to them, "Do you want me
to set 'the King of the Judeans' free for you?" (¹⁰You see, he
realized that the chief priests had turned him over out of
envy.) ¹¹But the chief priests incited the crowd to get Barabbas
set free for them instead. ¹²But in response Pilate again said
to them, "What do you want me to do with the man you
call 'the King of the Judeans'?" ¹³And they in turn shouted,
"Crucify him!" ¹⁴Pilate kept saying to them, "Why? What has
he done wrong?"

²¹And they conscript someone named Simon of Cyrene, who
was coming in from the country, the father of Alexander and
Rufus, to carry his cross.

Ordeal 14:65; 15:16–20; 15:29–30; 15:31–32; 15:36

14 ⁶⁵And some began to spit on him, and to put a blindfold
on him, and beat him, and say to him, "Prophesy!" And the
guards slapped him around as they took him into custody.

15 [16]And the <Roman> soldiers led him away to the courtyard of the governor's residence, and they summoned the whole company <of troops>. [17]And they dressed him in purple and crowned him with a garland woven of thorns. [18]And they began to salute him: "Greetings, 'King of the Judeans'!" [19]And they kept striking him on the head with a stick, and spitting on him; and they were getting down on their knees and bowing down to him. [20]And when they had made fun of him, they stripped off the purple and put his own clothes back on him. And they lead him out to crucify him.

[29]Those passing by kept taunting him, wagging their heads, and saying, "Well, well, well! You're the one who was going to destroy the temple and rebuild it in three days! [30]Save yourself and come down from that cross."

[31]Likewise the chief priests had made fun of him to one another, along with the scholars; they were saying, "He saved others, but he can't even save himself! [32]'The Anointed One,' 'the King of Israel,' should come down from the cross here and now, so that we can see for ourselves and believe!" Even those being crucified along with him were insulting him.

[36]And someone ran and filled a sponge with sour wine, stuck it on a stick, and offered him a drink, saying, "Let's see if Elijah comes to rescue him!"

Reactions 14:63; 15:5

14 [63]Then the chief priest tore his vestments and says, "Why do we still need witnesses?"

15 [5]But Jesus still did not respond, so Pilate was astonished.

Rescue 14:62

14 [62]Jesus replied, "I am! And you will see the Human One sitting at the right hand of Power and coming with the clouds of the sky!"

Vindication 12:10–11; 14:62; 15:38; 15:39; 16:4–7

12 [10]It seems you haven't read in scripture: A stone that the builders threw away has ended up as the keystone. [11]It was the Lord's doing, something we find amazing.

14 [62]Jesus replied, "I am! And you will see the Human One sitting at the right hand of Power and coming with the clouds of the sky!"

15 [38]And the curtain of the temple was torn in two from top to bottom!

[39]When the Roman officer in charge saw that he had died like this, he said, "This man really was God's son!"

16 [4]Then they look up and discover that the stone has been rolled away. (You see, the stone was very large.) [5]And when they went into the tomb, they saw a young man sitting on the right, wearing a white robe, and they grew apprehensive. [6]He says to them, "Don't be alarmed. You are looking for Jesus the Nazarene who was crucified. He was raised, he is not here. Look at the spot where they put him. [7]But go and tell his disciples, including 'Rock,' 'He is going ahead of you to Galilee. There you will see him, just as he told you.'"

Exaltation 14:62; 15:26

14 [62]Jesus replied, "I am! And you will see the Human One sitting at the right hand of Power and coming with the clouds of the sky!"

15 [26]And the placard, on which the charge against him was inscribed, read, "The King of the Judeans."

Investiture 15:17

15 [17]And they dressed him in purple and crowned him with a garland woven of thorns.

Acclamation 15:18; 15:26; 15:39

15 [18]And they began to salute him: "Greetings, 'King of the Judeans'!"

[26]And the placard, on which the charge against him was inscribed, read, "The King of the Judeans."

[39]When the Roman officer in charge saw that he had died like this, he said, "This man really was God's son!"

Reactions 15:39

> 15 ³⁹When the Roman officer in charge saw that he had died like this, he said, "This man really was God's son!"

Punishment 12:9; 12:36; 12:40; 13:2; 14:21; 15:38

> 12 ⁹What will the owner of the vineyard do? He will come in person, and massacre those farmers, and give the vineyard to others.

> ³⁶David himself said under the influence of the holy spirit, "The Lord said to my lord, 'Sit here at my right, until I make your enemies grovel at your feet.'"

> ⁴⁰They are the ones who prey on widows and their families, and then recite long prayers just to look good. These people will get what's coming to them, and more!

> 13 ²And Jesus replied to him, "Take a good look at these monumental buildings! Not a single stone will be left on top of another! Every last one will certainly be knocked down!"

> 14 ²¹The Human One departs just as the scriptures predict, but damn the one responsible for turning the Human One in! That man would be better off if he'd never been born!

> 15 ³⁸And the curtain of the temple was torn in two from top to bottom!

The writer of this narrative was not only adept at creating midrash for a scene or two, such as Mark 1. The writer also carefully crafts the pre-existing oral traditions—both sayings traditions as well as the linked healing stories.[11] But, in terms of the passion material, the writer took the extra step of forming all of this in overarching narrative. This complex narrative composition of the passion did not exist from the earliest days. As we have seen there is no evidence of such an extended structure. Neither was this narrative structure itself novel; the structure of the story goes back to the scribal activity of the mid second century BCE. The author of Mark chose to locate the fragments of the death of Jesus within a well-known space: the Tale of the Suffering Innocent One. In so doing the author has already sided with those who see that the death of Jesus was the ordeal of an innocent victim. The death of Jesus thus becomes not so much unique[12] as a further reiteration in the growing tradition of the death of the innocents.

Understanding that the death of Jesus has been placed within the orbit of the innocent sufferers tradition explains why the writer has joined this extended narrative to the story of Jesus' career. The Gospel of Mark is primarily concerned with its listeners who were awaiting the end of days. They saw themselves facing possible persecution. They had already experienced—even at a distance—the fall of the Temple. Some of them already may have perished. The composition of the story of Jesus' death comes from a concern to address the situation of the Markan community. The meaningfulness of the death of Jesus gave sense to their possible deaths before the end. Their fate was disclosed in his story. Just as the writer uses the stories about the disciples' misunderstanding to help the community understand what the death of Jesus means, so also does the writer use the story of Jesus' death to throw light on the meaning of their uncertain lives. The one whose blood was "poured out for many" (14:24) joins other innocent sufferers in solidarity. At the same time, the vindication of the "coming one" delivers hope for those who face the end of days.

One further point is this: the composition is a midrash, a fiction. The Tale of the Suffering Innocent One was not a historical description but a fictional narrative construction of scribes who trusted that the God of Israel would be faithful to the innocent sufferers. The stories of Daniel, Susannah, the three young men are all fictional responses to traumatic blows. The choice of using the Tale for the death of Jesus was a further instance of resorting to fiction to find meaning in the face of death and destruction.

The Temple Incident
—Fact or Fiction?

Mark 11 [15]They come to Jerusalem. And he went into the temple and began throwing the vendors and the customers out of the temple area, and he knocked over the currency exchange tables, along with the chairs of the dove merchants, [16]and he wouldn't even let anyone carry a container through the temple area. [17]Then he started teaching and saying to them, "Don't the scriptures say, 'My house shall be designated a house of prayer for all peoples? But you have turned it into 'a hideout for bandits'!"

[18]And the chief priests and the scholars heard this and kept looking for a way to destroy him. (You see, they were afraid of him because the whole crowd was astonished at his teaching.) [19]And when it grew dark, they were leaving the city.

The Temple incident (Mark 11:15–19; Matt 21:12–17; Luke 19:45–48; John 2:13–22) ignited much debate within the Jesus Seminar deliberations.[a] On three separate occasions the Seminar voted. The Fellows considered that Jesus had performed some anti-Temple act and spoke some word against the Temple. They ultimately reached a consensus that *there may be some historical basis for the Temple incident involving Jesus*. This confidence is somewhat undermined by the fact that the Fellows "had serious difficulties in pinpointing what Jesus actually did."[b] The final consensus agreed with the argument of John Dominic Crossan[c] as well as the contention of E. P. Sanders, who considers the act of Jesus in the Temple to be crucial for understanding the figure and fate of the historical Jesus.[d]

Yet, the lucid argument of Robert J. Miller, "Historical Method and the Deeds of Jesus: The Test Case of the Temple Demonstration," places the consensus of the Seminar in considerable jeopardy. First, he touches on the weak point of Sander's argument.

---

a. Funk and the Jesus Seminar, *The Acts of Jesus*, 121–22.
b. Funk and the Jesus Seminar, *The Acts of Jesus*, 121.
c. Crossan, *Who Killed Jesus*, 64.
d. Sanders, *Jesus and Judaism*, 305.

> Sanders determines the meaning of the temple demonstra-
> tion in much the same way as he establishes its historicity:
> by implicitly linking it to the threats Jesus allegedly made
> against the temple. Sanders presents no direct argument
> about the meaning, no investigation into the symbolic reso-
> nance of tables or act of overturning them. He concludes on
> different grounds that Jesus threatened the temple and uses
> this to interpret the symbolic act reported in the temple dem-
> onstration. But why overturning tables by itself portends de-
> struction he does not say. (Miller, "Historical Method," 9)

Having pointed out that Sanders moves quickly from Jesus'
Temple act to words attributed to him, Miller observes that
Sanders connects quickly the Temple action with the probable
cause of Jesus' death. The Temple incident was the decisive fac-
tor that "triggered"[e] the fate of Jesus.

It is interesting that Crossan's more nuanced argument
also depends on the words of Jesus as support for the Temple
act. Particularly Thomas 71 (Jesus said, "I will destroy [this]
house, and no one will be able to build it [...]") becomes crucial
for Crossan's argument. Crossan sees the saying in Thomas
as historical, and coupled with the reports of the false witnesses in Mark, it becomes evidence that Jesus did something
in the Temple which had the meaning suggested by the saying (Crossan, *Who Killed Jesus?* 59). Crossan couches all of this
within the larger socio-political framework of peasant revolt.
(Miller, "Historical Method," 19).

Miller, however, has some pointed comments.

> Crossan's argument comes up short when scrutinized in its
> light. Two conditions must be met: the saying must imply a
> deed and the saying must be historical. On the first condi-
> tion, Thomas 71 certainly can be read as Jesus' explanation of
> his temple demonstration, but it does not need the demon-
> stration to make sense. Thomas 71 can stand alone as a pro-
> phetic pronouncement. All it requires is for Jesus to be in the
> temple when he speaks it. As for the historicity of the saying,
> Crossan asserts it without presenting a convincing argument.
> The only evidence he cites, that Thomas has no interest in the

---

e. Sanders, *Jesus and Judaism*, 305.

95

passion, is ambiguous, as Crossan admits. (Miller, "Historical Method," 19)

Both Sanders and Crossan move to the imputed words of Jesus to argue for the meaning of the Temple act. Miller finds difficulty in each argument. But Miller puts his finger on a deeper issue: assumptions have preceded worked out arguments. Both Sanders and Crossan want to make the death of Jesus factually intelligible. Both want to give a reason for his fate. Miller delivers a telling blow to the desire to discover the "Big Connection":

> Nothing in the connection hypothesis is implausible. However, we should be cautious because its outline matches the plot of Mark's gospel. The connection hypothesis pictures Jesus being killed by those who knew what he stood for because of what he stood for. There is no evidence that this picture existed before Mark sketched it. Hence, to accept the connection hypothesis is to accept the essential historicity of the plot of Mark. The connection hypothesis assumes that Jesus' death requires an explanation based on well-formulated intentions of Jesus, his Jewish opponents, and the Roman authorities. (Miller, "Historical Method," 12)

What I find most interesting is this return to a Markan default. This seems to be the unspoken determinant behind both arguments. This situation becomes even murkier with the contention of Burton Mack:

> The temple act cannot be historical. If one deletes from the story those themes essential to the Markan plot, there is nothing left over for historical reminiscence. The anti-temple theme is clearly Markan and the reasons for it can be explained. The lack of any evidence for an anti-temple attitude in the Jesus and Christ traditions prior to Mark fits with the incredible lack of incidence in the story itself. Nothing happens. Even the chief priests overhear his "instruction" and do nothing. The conclusion must be that the temple act is a Markan fabrication. (Mack, *Myth of Innocence*, 292)

In fact, the Seminar has reached the consensus that *the Temple incident, the handing over of Jesus, and Jesus' arrest must have been linked, but our only linkage is a Markan creation and there-*

fore a fiction. This does not necessarily mean that the Seminar agrees completely with Mack, as its other votes indicate. But it does show that the Seminar was aware of the Markan hand. The lingering question is why the Seminar would opt for the possibility of some act that is not fully reflected in the text. My judgment is that the Markan default was at work, that the desire to discover some intelligibility in the death of Jesus pre-determined the final consensus.[f] In other words, the "facts" of the Temple incident have been determined by a prior "fiction." Indeed, the "fact of this fiction" grounds the consensus.

---

f. It also points out the inherent conservative nature of the Jesus Seminars scholars, despite the accusations that they were radical.

8

The Problem of Peter

The argument advanced in the previous chapter is that the passion material in the Gospel of Mark represents the first instance of the earliest passion narrative among the canonical gospels. But one piece of evidence still needs to be considered, namely, the Gospel of Peter.[a] To be sure, most New Testament scholars have either overlooked[1] it or consider it to be a "late" or derivative gospel.[2] In their estimation one does not have to deal with any material that comes after the canonical material.

However, in recent years Dominic Crossan and I independently re-examined the Gospel of Peter and concluded that, despite its brevity, the text contains an earlier version that preceded the Gospel of Mark.[3] Moreover, this earlier version ("Peter1") bears the characteristic elements of the Tale of the Suffering Innocent One. The literary format, discerned in Mark, already can be found in this earlier portion of Peter, and this material is the source of the Markan passion narrative. We therefore will consider this gospel before turning to the other remaining passion narratives (Matthew, Luke, John).

The Backstory of Peter

In 1886, in a monk's grave at Akhmim in Upper Egypt, French archeologists discovered a small papyrus codex. With this codex was found a fragmentary gospel narrative. It contained portions of a passion story, a miraculous epiphany, an empty tomb story, and the possible introduction to a resurrection story.

---

a. The Scholars Version translation of the Gospel of Peter is found in its entirety in appendix A. It would be good for the reader to read the fragment through before continuing. Please see Appendix B (p. 171). We shall concentrate in this chapter upon GosPet 1:1–8:6.

The cursive handwriting of the manuscript has been dated to the eighth or ninth century. The title of the gospel is derived from the mentioning of Simon Peter as the teller of the story (14:3; 7:2).

As soon as the transcription reached scholars in England and Germany, a fierce debate ensued over whether or not the gospel of Peter was dependent upon the canonical gospels. By the end of the first quarter of the twentieth century a consensus developed that Peter was dependent on the canonical gospels and could be dated no earlier than the first half of the second century.

Then a small fragment of papyrus (Oxyrhynchus Papyrus 2949) from the late second or early third century was published in 1972. The story of Joseph of Arimathea's request to Pilate for the body of Jesus can be detected on this fragment. Since this request appears to occur before Jesus' execution, it both contradicts the sequence in the canonical gospels and resembles the story in Peter 2:1–3a. This papyrus could either be an earlier version of Peter or from another independent passion narrative.[4]

During the twentieth century, scholarship gradually shifted in its appraisal of the gospels. Once seen simply as eyewitness accounts, the gospels have come to be understood as complex interpretive developments and constructions thanks to new work on the oral, literary, and editorial aspects of each gospel. The assumption that the canonical gospels were historical while the non-canonical gospels were not did not stand up under increasing criticism. Non-canonical gospels can no longer be ruled out as historical evidence in an *a priori* fashion because all the evidence from the ancient world has to be evaluated upon the same critical level. Once this happens, then the critical eye can detect some rather interesting possibilities within the Gospel of Peter and among extant gospel materials.

Opening up the Evidence
Detecting Possible layers
A critical reading of the fragment Gospel of Peter demands a close analysis of the evidence. As critical readers of the canonical gospels have done, I shall now pay attention to the apparent discrepancies, interruptions, and repetitions within the narrative. In so doing I can detect possible distinct layers even in this

fragmentary material. I shall concentrate in this analysis upon the material that can be best described as portions of a passion narrative (Pet 1:1–8:6).

Before we begin our analysis, since the Gospel of Peter is unknown to so many, let us read the text in question:

Gospel of Peter

1 ... but of the Judeans no one washed his hands, neither Herod nor any one of his judges. Since they were [un]willing to wash, Pilate stood up. ²Then Herod the king orders the lord to be [taken away], saying to them "Do to him what I commanded you."

2 Joseph, the friend of Pilate and the lord, stood there. When he realized that they were about to crucify him, he went to Pilate and asked for the lord's body for burial. ²And Pilate sent to Herod and asked for his body. ³And Herod replied, "Brother Pilate, even if no one had asked for him, we would have buried him, since the Sabbath is drawing near. ⁴For it is written in the Law, 'The sun must not set upon one who has been executed.'"

⁵And he turned him over to the people on the day before their festival, known as Unleavened Bread, began.

3 They took the lord and kept pushing him along as they ran; and they were saying, "Let's drag the son of God along, since we have him in our power." ²And they threw a purple robe around him and sat him upon the judgment seat and said, "Judge justly, king of Israel." ³And one of them brought a crown of thorns and set it on the head of the lord. ⁴And others standing about would spit in his eyes, and others slapped his face, while others poked him with a rod. Some kept flogging him as they said, "Let's pay proper respect to the son of God."

4 And they brought two criminals and crucified the lord between them. But he himself remained silent, as if in no pain.

²And when they set up the cross, they put an inscription on it, "This is the king of Israel." ³And they piled his clothes in front of him; then they divided them among themselves and gambled for them.

⁴But one of those criminals reproached them and said, "We're suffering for the evil that we've done, but this man,

who has become a savior of humanity, what wrong has he done to you?"

⁵And they got angry at him and ordered that his legs not be broken so he would die in agony.

5 It was midday and darkness covered the whole of Judea. They were confused and anxious for fear that the sun had set while he was still alive. <For> it is written,

> The sun must not set upon one who has been executed.

²And one of them said, "Give him vinegar mixed with something bitter to drink." And they mixed it and gave it to him to drink.

³And they fulfilled all things and brought to completion the sins on their head. ⁴Now many went around with lamps, and, thinking that it was night, they lay down.

⁵And the lord cried out, saying, "My power, <my> power, you have abandoned me." When he said this, he was taken up. ⁶And at that moment, the curtain of the Jerusalem temple was torn in two.

6 And then they pulled the nails from the lord's hands and set him on the ground. And the whole earth shook and there was great fear. ²Then the sun came out and it turned out to be three o'clock in the afternoon. ³Now the Judeans rejoiced and gave his body to Joseph so that he might bury it, since <Joseph> had observed how much good he had done.

⁴<Joseph> took the lord, washed <his body> and wound a linen <shroud> around him, and brought him to his own tomb, called "Joseph's Garden."

7 Then the Judeans and the elders and the priests perceived what evil they had done to themselves, and began to beat their breasts and cry out "Our sins have brought disasters down on us! The judgment and the end of Jerusalem are at hand!"

²But I began weeping with my friends. And quivering with fear in our hearts, we hid ourselves. (You see we were being sought by them as criminals and as people who wanted to burn down the temple.) ³As a result of all these things, we fasted and sat mourning and weeping night and day until the Sabbath.

8 When the scholars and the Pharisees and the priests had gathered together, and when they heard that all the people were moaning and beating their breasts, and saying, "If his death has produced these overwhelming signs, he must have been completely innocent!" ²They became frightened and went to Pilate and begged him, ³"Give us soldiers so that <we> can guard his tomb for three [days], in case his disciples come and steal his body and the people assume that he is risen from the dead and do us harm." ⁴So Pilate gave them the officer Petronius with soldiers to guard the tomb. And elders and scholars went with them to the tomb. ⁵And all who were there <with> the officer and the soldiers helped roll a large stone against the entrance to the tomb. ⁶And they put seven seals on it. Then they pitched a tent there and kept watch.

Almost at the start of the fragment Peter 2:1 interrupts the fragmented beginning.

1 ... but of the Judeans no one washed his hands, neither Herod nor any one of his judges. Since they were [un]willing to wash, Pilate stood up. ²Then Herod the king orders the lord to be [taken away], saying to them "Do to him what I commanded you." 2 *Joseph, the friend of Pilate and the lord, stood there.* When he realized that they were about to crucify him, he went to Pilate and asked for the lord's body for burial. ²And Pilate sent to Herod and asked for his body. ³And Herod replied, "Brother Pilate, even if no one had asked for him, we would have buried him, since the Sabbath is drawing near. ⁴For it is written in the Law, 'The sun must not set upon one who has been executed.'"

Not only is Joseph introduced as a new character in the narrative but also the concern for burial before the death of Jesus differs significantly from the Synoptic versions (see Luke 23:50–52, 54; John 19:38). Crossan has rightly suggested that the verses of Peter 6:3–4 are anticipated by this interpolation of Joseph material.[5]

6 ³Now the Judeans rejoiced and gave his body to Joseph so that he might bury it, since <Joseph> had observed how much good he had done. ⁴<Joseph> took the lord, washed <his

body> and wound a linen <shroud> around him, and brought him to his own tomb, called "Joseph's Garden."

I have two more points. First, Pilate and Herod no longer seem to be in the same place. The Tinkers to Evers to Chance[6] maneuver in Peter 2:1–2 would definitely suggest different locations for Joseph, Pilate ("and Pilate sent to Herod"), and Herod.[7] Yet, there is no hint of this in 1:2. Second, the concern for the burial of the body of the lord becomes a matter of legal observance in 2:3b ("we would have buried him, since the Sabbath is drawing near ..."). Indeed, we find in 2:3b the only explicit use of scripture in Peter. This recurs in 5:1b,c,

> [1b]It was midday and darkness covered the whole of Judea. They were confused and anxious for fear that the sun had set while he was still alive. <For> it is written, "The sun must not set upon one who has been executed."

and is implied in 6:2, 3a:

> [2]Then the sun came out and it turned out to be three o'clock in the afternoon.[3]Now the Judeans rejoiced and gave his body to Joseph so that he might bury it, ...

These observations become even more curious when we bring POxy 2949 into play.[8] The Oxyrhynchus Papyrus 2949 is truly a fragment, where only the middle of the page is legible. Frag 1 and Frag 2 are two sides of the same papyrus.

Frag 1
Line 5 ... the friend of Pilate ...   Pet 2:1
Line 6 ... that he ordered ...   Pet 2:1
Line 7 ... came to Pilate ...   Pet 2:2
Line 8 ... [the] body for burial ...   Pet 2:2
Line 9 ... asked [Herod] ...   Pet 2:2
Line 10 ... said ...   Pet 2:3
Line 11 ... asked ...   Pet 2:3
Frag 2
Line 15 ... Pil[ate] ...
Line 16 ... one of [them] ...   Pet 3:3

From this quite fragmentary material some very interesting similarities with Peter 2:1–3 emerge. The material is not exactly the same material.[9] Nor is there any indication of the scriptural citation found in Peter 2:3. As noted by G. M. Browne, R. A. Coles[10] is correct that this material does seem to indicate a petition for the body before the execution. What I would conclude from all this is that 2:1–2 represents a fragment of an independent tradition of which POxy 2949 is a variant. Moreover, the Joseph material appears to have circulated originally as a whole (such as is found in Mark 15:42–47) but with the differences in the time of the petition for the body and the role of Herod. If that is so, we may well see in Peter 2:1–2; 6:3–4 an editorial split of previously united material called the "Joseph Fragment" here and below. Furthermore, because of the points just advanced, I would also contend that Peter 2:3a,b represent a further addition to this editorial activity.

> 2 ³And Herod replied, "Brother Pilate, even if no one had asked for him, we would have buried him, since the Sabbath is drawing near."

As we move from 2:3b we can discern a rather curious phenomenon. With the exception of the title "the lord" (3:1, 3; 4:1; 5:5; 6:1) no other instance of proper names or titles occurs until 6:3. The antagonists of the lord are presented in a fashion quite similar to those anonymous antagonists of the Just One in WisSol 2:12, 17–20.

> 2 ¹²let us lie in wait for the just man,
> because he is inconvenient to us and opposes our actions …
> ¹⁷Let us see if his words are true,
> And let us test what will happen at the end of his life;
> ¹⁸For if the just man is God's child, he will help him,
> And will deliver him from the hand of his adversaries.
> ¹⁹Let us test him with insult and torture,
> So that we may find out how gentle he is,
> And make trial of his forbearance.
> ²⁰Let us condemn him to a shameful death,
> For, according to what he says, he will be protected.
> (HarperCollins trans.)

Moreover, in 5:1b,c the concern for the burial according to religious convention (cf. 2:3) resumes. If this is from the same hand as 2:3a,b, then we should also remove this as a later editorial level.

Next, note the various reactions to the death of the lord.

- seismic shocks (5:6; 6:1)
- "the Judeans rejoicing" that the sun had not set in 6:3a
- the "Judeans, elders and priests" considering the implications of their deed (7:1)
- the weeping and hiding of Simon Peter and company (7:2)
- the report of the "scribes, Pharisees and priests" of the repentance of the people (8:1)

I would argue that 6:3a ("Now the Judeans rejoiced") is from the same editorial hand as found in 2:3a,b, and 5:1b,c. The removal of 6:3a would not interrupt the Joseph legend material. Indeed, the original subject who "gave" the body to Joseph could have been either Herod or Pilate. (Does POxy 2949 l. 10 above have any bearing on this?) Moreover, the presence of 6:2 ("Then the sun came out and it was found to be the ninth hour") may be there simply for the reaction of 6:3a, in light of what was said in 5:1a ("It was midday and darkness covered the whole of Judea."). Denker[11] has quite rightly argued for a prophetic background for 5:1a (cf. Amos 8:9–10); 6:2; however, he moves beyond this to a more historicized description. I would thus connect 6:3b–4 with 2:1–2 and separate this out as a later editorial level.

The text of Peter 7:1 deserves consideration.

> Then the Judeans and the elders and the priests perceived what evil they had done to themselves, and began to beat their breasts and cry out "Our sins have brought disasters down on us! The judgment and the end of Jerusalem are at hand!"

This contradicts the reaction of 6:3a:

> Now the Judeans rejoiced and gave his body to Joseph so that he might bury it, since <Joseph> had observed how much good he had done.

Yet at the same time it is quite different from the other reaction indicated in 8:1a, 2ff.

> When the scholars and the Pharisees and the priests had gathered together, and when they heard that all the people were moaning and beating their breasts, and saying, "If his death has produced these overwhelming signs, he must have

been completely innocent!" [2]They became frightened and went to Pilate and begged him.

The explicit mentioning of the end of Jerusalem may well give us a basis for the dating of this material (7:1). At this point this reaction not only appears different but also suggests another editorial level. The text of 7:2–3 also interrupt the narrative with the introduction of the first person singular and plural.

> 7 [2]But I began weeping with my friends. And quivering with fear in our hearts, we hid ourselves. (You see we were being sought by them as criminals and as people who wanted to burn down the temple.) [3]As a result of all these things, we fasted and sat mourning and weeping night and day until the Sabbath.

This is repeated in 14:2–3.

> [2]But I began weeping with my friends. And quivering with fear in our hearts, we hid ourselves. (You see we were being sought by them as criminals and as people who wanted to burn down the temple.) [3]As a result of all these things, we fasted and sat mourning and weeping night and day until the Sabbath.

This is the first time we have had any indication of the disciples of the lord. We should also note that 7:2b may well be linked to the previous verse. The suspicion of "wishing to burn down the Temple" would place it within the same range as 7:1.[12]

By removing 6:2–7:3 as a later addition, 8:1 becomes the reaction to the events surrounding the crucifixion. I would argue that 8:1b is part of original layer, with all the people murmuring and beating their breasts, saying, "If his death has produced these overwhelming signs, he must have been entirely innocent!" with 8:1a being an editorial tie. "The people" repent at seeing the "overwhelming signs" which had been given in 5:1a, 4, 6; 6:1. Further, the term "the people" mentioned at the end of the passion events also comes at the beginning of the passion material (2:3c, "And he turned him over to the people ...").

By paying attention to the various discrepancies, interruptions, and repetitions within the narrative, we have detected distinct layers even in this fragmentary material. We have gotten to Peter1, the earliest level of the Gospel of Peter.

9

The Earliest Layer
of Peter

Detecting a Pattern

I can now present what I argue to be the earliest level of the Gospel of Peter:

2 ³cAnd he turned him over to the people on the day before the Unleavened Bread, their feast.

3 They took the lord and kept pushing him along as they ran; and they would say, "Let's drag the son of God along, since we have him in our power." ²And they threw a purple robe around him and sat him upon the judgment seat and said, "Judge justly, King of Israel." ³And one of them brought a crown of thorns and set it on the head of the lord. ⁴And others standing about would spit in his eyes, and others slapped his face, while others poked him with a rod. Some kept flogging him as they said, "Let's pay proper respect to the son of God."

4 And they brought two criminals and crucified the lord between them. But he himself remained silent, as if in no pain. ²And when they set up the cross, they put an inscription on it, "This is the king of Israel." ³And they piled his clothing in front of him; then they divided it among themselves, and gambled for it. ⁴But one of those criminals reproached them and said, "We're suffering for the evil that we've done, but this fellow, who has become a savior of humanity, what wrong as he done to you?" ⁵And they got angry at him and ordered that his legs not be broken so he would die in agony.

5 It was midday and darkness covered the whole of Judea. They were confused ²And one of them said, "Give him vinegar mixed with something bitter to drink." And they mixed it and gave it to him to drink. ³And they fulfilled all things and brought to completion the sins on their head. ⁴Now many went about with lamps, and, thinking that it was night, they laid down. ⁵And the lord cried out, saying, "My power, (my) power you have abandoned me." When he said this, he was taken up. ⁶And at that moment, the veil of the Jerusalem temple was torn in two.

6 And then they pulled the nails from the lord's hands and set him on the ground. And the whole earth shook and there was great fear. … 8 ¹ᵇEverybody was moaning and beating their breasts, and saying "If his death has produced these overwhelming signs, he must have been entirely innocent."

In light of our analysis it is now important to concentrate on the material still intact (2:3c–5:1a, 5:2–6:1, 8:1b). This is an early passion narrative, which recounts the death and exaltation of the lord through the employment of the genre of the story of the Tale of the Suffering Innocent One. While I agree with Crossan[1] that the observations of Nickelsburg are most appropriate for the Gospel of Peter, I maintain that a level, earlier than the first level presented by Crossan, can be detected.[2] I call this earliest level "Peter1." Nickelsburg's list of generic components of the Tale of the Suffering Innocent One allows us to do two things:

- discern a basic pattern
- explain how and why the various secondary elements have been inserted into the Gospel of Peter

The following breakdown follows Nickelsburg's narrative elements or components, most of which describe "actions," while a few of them present "emotions." The components perform particular functions within the flow and logic of the story.[3]

Condemnation
Here the protagonist is formally condemned to death.

And he turned him over to the people on the day before the Unleavened bread, their feast. (Pet1 2:3c)

Ordeal

The protagonist's imminent destruction becomes a test of his claims or validity. This component includes some expression by the antagonists such as, "Let us (or we will) see ..."

> They took the lord and kept pushing him along as they ran; and they would say, "Let's drag the son of God along, since we have him in our power." (Pet1 3:1,2a)

Investiture, Acclamation

In the usual format the investiture comes upon the vindication and exaltation of the protagonist. The character is appropriately invested with royal robes. The new status of the protagonist is then acclaimed. Here, however, we have in ironic fashion an "enthronement." The acclamation may also be an indirect indication of the accusation, which we do not have in this fragment.

> And they threw a purple robe around him and sat him upon the judgment seat and said, "Judge justly, king of Israel." And one of them brought a crown of thorns and set it on the head of the lord. (Pet1 3:2b, 3)

Ordeal

The testing continues. This is quite reminiscent of the Servant Songs and its revision in Wisdom of Solomon. The testing of a "son of God" is paramount.

> and others standing about would spit in his eyes and others slapped his face, while others poked him with a rod. Some kept flogging him as they said, "Let's pay proper respect to the son of God." And they brought two criminals and crucified the Lord in between them. (Pet1 3:4, 4:1a)

Reaction

Reactions, both positive and negative, in this genre occur at different points and in different fashions. Here the reaction of the lord suggests the trust and obedience of the just sufferer.

> But he himself remained silent, as if in no pain. (Pet1 4:1b)

Acclamation

In contrast to the usual format, an ironic angle is present in the superscription. We may have another intimation of the accusation.

And when they set up the cross, they out an inscription on (it): "This is the king of Israel." (Pet1 4:2)

Reaction
Here we see the varied reactions to the fate of the just one.

> And they piled his clothing in front of him; then they divided it among themselves, and they gambled for it. But one of those criminals reproached them and said, "We're suffering for the evil that we've done, but this fellow, who has become a savior of humanity, what wrong has he done to you?" And they got angry at him and ordered that his legs not be broken so that he would die in agony. (Pet1 4:3–5).

Punishment
The corollary of the vindication of the righteous one is the punishment and destruction of the antagonists. Just as the investiture is anticipated here so also is the reaction of nature (cf. WisSol 5:17, 20).

> It was midday and darkness covered all Judea. They were confused (Pet1 5:1a)

Ordeal
This may well be the *coup de grace* (could the drink be understood as poisonous?).

> And one of them said, "Give him vinegar mixed with something bitter to drink." And they mixed it and gave it to him to drink." (Pet1 5:2)

Punishment
Further indications of the punishment towards the antagonists are made. These also are anticipations (cf. WisSol 4:20).

> And they fulfilled all things and brought to completion the sins on their head. Now many went about with lamps, and thinking that it was night, they laid (fell) down. (Pet1 5:3,4)

Prayer
Within this genre the righteous one expresses his innocence, frustration, or trust in prayer. Here the cry of abandonment can be seen as a prayer for deliverance.

> And the lord cried out, saying, "My power, <my> power, you have abandoned me." (Pet1 5:5a)

Rescue

Usually the protagonist is delivered at the very brink of death. Only in Wisdom of Solomon 3:2–4 and 2 Maccabees 7 are there "post mortem" rescues. Here the rescue is combined with an exaltation, which in most cases occurs in a court setting.

> When he said this, he was taken up. (Pet1 5:5b)

Vindication

In this component the protagonist is shown to have been right or innocent. The vindication, as is the case here, may be demonstrated by the turn of events.

> And at that moment, the veil of the Jerusalem Temple was torn in two. And then they pulled the nails from the lord's hands and set him on the ground. And the whole earth shook and there was great fear. (Pet1 5:6–6:1)

Reaction/Acclamation

The antagonists' wonder and astonishment over the rescue and vindication of the protagonist are noted. This surprise is a consequence of the antagonists' assumptions suggested in the ordeal. The people, upon witnessing the seismic events, declare the lord to be "just" and repent of their action.

> All the people were moaning and beating their breasts, and saying, "If his death has produced these overwhelming signs, he must have been entirely innocent!" (Pet1 8:1b)

This reconstructed narrative manifests much of the generic components of the story of persecution and vindication. In contrast to the prevailing style of this tradition (e.g., 2 Maccabees 7, where specific characters are given for protagonists and antagonists), this story apparently follows more closely the narrative style of the Wisdom of Solomon, where the only one entitled is the "just one", the "son of God." With the use of the title "the lord" we are only one step removed from a reading of the story of the righteous one as a type.

The literary components of the Tale of the Persecution and Vindication of the Innocent One are exhibited here. This is not a factual report but an interpretive rendering of the death of Jesus. The writer of Peter1 has chosen to use the imaginative locus or topos of the Tale of the Innocent One. The succeeding gospel accounts (including the later levels of Peter) continue to build upon the structure of this Tale. They fill in the skeletal structure with more and more details, including large blocks of Resurrection and Tomb material.

The Midrashic Composition

The Jewish creative process of midrash was the taking of a verse or verses of scripture as the launching pad for a story's construction. While the pre-Pauline traditions used a single verse to make sense of the fate of Jesus (the citation tradition), midrash moves beyond this to deliver a narrative. The cameo essay, "A New Testament Example of Midrash" illustrates in Acts 2 such a constructive process, whereby the post mortem scenario described in Peter's speech comes about through the use of scriptural citations. The scenario envisioned emerges out of these verses. We have also noted in the passion material in Mark that specific verses from the Jewish writings were strategically employed to fill out the meaning of the narrative.

Peter1 engages in the midrashic compositional process and, perhaps, is the bridge from the use of scriptural citations to the development of a connected narrative. Denker, Koester, and Crossan have argued that early traditions upon which Mark drew were based upon the Tale of the Suffering Innocent One. The German scholar Denker argued that Peter depended on the traditions of interpreting the materials from the Hebrew Scriptures for the description of Jesus' suffering and death.[4] The German-American scholar Helmut Koester has also argued that scriptural passages form the basis of the Petrine narrative.[5] But it is Crossan who pushed the argument further.[6] He thoroughly explored the possibilities of scriptural memory to make his case that the Gospel of Peter was prophetic material "historicized."

The basis for such arguments come from what Denker originally disclosed, namely, that verses from Peter were generated from the Hebrew Writings. The chart on the Petrine Midrash lays out how Denker sees Peter employing Hebrew Scripture.

Significantly this "prophetic layer" (with the exception of Pet 1:1) is found completely in the material that I have isolated as the earliest layer of Peter. None of the arguments of Denker, Koester, and Crossan assumes that there is some historical kernel behind the words. Rather, the combination of creative prophetic "recalling" with the Tale of the Suffering Innocent One would have provided sufficient framing for the rather meager information available. Even in the earliest fragment of

Petrine Midrash

Pet 1:1 … but of the Judeans no one washed his hands, neither Herod nor any one of his judges. Since they were [un]willing to wash, Pilate stood up.

Ps 2:1 (RSV) Why do the nations conspire, and the peoples plot in vain?

Pet 3:4 And others standing about would spit in his eyes, and others slapped his face, while others poked him with a rod. Some kept flogging him as they said, "Let's pay proper respect to the son of God."

Isa 50:6 I gave my back to the smiters, and my cheeks to those who pulled out the beard; I hid not my face from shame and spitting. [7]For the Lord GOD helps me; therefore I have not been confounded; therefore I have set my face like a flint, and I know that I shall not be put to shame;
Zech 12:10 "And I will pour out on the house of David and the inhabitants of Jerusalem a spirit of compassion and supplication, so that, when they look on him whom they have pierced, they shall mourn for him, as one mourns for an only child, and weep bitterly over him, as one weeps over a first-born.

Pet 4:1a And they brought two criminals and crucified the lord between them.

Isa 53:12 Therefore I will divide him a portion with the great, and he shall divide the spoil with the strong; because he poured out his soul to death, and was numbered with the transgressors; yet he bore the sin of many, and made intercession for the transgressors.

Pet 4:1b But he himself remained silent, as if in no pain.

Isa 50:7 For the Lord GOD helps me; therefore I have not been confounded; therefore I have set my face like a flint, and I know that I shall not be put to shame;
Isa 53:7 He was oppressed, and he

	was afflicted, yet he opened not his mouth; like a lamb that is led to the slaughter, and like a sheep that before its shearers is dumb, so he opened not his mouth.
Pet 4:3 And they piled his clothing in front of him; then they divided it among themselves, and gambled for it.	Ps 22:18 They divide my garments among them, and for my raiment they cast lots.
Pet 5:1 It was midday and darkness covered the whole of Judea. They were confused and anxious for fear the sun had set since he was still alive. <For> it is written that, "The sun must not set upon one who has been executed."	Amos 8:9 "And on that day,"says the Lord GOD, "I will make the sun go down at noon, and darken the earth in broad daylight."
Pet 5:2 And one of them said, "Give him vinegar mixed with something bitter to drink." And they mixed it and gave it to him to drink	Ps 69:21 They gave me poison for food, and for my thirst they gave me vinegar to drink.
Pet 5:5a And the lord cried out, saying, "My power, <my> power, you have abandoned me."	Ps 22:1 My God, my God, why hast thou forsaken me? Why art thou so far from helping me, from the words of my groaning?

the Passion tradition we find evidence of Crossan's apt phrase "prophecy historicized" not "history remembered."[7] Beyond a simple uncovering of sources, these midrashic moves have been made within the locus or structure of the Tale of the Suffering Innocent One. Both foci of our critical perspectives here come together. Earlier, isolated citations of scripture to render the fate of Jesus meaningful have now been gathered together into the overarching narrative of the Tale of the Suffering Innocent One. A significant step in the memory of the early Jesus community has been achieved. Now we know why these verses "hang together."

We can now clearly lay out the steps in the development of the Gospel of Peter. The earliest level of Peter in one aspect deviates from the prevailing style of this tradition where typically specific protagonists and antagonists are named (e.g., 2 Macc 7). The story in Peter follows more closely the narrative style of the Wisdom of Solomon, where the main character is entitled the "just one," the "son of God," but is never named.

> WisSol 2 [17]"Let us see if his words are true, and let us test what will happen at the end of his life; [18]for if the just man is God's son, he will help him, and will deliver him from the hand of his adversaries. [19]Let us test him with insult and torture, that we may find out how gentle he is, and make trial of his forbearance. [20]Let us condemn him to a shameful death, for, according to what he says, he will be protected."

With the use of the title "the lord" we are only one step removed from reading the story of the just one as a type. On the other hand, the character of Jesus in Mark has been greatly developed beyond the simple type. We can see that this material from Peter moves beyond the citation tradition as well as the allusive construction on the Sayings Gospel Q, with a connected narrative concerning the suffering of the Innocent One. Clearly, it is more primitive than what we find in the Markan narrative.

The Social Location of Peter1

The midrashic character of the narrative fits well the situation of a mixed Hellenistic community such as in Antioch. The citations and the memorial meal tradition originated in such Jewish Jesus communities. The Syrian Jesus communities' recasting of the catastrophe of Jesus' crucifixion into a hero's death may have centered in the meal experience. The meal experience provided the occasion to move from a citation tradition to a narrative. The communities mixed composition of Jewish and non-Jewish members drove the need for a narrative to unify both sides.

Peter1 assigns no blame for the killing of Jesus to any of the authorities. Of course, people would know that Jesus died from a Roman execution. But the issue before them was not the assignment of historical blame. On the contrary, in this earliest layer, the fact that the "people" are responsible for the death of Jesus points to the construction of this Tale. Also the vindication of the victim occurs at death, where the lord is "taken up." The rhetorical effect of the early fragment is twofold: to convince the audience that the lord is innocent (*dikaios*) and that the "people" are sinful, yet able to repent (8:1b). The example of the lord who is nobly patient to the end delivers narrative proof of his fidelity (*pistis*).

The heroic allusions noted earlier in the early pre-Pauline traditions are fleshed out. The rescue of his spirit by God and the accompanying tremors substantiate the validity of such a virtuous one. Not only is this man sarcastically dubbed a son of God and ironically entitled "King of Israel," but he is declared, in the midst of his humiliating ordeal, a "savior[8] of humanity." This narrative can appeal to two different audiences: Jews and Gentiles. By virtue of carrying the social stigma or blame of inferiority (vis-à-vis God's people the Jews), the non-Jews would be able to identify with the victim so humiliated. The role of the "people" in this narrative would startle the Jewish audience. But the people, at first caught up in the persecution and execution of the Innocent One, after decisive signs of divine approval, repent offering the audience a model of reconsidering their stance and status. Both sides can identify with the "just one." The midrashic fabulation creates the deep mythic grounds for a mixed and reconciled association. The title of "lord" is woven into the narrative threads of the vindicated just one, whose beneficial function for humanity unites listeners of the story in a novel association around a meal.

Turning a mixed community into a new association removes the social stigma and shame that went hand in hand with social negotiation in the first century. The full-bodied telling of the story of the vindicated Innocent One concretizes the possibility of imaginatively crossing social boundaries first in the narrative and then in social interaction. Those who saw themselves as inferior, within the pyramidal power structure of the Roman world, who were understood as less than human, saw in such constructions a way to reframe *their* existence and future. It was never a question of reporting the story of the death of Jesus. No one was interested in handing on some factual account for posterity. Rather, the construction of the story of the fate of Jesus breached the mythoi that dominated the social world of the first century.

The Priority of Peter1

How does Peter1 relate to the Gospel of Mark? We have already established that Mark is the probable source of the passion narrative of the other canonical gospels. Brown, among others, contended that Peter is an unwieldy collage assembled from the echoes of the canonical gospels. However, such a position stems from a reluctance to consider the possible layering of Peter and a prejudice in favor of the canonical gospels that dismisses the non-canonical. As demonstrated above, an early layer can be detected and reconstructed.

Such a reconstruction raises some interesting connections.

1. First, this early layer (Peter1) illuminates the critical conversation about the development of the early Jesus traditions.
2. The narrative order found in Peter1 coincides with the order found in the other passion narratives.
3. The central figure of the narrative is known only as "lord." Such an entitlement stands midway between the anonymous narrative "son of god" in the Wisdom of Solomon and the named Jesus in the Gospel of Mark. A tradition develops and an ever greater Christological focus comes into play.
4. Jewish scriptural verses have been turned into a connected narrative. The citations tradition moves beyond singular citations to a story structure. At the same time, this material in Peter1 is less developed than in Mark. This again speaks to the primitive aspect of Peter1 over Mark.
5. There is no indication in Peter1 of the devastation of the Jewish War. Rather, Peter1 attempts to bring Jews and non-Jews together, thereby reflecting an earlier communal situation, as one would find among the Syrian Jewish Jesus community.
6. In Peter1 a variety of later concerns, including an antipathy towards the "Judeans" is missing. Again, this would indicate a time earlier than that envisioned by the Markan community.

For all these reasons, Peter1 is prior to Mark. Furthermore, since all the passion narratives utilize one overarching order, the inevitable conclusion is that Peter1 was the original commonplace in which the fragments about the death of Jesus were stored and rewoven.

We can illustrate this new relationship among the passion narratives. Note that both Peter1 and the later version of the Gospel of Peter are given.

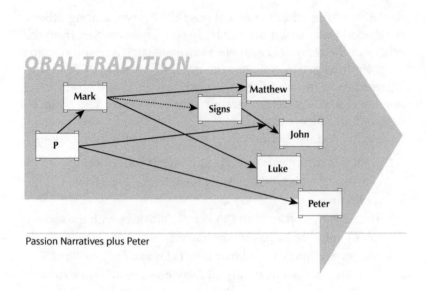

Passion Narratives plus Peter

The original passion narrative was not a factual report but a creative construction of a commonplace that attempted to make sense of the death of Jesus for the community of Peter1. The resources and strategies of ancient memory provide what we now call the passion narrative.

10

The Death Story of Jesus in Matthew

The Gospel of Matthew emerged in the last quarter of the first century as surviving Jews were attempting to recover and rebuild from the catastrophe of the Jewish War against Rome. Not only was the Temple destroyed but Jewish leadership came into question. While the Pharisees gathered at Jamnia in northwest Israel, regrouping, reconstituting the identity of Israel, as they recollected the oral traditions through the composition of the Mishnah, for the community of Matthew their memories of the words and deeds of Jesus provided the basis of what they held to be the true interpretation of Torah. For them Jesus the Anointed, the embodiment of God's Wisdom, was the prism through which they interpreted the traditions (5–7; 22:34–40). In that light the Matthaean community saw the Pharisees as the primary competition for Jewish leadership. The polemic of Matthew 23 comes from that perceived threat.[1] Moreover, the Matthaean passion account likewise functions within this competitive Jewish context. The writer of Matthew retells the story of the fate of Jesus to throw light upon his community's situation. A close comparison of the passion narratives clearly reveals that the writer of Matthew follows the Markan narrative in great detail.

How Matthew Follows Mark

Provocation   Mark 11:15–17; 12:12; Matt 21:18–19
Conspiracy   Mark 11:18; 12:12–13; 14:1–2; 14:10–11;
               Matt 12:46; 26:1–5; 26:14

Decision	Mark 14:6–8; 14:35–36; 14:41–42; Matt 26:10–13; 26:45–46
Trust	Mark 14:35–36; Matt 26:39
Obedience	Mark 14:3–9; 14:35–36; Matt 26:6–13, 39
Accusation	Mark 14:57–61; 15:2–3; Matt 26:60–63; 27:11–12
Trial	Mark 14:53–64; 15:1–15; Matt 26:57–68; 27:1–26
Condemnation	Mark 14:64; 15:15; Matt 26:65; 27:26
Protest	Eliminated when accusation is true.
Prayer	Mark 14:35–36; 15:34; Matt 26:39; 27:46
Assistance	Mark 15:9–14; 15:21; Matt 27:17–24; 27:32
Ordeal	Mark 14:65; 15:16–20; 15:20b–21; 15:22–26; 15:29–30; 15:31–32; 15:33–37; Matt 26:67; 27:27–31a; 27:33–37; 27:38–40, 41–44; 45–50
Reactions	Mark 14:63; 15:5; Matt 26:65–66; 27:14
Rescue	Mark 14:62; Matt 26:64
Vindication	Mark12:10–11; 14:62; 15:38; 15:39; 16:4–7; Matt 21:42; 26:64
Exaltation	Mark 14:62; 15:26?; Matt 26:64; 27:37?
Investiture	Mark 15:17; Matt 27:28–29
Acclamation	Mark 15:18; 15:26; 15:39; Matt 27:29
Reactions	Mark 15:39; Matt 27:54
Punishment	Mark 12:9; 12:36; 12:40; 13:2; 14:21; 15:38; Matt 21:41; 22:44; 20:42–43; 24:2; 26:24; 27:3–10; 27:51–53

Many have noted that Mark is the principal source of Matthew's passion material.[2] Indeed, since the Markan narrative comes out of the Jewish literary tradition of the Tale of the Suffering Innocent One, it is not unusual for Matthew to continue in the same vein. But Matthew does more than simply repeat the Markan source. The writer of Matthew is self-conscious in his appropriation of the Markan narrative material, as becomes evident when one inspects what Matthew has done to his source material. Close observation shows that the writer not only knew of the elements that went into the composition of the Tale of the Innocent One but also intensified and underlined these thematic portions. The writer adds very specific material to the passion narrative. The story pattern of the Suffering Innocent One has become a generative locus for another telling of the fate of Jesus.

The Matthaean Insertions

Let us note each addition Matthew makes to determine how the writer was intensifying the story of the Innocent One.

26:3, 57 The writer of Matthew takes over Mark's description of the conspiracy against Jesus (Mark 14:1b) and adds some specificity by noting that the conspirators "gathered in the courtyard of the chief priest, whose name was Caiaphas." This anticipates the trial scene before Caiaphas in 26:57. Such an addition underscores the opposition to the Innocent One.

26:15 The mentioning of "thirty silver coins" reinforces the betrayal of the Innocent One.

26:25 The one who betrays Jesus voices his duplicity: Judas, the one who was going to turn him in, responded, "You can't mean me, can you, Rabbi?"

26:28c The heroic covenant, "poured out for many" is further refined by the phrase "for forgiveness of sins." The hero's intent is laid bare for the listening audience.

26:50 But Jesus said to him, "Friend, do what you came to do." This touching line, reinforces the perfidy of betrayal.

26:52–54 These verses not only reinforce the innocence of the victim but also underscore the critique against those who warred against Rome. The Matthaean tendency to rely upon the Jewish Scriptures is alluded to at the end:

> [52]Then Jesus says to him, "Put your sword back where it belongs. For everyone who takes up the sword will be destroyed by the sword. [53]Or don't you think I can call on my Father, who would put more than twelve legions of heavenly messengers at my disposal? [54]But then how would the scriptures that say these things are inevitable be fulfilled?"

27:3–10 This insertion, detailing the death of Judas, reinforces the judgment upon the one who opposed the Innocent One:

> [3]Then Judas, who had turned him in, realizing that Jesus had been condemned, was overcome with remorse and returned the thirty silver coins to the chief priests and elders. [4]He said, "I've made a serious mistake in turning in this blameless man." But they said, "What do we care? That's your business." [5]And hurling the silver into the temple he

slunk off, and went out and hanged himself. ⁶The chief priests took the silver and said, "It wouldn't be right to put this into the temple treasury, since it's blood money." ⁷So they devised a plan and bought the potter's field as a burial ground for foreigners. ⁸As a result, that field has been called Bloody Field even to this day. ⁹Then the prediction spoken through Jeremiah the prophet was fulfilled: "And they took the thirty silver coins, the price put on a man's head (this is the price they put on him among the Israelites), ¹⁰and they donated it for the potter's field, as my Lord commanded me."

27:19 This brief insertion further underscores the innocence of the victim:

¹⁹While he was sitting on the judgment seat, his wife sent a message to him: "Don't have anything to do with that innocent man, because I have agonized a great deal today over a dream about him."

27:24–25 Once more the innocence of the victim is maintained, along with the dramatic irony of the scene.

²⁴Now when Pilate could see that he was getting nowhere, but that a riot was starting instead, he took water and washed his hands in full view of the crowd and said, "I'm not responsible for this man's blood. That's your business!" ²⁵In response all the people said, "So, smear his blood on us and on our children."

27:40b, 43 Those who oppose the victim taunt him with the sarcastic use of the title of "God's son." This title reflects the material in Wisdom of Solomon 2.

⁴⁰ᵇ"If you're God's son … ⁴³He trusted God, so God should rescue him now if he cares about him. After all, he said, 'I'm God's son.'"

27:51b–53 This insertion further elaborates the reaction to the death of the Innocent One.

⁵¹ᵇand the earth quaked, rocks were split apart, ⁵²and tombs were opened and many bodies of sleeping saints came back to life. ⁵³And they came out of the tombs after his resurrection and went into the holy city, where they appeared to many.

27:62–66 While this scene reiterates the continued opposition even as the Innocent One's death, it may also reflect a later redactional layer that deals with the proclamation of a raised Jesus.[3]

> [62]On the next day, which is the day after preparation, the chief priests and the Pharisees met with Pilate. [63]"Your Excellency, we remember what that deceiver said while he was still alive: 'After three days I'm going to be raised up.' [64]So order the tomb sealed for three days so his disciples won't come and steal his body and tell everyone, 'He has been raised from the dead.' If that were to happen, the last deception will be worse than the first." [65]Pilate replied to them, "You have guards; go and secure it as you think best." [66]They went and secured the tomb by sealing <it with a> stone and posting a guard.

The employment of these insertions fundamentally reinforces the structure of the Tale inherited from Mark. Matthew continues to explore and exploit the memory locus of the Tale of the Innocent Sufferer. More characters are introduced as opponents/aids (Caiaphas, Pilate's wife). Further details are given ("palace of Caiaphas," "thirty pieces of silver," Judas' death, Pilate's wife's dream). Throughout the innocence of Jesus is further underscored.[4]

Carruthers has noted that the function of the ancient memory place (*locus/topos*) was not to repeat mimetically but to deliver heuristic possibilities. The memory space allows, engenders, or authorizes new versions of the story. Matthew is at home with this memory space. The ancient writer was not interested in passing on "the facts" but in determining what was meaningful for his community. Just as the writer of Mark told the story of Jesus' death to help make sense of the deaths of those within his community, so also does the writer of Matthew redeploy the story for his community as they compete for the attention of their fellow Jews.

"If We Only Knew"
An Addition—Lethal and Lingering

This competitive situation throws light on the "blood curse," a Matthaean addition. These verses have aided and abetted, indeed, have justified the growth and maintenance of anti-Judaism and anti-Semitism.[a] The "blood curse" passage is found in Matthew 27:24b–25. These additional verses appear in the Markan scene where the crowd is asked to choose between Barabbas and Jesus.

We have already argued that the entire Markan scene is historically implausible and a literary fiction (see cameo on, "A Case of True Fiction," pp. 87–88). As a fiction, however, it does convey a primary historical insight of what was the real power in play. Jews were offered a humiliating choice over which fellow Jew to execute. It was a display of Roman dominance understandable particularly after the fall of the Temple.

The Blood Curse

Mark 15:6–15	Matthew 27:15–26
[6]At each festival it was the custom for <the Roman governor> to set one prisoner free for them, whichever one they requested. [7]And one called Barabbas was being held with the insurgents who had committed murder during the insurrection.	[15]At each festival it was the custom for the governor to set one prisoner free for the crowd, whichever one they wanted. [16]<The Romans> were then holding a notorious prisoner named Jesus Barabbas.
[8]And when the crowd arrived, they began to demand that he do what he usually did for them.	[17]When the crowd had gathered,
[9]And in response Pilate said to them, "Do you want me to set 'the King of the Judeans' free for you?"	Pilate said to them, "Do you want me to set Jesus Barabbas free for you or Jesus who is known as 'the Anointed One'?"

---

a. Anti-Judaism is a dislike of Jews due to a literal reading of scriptural texts. This is not the xenophobia prevalent throughout the Roman world. It is distinctly linked to the way in which specific texts of the Christian communities were interpreted. Once the Jesus followers began to leave their original Jewish matrix, what would have been seen as in-house arguments became "us vs. them" battlefronts. Certainly this was in play by the mid to end of the second century ce. Anti-Semitism, a relatively modern phenomenon, is a hatred of Jews simply because they are Jews.

(¹⁰You see, he realized that the chief priests had turned him over out of envy.)

(¹⁸You see, he knew that they had turned him over out of envy.)

¹⁹While he was sitting on the judgment seat, his wife sent a message to him: "Don't have anything to do with that innocent man, because I have agonized a great deal today over a dream about him."

¹¹But the chief priests incited the crowd to get Barabbas set free for them instead.

¹²But in response Pilate again said to them, "What do you want me to do with the man you call 'the King of the Judeans'?"

²⁰The chief priests and the elders induced the crowds to ask for Barabbas but to have Jesus executed. ²¹In response <to their request> the governor said to them, "Which of the two do you want me to set free for you?" They said, "Barabbas!"

²²Pilate says to them, "What should I do with Jesus, known as 'the Anointed One'?"
Everyone responded, "Have him crucified!"
²³But he said, "Why? What has he done wrong?" But they would shout all louder, "Have him crucified!"

¹³And they in turn shouted, "Crucify him!"

¹⁴Pilate kept saying to them, "Why? What has he done wrong?" But they shouted all the louder, "Crucify him!"

²⁴Now when Pilate could see that he was getting nowhere, but that a riot was starting instead, he took water and washed his hands in full view of the crowd and said, "I'm not responsible for this man's blood. That's your business!"
²⁵In response all the people said, "So, smear his blood on us and on our children."

¹⁵And because Pilate was always looking to satisfy the crowd, he set Barabbas free for them, had Jesus flogged, and then turned him over to be crucified.

²⁶Then he set Barabbas free for them, but had Jesus flogged, and then turned him over to be crucified.

Matthew intensifies the scene in a number of ways. Pilate gives the choice between "Jesus Barabbas" or Jesus "known as the Anointed One" (Matt 27:17). Pilate's wife sends a message underscoring the innocence of Jesus (Matt 27:19). Then the writer portrays Pilate as washing his hands, thereby declaring he is "not responsible for this man's blood" (Matt 27:24). All the people in the crowd respond, "So, smear his blood on us and on our children" (Matt 27:25). From the perspective of Matthew's community the people have not chosen wisely. They have not perceived the innocence of Jesus. Instead they chose the wrong "Jesus," "a notorious prisoner" (Matt 27:16). They have rejected the "Anointed One" for an unlikely stand-in. Even the Roman official declared Jesus' innocence. To which the people ironically state that they will be responsible for Jesus' death.[b] From the point of view of Matthew's community in the period after the Jewish War, it would be quite obvious that indeed the people had received retribution for Jesus' execution. The Temple had been destroyed and Jerusalem taken in the lifetime of the crowd and their children. The Gospel of Mark had already linked the death of Jesus to the destruction of the Temple. In Matthew this connection is maintained and refined. Matthew has begun to lessen Roman involvement in Jesus' death with Pilate's washing of his hands. At the same time, the onus of responsibility is placed not only on the leaders of the Jews but also on the people themselves. The people within the scene have unknowingly implicated themselves in the fate of Jesus.

Clearly the Jews in this scene bear the responsibility for the death of Jesus. It was on their very lips. Those who read this text literally and without a sense of historical context continue to use this text as proof of Jewish guilt and a reason why Jews throughout history are "cursed." They cursed themselves when they said, "So, smear his blood on us and on our children." They knowingly rejected Jesus and for that they continue to suffer from a cursed condition.

But is it that clear? On a simple literal level, the "cursed" condition would have applied to the crowd (and their children) before Pilate at that time. By the time Matthew was written the "judgment" had been rendered on those who experienced the

---

b. Within this scene the people sarcastically declare that they will be responsible for Jesus' death. They do not see what Matthew's community holds: that Jesus was innocent.

fall of Jerusalem. In other words, the people had "taken their hit." A literal interpretation of the scene actually misses the dramatic capacity of the material.

Mark had already infused with irony this dramatic scene before Pilate. Matthew carries this irony forward. The crowd in Mark and Matthew do not perceive the implications of their judgments. However, from the perspective of the Markan and Matthaean communities, the crowd appears to miss what the later Jesus communities got, namely, that Jesus is the Innocent One. The declaration of the crowd in Matthew further underscores this ironic position which is intensified even more when one considers how this sounds after the destruction of Jerusalem.

Why does Matthew intensify this dramatic irony?

- Is Matthew "rubbing it in" against fellow Jews who did not share the conviction that Jesus was the Anointed One?
- Is this gospel the beginning of an inter-Jewish dispute that will ultimately develop into anti-Judaism and then anti-Semitism?
- Is Matthew trying to spin the death story of Jesus away from any Roman involvement?[c]

Two major factors must be considered. First, Matthew consciously uses the story frame of the Suffering Innocent One. The intensification of this story pattern becomes a possible clue to the writer's intent. The writer has focused quite sharply on "the people." Does this focus not mean that we have evidence of one Jewish group condemning those who disagree with them over the Anointed One? It would appear so, except for the very words put on the people's lips by the writer: "So, smear his blood on us and our children." We have already noted that dramatic irony. The crowd does not know what they are saying. But there is more here than simply realizing that the words presaged the tragic fall of Jerusalem. The people called for Jesus'

---

c. The fact that Pilate declares Jesus innocent and washes his hands of the matter is an attempt by the writer of Matthew to reframe the death of Jesus. Historically the death of Jesus was a Roman execution. Years later, when the two Jewish groups, the Pharisees and the Matthaean community, competed to speak for the vanguard of what was left of the Jewish people, the Jesus followers sought to downplay the fact that the original leader of the Jesus Movement was executed by the Romans, who would decide who would speak for the Jews, and who would hardly turn to a community whose leader they had liquidated.

blood to be smeared on them. On first blush it means that they will be responsible for his life. Yet we cannot forget that this gospel carried echoes of its oral performance. In fact, the last time that blood was mentioned before this section came at the final meal of Jesus and his disciples.

> Matt 26 [27]He also took a cup and gave thanks and offered it to them, saying, "Drink from it all of you, [28]for this is my blood of the covenant which has been poured out for many for the forgiveness of sins."

Matthew alone adds the phrase "for the forgiveness of sins" (Matt 26:28c). Matthew has taken over the Markan language wherein the death of Jesus has been cast as a hero's death. The Markan Jesus dies, like other Jewish heroes, for many. But in Matthew the outpouring of Jesus blood, that is, his death, brings the possibility of forgiveness. This outpouring in blood echoes the scene in Exodus, where Moses seals the people in God's covenant:

> Exod 24 [8]Moses took the blood and dashed it on the people, and said, "See the blood of the covenant that the Lord has made with you in accordance with all these words."

Matthew's Jewish perspective implies a second irony embedded in this passage. Not only do the people fail to see what they are saying but, from Matthew's community's vantage, the people are unwittingly calling for the blood of Jesus, that is, *the forgiveness of the covenant*, to fall on them. The writer of Matthew is actually offering to his fellow Jews the opportunity to recognize in those ironic words the possibility of life and forgiveness. The emphasis of this scene is not upon a harsh condemnation of fellow Jews but an offer of forgiveness and reconciliation. The Matthaean community is trying to win over fellow Jews to the Jesus cause. Their refusal to accept Jesus could be turned around and his death could become their occasion of God's forgiveness.

Sadly, there is a third ironic note to be heard from this scene. When the readers of Matthew's gospel are no longer Jewish but Gentile, the reading becomes very different. From the perspective of the subsequent history of Jewish-Christian relations, the attempt at reconciliation by the Matthaean community with fellow Jews was a failure. The very scene used by the Matthaean community to suggest the possibility of reconciliation actually became one of the foundation stones in the bastion of anti-Judaism. What was once a literary instrument employed to speak subtly to fellow Jews soon became a lethal weapon with which to justify the hatred and killing of Jews.

Coda
Signals of Solidarity

From its inception the Tale of the Suffering Innocent One has been a Jewish response to the question of the justice of God. The fact that pious Jews faithful to their traditions were persecuted and put to death by the Seleucid Monarch Antiochus Epiphanes IV led not only to the Maccabean revolt but to a radical question: How can the God of Israel be just if the innocent suffer so? The scribal response was to tell a story.

This haunting question has continued through time. The question has been raised and entered into by a variety of voices. Indeed, in the twentieth century, rocked by world-engulfing wars and increasing waves of genocide, iterations of the Tale still appear. Examples of this can be found in the works of two great artists of the twentieth century who have extended this narrative conversation: Marc Chagall and Eli Wiesel.

Both of these artists call us back not only to our humanity but to the presence of mystery in our midst. We need all the imagination and honesty possible to take seriously their visions—such as Wiesel's *Night* and Chagall's *Exodus*.

See, for example, the courage and the continued conversation of Elie Wiesel's *Night*. In that staggering scene where the concentration camp is forced to watch the hanging of a child, the narrator remembers hearing a man asking, "Where is God now?" And the narrator adds, "I heard a voice within me answer him: ... Here He is—He is hanging here on this gallows." He then notes that he cannot pray as the inmates later celebrate Rosh Hashanah. In his haunting style Wiesel writes:

> How could I say to Him: Blessed be Thou, Almighty, Master of the Universe, who chose us among all nations to be tortured day and night, to watch as our fathers, our mothers, our brothers end up in the furnaces? ... But now, I no longer pleaded for anything. I was no longer able to lament. On the

contrary, I felt very strong. I was the accuser, God the accused.

This scene is part of an extended conversation that began so long ago. The Tale of the Suffering Innocent One has been taken up again, as it was by Andre Schwartz Bart in *The Last of the Just*. The writer of the passion of Mark was an earlier interlocutor of this centuries-long conversation, or perhaps better, lament. The echoes of these stories tremble across time and space. They reinforce and cross-examine each other. Both the agony of the suffering of the innocent and the question of the justice of God are again and again placed before us. Wiesel refuses to provide a pat response to the torture of the innocent. He stops us from moving away from the scene of the crime.

Much of the same can be said of the painter Marc Chagall. While many are taken by the brilliance and courage of his haunting *White Crucifixion*, I would mention Chagall's often overlooked *Exodus*. In the manner of James Joyce's *Finnegan's Wake*, one can describe this painting as "Here comes Everybody!" Chagall gives us a rush of Jews in exodus, with Moses, holding the sacred tablets on the right side of the picture; fleeing mothers cradling children at the center; a synagogue in flames to the left; the ever-present signature rooster aloft; and a crucified Jesus in the back, embedded with the people, with his arms extended on the cross that seems to encompass all in this frantic movement.

Chagall undermines the work of centuries of artistic and theological domination that have turned the crucified one into a macabrely majestic enthronement scene. The Jewish figures in this rush of freedom reclaim their own upon the cross, as the crucified One enfolds them in solidarity. No one dies alone here. No one flees alone here. No one escapes alone here. All are part of this tremulous painting.

Both of these artists carry forward the conversation of the Suffering Innocent One. Neither would stop this conversation from continuing. In fact, the task is still before us. Can we face this question of innocent suffering in our midst again? How shall we respond? Will we remember that there are ways of telling the story? Will we dare look innocent suffering in the face? Who now are the innocent ones who cry out for some signal of solidarity?

11

The Lukan Retelling

The Gospel of Luke continues to utilize the narrative memory frame of the Tale of the Suffering Innocent One, but, as Matthew does, the writer modifies the material in an attempt to take the story into another direction. Once again we see in this modification an instance of the growth and diversity of the Jesus movement as well as the generative possibility of the Suffering Innocent memory structure.

Luke presents a unique witness to the developing Jesus traditions, for the writer also authored the Acts of the Apostles. Such an addition represents a remarkable change in perspective for the early Jesus materials. The author of this two-volume enterprise takes a longer view of time (from Adam to the End) that contains particular periods, including the "golden age" of Jesus' public career and the beginning of the fledgling movement. The "*bios*" or life of Jesus found in Mark has become transformed into a far-ranging historical narrative that fits the ancient genre of romance. Written most likely in the early second century (and thus after the age of the apostles),[1] this gospel was addressed to followers who were acquainted with and appreciated the Jewish traditions,[2] probably a mixed community of Jews and Gentiles. This two-volume work creates what we today would call a "foundation myth" for the developing Jesus Movement. It not only locates this movement with the history of Israel but also makes the argument that it has become the new Israel.[a]

---

a. Indeed, the beginning of supersessionism can be found here. The argument that the Jesus Movement is the "new Israel" comes out of the competitive battle for identity and survival within the Imperial world. The incalculable damage this battle has wreaked over the centuries against Jews cannot be overlooked.

At the same time, it speaks to followers who would have been considered at odds with the Roman Empire.

The location of the gospel is disputed. Antioch would be a possible site, but it is more likely that Ephesus claims the honor. The two-volume work shows far more direct awareness of local landmarks and events in the Aegean.[3] The gospel, moreover, takes a long-range view, unlike the frenetic vision of the Markan text. The end of the world is not fast approaching; the community is not the final one.[4] Rather, the Lukan material is concerned with how the followers of Jesus are carrying on within an imperial world.

This new situation shapes the character of Jesus in this gospel. Jesus here becomes a teacher and healer; indeed, the unique structure of his journey to Jerusalem (9:51–19:28)[5] delivers an extensive course on discipleship. For the words and deeds of Jesus instruct and illustrate how to live "on the way." The listeners to this material are encouraged to imitate the example and embody the wisdom of Jesus. The passion narrative's retelling underscores this project of imitation.

Luke, like Matthew, is indebted to Mark. The writer continues the narrative structure found in Mark.

How Luke Follows Mark

Provocation	Mark 11:15–17; 12:12; Luke 19:45–46
Conspiracy	Mark 11:18; 12:12–13; 14:1–2; 14:10–11; Luke 19:47–48; 20:19–20; 22: 2, 3–6
Decision	Mark 14:6–8; 14:35–36; 14:41–42; Luke 22:41–42
Trust	Mark 14:35–36; Luke 22:41–42
Obedience	Mark 14:3–9; 14:35–36; Luke 7:36–39; 22:1–42
Accusation	Mark 14:57–61; 15:2–3; Luke 22:67; 23:3, 5
Trial	Mark 14:53–64; 15:1–15; Luke 22:54–71; 23:1–25
Condemnation	Mark 14:64; 15:15; Luke 22:71; 23:24
Protest	Eliminated when accusation is true.
Prayer	Mark 14:35–36; 15:34; Luke 22:42; 23:46
Assistance	Mark 15:9–14; 15:21; Luke 23:14–16; 23:20; 23:26; 23:27
Ordeal	Mark 14:65; 15:16–20; 15:20b–21; 15:22–26; 15:29–30; 15:31–32; 15:33–37; Luke 22:63–64; 23:10–11; 23:26; 23:32–34; 23:35–38, 23:39; 23:44–46
Reactions	Mark 14:63; 15:5; Luke 22:71; 23:11; 23:27

Rescue	Mark 14:62; Luke 22:69
Vindication	Mark 12:10–11; 14:62; 15:38; 15:39; 16:4–7; Luke 20:17; 22:69
Exaltation	Mark 14:62; 15:26; Luke 22:69; 23:38
Investiture	Mark 15:17; Luke —
Acclamation	Mark 15:18; 15:26; 15:39; Luke —
Reactions	Mark 15:39; Luke 23:47
Punishment	Mark 12:9; 12:36; 12:40; 13:2; 14:21; 15:38; Luke 21:6; 22:22; 23:28–31

Where Luke Differs from Mark

In contrast to the Gethsemane scene in Mark, the Lukan version (22:39–46) focuses directly on the Innocent One, who is about to undergo the agony of martyrdom. No mention is made of the names or drowsiness of the disciples. The writer has reduced the scene to its essentials so that the listening audience can learn well how a person is to face with resolution and trust the prospect of a martyr's fate.

Luke also colors the period of the passion as a special time within his overarching temporal sequence. The public career of Jesus in Luke is remarkable for being a "Satan-free" time. Luke notes that Satan, thwarted by Jesus' refusal in the desert, leaves Jesus alone "for the time being" (4:14). Only at the beginning of the passion narrative does Satan re-enter the picture: "Then Satan took possession of Judas" (22:3). The "golden age" of Jesus' public career occurs within those boundaries. At the same time, the travel narrative (9:51–19:28) set in this "golden period" provides the educational direction and momentum for the listeners to see that the passion narrative that follows continues to deliver an example to be imitated.

The Lukan insertions into the Markan frame are telling. Again and again these new materials declare Jesus' innocence.

In Luke 23:4 we find:

And Pilate said to the chief priests and the crowds, "In my judgment there is no case against this man."

In 23:14–15 Pilate again, this time before Herod, declares:

Now look, after interrogating him in your presence, I have found in this man no grounds at all for your charges against him. Nor has Herod ...

Verse 23:22 reiterates Pilate's estimation of Jesus before the crowds: "In my judgment there is no capital case against him."

One of the crucified criminals points out the injustice of Jesus' execution: "We are getting justice, since we are getting what we deserve. But this man has done nothing wrong" (23:41). Most dramatic is the exclamation of the Roman officer at the moment of Jesus' death: "This man really was innocent!" (23:47).

The note of repentance on the part of those returning home after Jesus death further reiterates his innocence.

And when the throng of people that had gathered for this spectacle observed what had transpired, they all returned home beating their chests[6] (23:48).

Other elements of the Innocent Sufferer Tale[7] crop up too. The additional scene before Herod adds to the ordeal of Jesus as an innocent sufferer (23:5–12). The lament of the women on the way to the place of crucifixion presents another echo of Jesus' innocence as well as an intimation of punishment (23:27–31). Furthermore, in the final scene on the cross we find that many manuscripts include the line: "Father, forgive them because they don't know what they are doing" (23:34). This prayer certainly would reinforce the trust and innocence of the Suffering One.[8]

An echo of this scene occurs in Acts 7. The death of Stephen greatly resembles that of Jesus in Luke 23. Stephen offers up his spirit (Acts 7:59) just as does Jesus (Luke 23:46). Both utter words of forgiveness for their killers (Acts 7:60; Luke 23:34). This literary resemblance goes beyond an intended typology. The writer of Luke-Acts wishes his audience to learn from the scenes, to discover how to imitate them in their own life situation. The story of Stephen provides a concrete instance of what can be done. The *Imitatio Christi* tradition begins with this two-volume narrative.

A final difference in the Lukan retelling of the Tale of Persecution and Vindication of the Innocent One is this: the post-mortem appearances of Jesus take place in and around Jerusalem. Even the appearance at Emmaus sends the disciples back to the city (24:13–33). There is a reason for this difference.

Acts begins its progress from Jerusalem throughout the Roman world. Once more the overarching historical frame refines the Tale of the Suffering Innocent One. It is no longer a tale of one life alone; now it is a story that continues to grow and replicate to the end of time and the world.

The death story of Jesus in Luke continues in the narrative sound chamber of the Suffering Innocent One. It goes beyond answering the Markan community's question regarding how to find meaning in the deaths of those who were executed. The Lukan version offers its listeners a pattern for survival in the imperial world. The suffering and death of Jesus (as well as that of Stephen) present a pattern for action and behavior, continuing the ancient method of learning through imitation (*mimesis*). The story gives disciples a way through the harshest trauma of human existence. In imitating their master unto death they can face the unknown with resilience and confidence for they are part of a movement that has just begun to grow.

Coda
A Practical Query

Often during Lent a number of pastors have asked what to do on Palm Sunday. Since the gospel reading is quite extensive, there is little time for any sort of a developed sermon. Should the pastor still preach?

In order to break up the tedium of a single voice, some communities actually divide the narrative into distinctive voices, such as the "Crowd," "the Leading Priests," "Pilate," and "Jesus." Quite often members of the congregation play the role of the crowd calling for Jesus' death. There have been pastors who intentionally reversed the roleplay and have taken the part of the crowd.

Such a partition of voices does more than break up the tiresome drone of a single reader. Uncomfortable aspects of the narrative begin to gain greater notice. When pastors and community have become sensitive to the problem that the virus of anti-Semitism often has used these scenes to energize Jewish pogroms and to maintain the advance of that prejudice, conscientious people begin to question whether the offensive passages should be surgically removed.

Before getting out the scissors, it might be better to remind one another of the historical aspects of this narrative material. First, scripture scholarship has for some time now noted that the gospels are only indirect witnesses to the historical Jesus. Each gospel reflects, rather, the time and concerns of that later community. Secondly, when the passion narratives are considered, they have been written out of a particular format—The Tale of the Suffering Innocent One. Such a story format emerged from Jewish scribes' attempt to make sense of the suffering of innocent Jews, persecuted during the rule of Antiochus Epiphanes IV. The question of how the God of Israel could be just if those who kept the traditions suffered so was uppermost in their minds. Their response was the construction of the Tale of the Suffering Innocent One. Here the scribes communicated their conviction that the God of Israel will not forget those who have fallen. They will be vindicated. Out of that narrative tradition the early Jesus writers crafted the passion story of Jesus. This was not created to condemn Jews; rather it was an attempt to do two things simultaneously: to make sense of both the deaths of those community members and that of Jesus. Indeed, by the very nature of the story pattern, Jesus dies as one of the many innocent victims. Jesus' death is a death in solidarity with those whom history would forget. Moreover, this telling of the death of Jesus was not separate from a Jewish context. It was not meant to set Jews against Christians (since Christians did not exist as such), but to make sense of the lost through the application of this story pattern.

The answer to the pastors' initial question rests on how we hear the passion narrative. Go back to the experience and the question that spawn this narrative tradition. Let everyone ask oneself: *Have I ever experienced the suffering of an innocent?* Take some time. For there are very few who have not had that experience, or who will forget the anger that still seethes over it. In fact, the question of the justice of God quickly becomes a major issue. The key for those engaged in the Palm Sunday services is to begin with that fundamental question. Do not put it or the attendant feelings aside. But hear the passion narrative in that fashion. Pastors do not need to say more than this: there are images and stories into which we can only enter through suffering and this narrative is such. Simply ask the community to recall their experience of innocent suffering. As the words of the narrative wash over them they may well discover a vein of sympathy and solidarity. The story does not remove the pain, but it opens listeners up to find something deeper, where there no longer is isolation but a tragic company of millions of innocents.

A contemporary Russian, Valentin Rasputin, captures much of this in his novel:

> Death seems terrible, but it sows the most kind and useful harvest in the souls of the living, and from the seed of mystery and decay develops the seed of life and understanding. Look, think, and have ceremonies and rites! Man is not alone. There are many countrymen in his skin, like men in a boat rowing from shore to shore, and the true person appears perhaps only in the moments of parting and torment—here he is, remember him. (*Farewell to Matyora*)

12

The Gospel of John
The Twice Remembered Death

The Gospel of John both continues and radically revises the format of the Tale of the Persecution and Vindication of the Innocent One. From a basic comparison with Mark we can see how far the Fourth Gospel follows the First Gospel.

How John Follows Mark

Provocation	Mark 11:15–17; 12:12; John 2:13–16
Conspiracy	Mark 11:18; 12:12–13; 14:1–2; 14:10–11; John —
Decision	Mark 14:6–8; 14:35–36; 14:41–42; John 12:7–8; 12:27; 18:11b
Trust	Mark 14:35–36; John 12:27; 18:11b
Obedience	Mark 14:3–9; 14:35–36; John 12:1–8; 12:27; 18:11b
Accusation	Mark 14:57–61; 15:2–3; John 2:19; 18:33–37
Trial	Mark 14:53–64; 15:1–15; John 18:12–13, 19–24, 28–40
Condemnation	Mark 14:64; 15:15; John 19:1, 16
Protest	Eliminated when accusation is true.
Prayer	Mark 14:35–36; 15:34; John 12:27; 19:30
Assistance	Mark 15:9–14; 15:21; John 18:38b; 19:12–13; 19:25–27
Ordeal	Mark 14:65; 15:16–20; 15:20b–21; 15:22–26; 15:29–30; 15:31–32; 15:33–37; John 19:1–3; 19:16–24; 19:28–30
Reactions	Mark 14:63; 15:5; John —
Rescue	Mark 14:62; John —
Vindication	Mark 12:10–11; 14:62; 15:38; 15:39; 16:4–7; John —

Exaltation	Mark 14:62; 15:26; John 19:19
Investiture	Mark 15:17; John 19:2–3
Acclamation	Mark 15:18; 15:26; 15:39; John 19:3
Reactions	Mark 15:39; John —
Punishment	Mark 12:9; 12:36; 12:40; 13:2; 14:21; 15:38; John —

While John follows the Markan sequence, significant differences crop up when we compare specific passages. The writer of the Fourth Gospel does more than make additions to the passion narrative, as in Matthew or Luke. A rather distinct voice reconstructs the tradition. This is not just the case in regard to the passion material. Literary and historical analyses have demonstrated that the Fourth Evangelist throughout the gospel revises earlier traditions and understandings of Jesus.[1] This revision of traditions came out of the maturing experience of the Johannine community.[2]

The Fourth Gospel re-envisions the earlier traditions through a creative use of memory and the presence of the "advocate or paraclete." We can equate memory in the Gospel of John with "doing theology" today. The community re-read Jesus' words and deeds, that had been handed down, in light of their sacred writings and growing experience (2:22).

> John 2 [18]To this the Judeans responded, "What sign can you show us to justify doing all this?" [19]Jesus replied, "Destroy this temple and I'll raise it in three days." [20]"It has taken forty-six years to build this temple," the Judeans said, "and you're going to raise it in three days?"

> ([21]However, he was referring to his body as a temple. [22]When he had been raised from the dead his disciples remembered that he had made this claim, and so they came to believe both the word of scripture and the word Jesus had spoken.)

The presence of the "advocate or paraclete" (Spirit) enables this new re-reading or interpretation (14:26):

> [26]Yet the advocate, the holy spirit the Father will send in my name, will teach you everything and remind you of everything I told you.

The entire Fourth Gospel is a twice-remembered tale. The Johannine Jesus followers believe that they can, through the presence of the "advocate,"[3] re-read all the words and deeds of Jesus along with the Jewish Scriptures in a new perspective. Earlier traditions and texts can be and are revised. This ability to re-read, for example, enabled the Fourth Evangelist to reconstruct an earlier tradition of wonder stories. Scholars have called this earlier collection of healings and wonders the "signs tradition or sign gospel."[4] The writer of John revised this tradition and brought it to a new level. What were once wonder stories told by wandering Jesus followers became an epiphany into the identity of the one performing these deeds. The author of the Fourth Gospel places all that has come before within a concentrated Christological focus. This concentrated focus on the identity of the Johannine Jesus comes across especially in the dialogues of the gospel. As an interlocutor, the Johannine Jesus constantly pushes his listener to deeper and deeper levels of meaning in regard to the identity of the interlocutor. The drawn-out story of the raising of Lazarus is a wonderful example of this deepening technique. The story functions as a teaching model to move the listener to understand that the true encounter with the Johannine Jesus comes not at the end of time but right now in the present.[5]

Even the death of Jesus in John is reread in the Johannine fashion. The death of Jesus is actually introduced in the Book of Signs (3:14; 8:28; 12:33). Three brief passion sayings prepare the listener for the final death story. Unlike the passion predictions found in Mark (see chapter 2, "Passion Predictions" above, pp. 21–23), John's sayings revise the fate of Jesus from "suffering and rising" to "being elevated."

> 3 [14]In the desert Moses elevated the snake; in the same way the Human One is destined to be elevated, [15]so that every one who believes in him can have unending life.

> 8 [28]"When you elevate the Human One. Then you'll know that 'I am,' and that I do not act on my own."

> 12 [32]"And if I am elevated from the earth, I'll take everyone with me." ([33]He said this to show what kind of death he was going to die.)

The "lifting up" (a first century euphemism for crucifixion) of Jesus (3:14) is seen in the Fourth Gospel as the occasion for the epiphany of the divine ("I Am," 8:28) with implications for all (12:33). By the time the listener stands at the cross all the echoes of those premeditated sayings hit home (19:18–30). The death scene of Jesus in John no longer is the locus of a martyr's death but a revelation of something deeper than the violent structures of the first century. In the very midst of utter degradation and ultimate diminishment the presence of God shines through.

The Revised Narrative

Two Instances

Let us now turn to two instances of the Johannine revision of the passion narrative material. The writer is quite aware of the earlier format but goes beyond this basic structure. His dramatic style reworks the material to great effect, intensifying irony and insight in the process.

In comparing the scene in which the crowd is offered the choice of Barabbas or Jesus (see pp. 124–31) in Mark and Matthew, we saw how Matthew has intensified the scene, as well as adding the irony of the "blood curse." The Johannine parallel goes far beyond a simple addition. The writer of the Fourth Gospel has rewritten the scene in such a way that we can actually sketch out the dramatic pattern in the material (18:28–19:16). The writer sets the action in two locations (outside, in view of the crowds; inside, Pilate's courtroom). If we pay attention to the way in which the individual scenes shift from "outside" to "inside" we can determine that there are seven interlocking scenes in this section constructed in chiastic fashion.[6]

Overview of Chiasm

    a 18:28–32 outside/charge/Jesus must die/irony
      b 18:33–37 inside/interrogation/kingship/irony with Pilate
        c 18:38b–40 outside/innocence/Barabbas/irony/title
          d 19:1–3 inside/scourging/mocking/king
        c' 19:4–8 outside/innocence/ecce homo/irony
      b' 19:9–12 inside/interrogation/power/irony of power
    a' 19:13–16 outside/verdict/paradox: true king handed over, law forsaken

Chiasm in Detail

    a 18:28–32 outside/charge/Jesus must die/irony

> [28]They then take Jesus from Caiaphas' place to the governor's residence. By now it was early morning. (They didn't actually go into the governor's residence; or else they would become unclean, and unable to eat the Passover

meal.) ²⁹So Pilate came out and says to them, "What charge are you bringing against this man?" ³⁰"If he hadn't committed a crime," they retorted, "we wouldn't have turned him over to you." ³¹"Deal with him yourselves," Pilate said to them. "Judge him by your own law." "But it's illegal for us to execute anyone," the Judeans said to him. (³²They said this so Jesus' prediction of how he would die would be fulfilled.)

b 18:33–37 inside/interrogation/kingship/irony with Pilate

³³Then Pilate went back into his residence. He summoned Jesus and asked him, "*You* are 'the King of the Judeans'?" ³⁴"Is this what you think," Jesus answered, "or what other people have told you about me?" ³⁵"Am I a Judean?!" countered Pilate. "It's your own people and the chief priests who have turned you over to me. What have you done?" ³⁶To this Jesus responded, "My empire is not part of this world. If it were, my people would be fighting to keep me from being turned over to the Judeans. But the truth is, my empire does not belong here. ³⁷"So you are a king!" said Pilate. "You're the one saying I'm a king," responded Jesus. "This is what I was born for, and this is why I came into the world: to testify to the truth. Everyone who belongs to the truth listens to my voice." ³⁸"What is the truth?" says Pilate.

c 18:38b–40 outside/innocence/Barabbas/irony/title

^{38b}When he had said this, he again went out to the Judeans. "In my judgment there is no case against him," he says to them. ³⁹"But it's your privilege at Passover to have me free one prisoner for you. So, do you want me to free 'the King of the Judeans' for you?" ⁴⁰At this they shouted out again, "Not this guy—Barabbas!" (Barabbas was an insurgent.)

d 19:1–3 inside/scourging/mocking/king

Then Pilate had Jesus taken away and flogged. ²And the soldiers wove a crown out of thorns and put it on his head; they also dressed him up in a purple robe.³They began marching up to him and saying: "Greetings, 'King of the Judeans,'" as they slapped him in the face.

c′ 19:4–8 outside/innocence/ecce homo/irony

4Pilate went outside once more. "See here," he says, "I'm bringing him out to make it clear to you that in my judgment there is no case against him." 5Now Jesus came outside, still wearing the crown of thorns and the purple robe. Pilate says to them, "Look at the man." 6When the chief priests and the police saw him, they screamed, "Crucify! Crucify!" "Deal with him yourselves," Pilate tells them. "You crucify him. I have told you already: I don't find him guilty of any crime." 7"We have our law," the Judeans answered, "and our law says that he must die because he has made himself out to be God's son." 8When Pilate heard this kind of talk he was even more afraid.

b′ 19:9–12 inside/interrogation/power/irony of power

9He went back into his residence. "Where are you from?" he asks Jesus. But Jesus didn't answer him. 10"You won't speak to me?" says Pilate. "Don't you get it? I have the power to free you, and I have the power to crucify you." 11"You would have no power of any kind over me," said Jesus, "unless it was given to you from above. That is why the one who turned me in to you has committed the greater sin." 12At this, Pilate began to look for a way to release him. But the Judeans screamed at him, "If you free this man, you're no Friend of Caesar! Every self-appointed king is in rebellion against Caesar."

a′ 19:13–16 outside/verdict/paradox: true king handed over, law forsaken

13Pilate heard all this, but still he brought Jesus out and sat him on the judge's seat in the place called Stone Pavement (Gabbatha in Hebrew). 14(It was now about twelve noon on the day of preparation for Passover.) He says to the Judeans, "Look, here's your king." 15But they only screamed, "Get him out of here! Crucify him!" "Am I supposed to crucify your king?" asks Pilate. The chief priests answered him, "The only king we have is Caesar!" 16And so, in the end, Pilate turned him over to them to be crucified.

The Tale of the Suffering Innocent One continues but with significant transformation. There are still accusers of the Innocent One: the chief priests and the Judeans. Pilate not only declares him innocent but also goes out of his way to render Jesus pitiable to the Judeans. The dramatic choice of Barabbas that we saw in Mark has almost been overlooked (18:40). Instead, the "ecce homo" scene (19:13–16) replaces it with stunning effect. In comparison with Mark's rendering, this scene shows a hand that is familiar with the dramatic techniques of the ancient drama.[7] Not only do the scenes shift from outside to inside and back but also the dialogue works along what has been called the "law of stage duality." In ancient drama only two characters at most would be speaking to one another at one time. Pilate converses with the accusers of Jesus, then with Jesus, then outside with the Judeans, then back to Jesus and so on. From the perspective of the writer a savage irony unfolds. The one considered by the Johannine community to be the true king is condemned to death; the official responsible for law and order caves into the demands of the Judeans; the Judean leaders forget their Torah and declare they have only the law of Caesar. The relatively simple irony of Mark's scene has been twisted into a refined dramatic production. Throughout the entire Passion Narrative of John contradictions compound as the listeners of this gospel experience a variety of characters acting in ignorance of their true condition.

A second example of the dramatic capacity of the writer of John can be found in the next major section of the passion narrative. The structure of John 19:16b–37 becomes quite evident when one notes that the crucifixion scenario forms another chiastic pattern (a, b, c, d, c', b', a').

Overview of Chiasm

    a 19:16b–19 Crucifixion site, two other victims, titulus cited
      b 19:20–22 Judeans, Pilate
        c 19:23–24 Crucifixion site, clothes, scripture citation
          d 19:25–27 Crucifixion site, Mother, Beloved Disciple
        c' 19:28–30 Crucifixion site, thirst, death, scripture
          mentioned
      b' 19:31 Judeans, Pilate
    a' 19:32–37 Crucifixion site, crurifragium, scripture cited

Chiasm in Detail

a 19:16b–19 Crucifixion site, two other victims, titulus cited

So they took Jesus, [17]who carried the cross for himself, out to the place called Skull (known in Hebrew as Golgotha). [18]There they crucified him, and with him two others—one on each side, with Jesus in the middle. [19]Pilate also had a notice written and posted it on the cross; it read: "Jesus the Nazorean, the King of the Judeans."

b 19:20–22 Judeans, Pilate

[20]Many of the Judeans read the notice, since Jesus was crucified near the city and it was written in Hebrew, Latin, and Greek. [21]The chief Judean priests tried protesting to Pilate: "Don't write, 'The King of the Judeans,' but instead, 'This man said, "I am King of the Judeans."'" [22]Pilate answered them, "What I have written stays written."

c 19:23–24 Crucifixion site, clothes, scripture citation

[23]When the soldiers had crucified Jesus, they took his clothes and divided them into four shares, one share for each soldier. But his shirt was woven continuously without seam.[24]So they said to each other, "Let's not tear it, but toss to see who gets it." This happened so that the scripture would be fulfilled that says, "They divided my garments among them, and for my clothes they cast lots." So this is what the soldiers did.

d 19:25–27 Crucifixion site, Mother, Beloved Disciple

[25]Meanwhile Jesus' mother, his mother's sister, Mary the wife of Clopas, and Mary of Magdala stood near his cross. [26]When Jesus saw his mother, and the disciple he loved standing nearby, he says to his mother, "Lady, here is your son." [27]Then he says to the disciple, "Here is your mother." And from that moment the disciple made her part of his family.

c' 19:28–30 Crucifixion site, thirst, death. scripture mentioned

²⁸Then, since Jesus knew that everything was now completed, he says (in order to fulfill scripture), "I'm thirsty." ²⁹A bowl of sour wine was sitting there, and so they filled a sponge with wine, stuck it on some hyssop, and held it to his mouth. ³⁰When Jesus had taken some wine, he said, "Now it's complete." Lowering his head, he handed over his spirit.

b′ 19:31 Judeans, Pilate

³¹Since it was the day of preparation, the Judeans asked Pilate to have the legs of the three broken and the bodies taken away. Otherwise their bodies would remain on the cross during the Sabbath day. (You see that Sabbath was a high holy day.)

a′ 19:32–37 Crucifixion site, crurifragium, scripture cited

³²So the soldiers came and broke the legs of the first man, and then of the other who had been crucified with him. ³³But when they came to Jesus, they could see that he was already dead, so they didn't break his legs. ³⁴Instead, one of the soldiers jabbed him in the side with his spear, and right away blood and water came pouring out. (³⁵The one who observed this has given this testimony and his testimony is true. He knows he is telling the truth, so you too will believe.) ³⁶This happened so the scripture that says, "No bone of his shall be broken," would be fulfilled, ³⁷as well as another scripture that says, "They shall look at the one they have pierced."

The initial scene (a) places Jesus and the criminals at the crucifixion site. The "titulus" on the cross provides a climax to the scene and brings the Judeans in protest to Pilate. Scenes b and b′ are set away from the crucifixion site with the Judeans making requests of Pilate. Scenes c and c′ bring the focus back to the crucifixion site, touching on the action of the soldiers and noting that this is in fulfillment of scripture. Only scene d is unique. It has no connection with what is "written," nor with the "Judeans" and Pilate. This midmost scene, the pivot of the chiasm, provides a central point to the overall construction, focusing upon the self-giving ideal of mother and son in the face of death. As many scholars have pointed out, this scene allows the Johannine community to stand in witness in the persona of the anonymous disciple (see 19:35). The final section (19:32–37) not only frustrates the Judeans' attempt to get rid of the troublesome Jesus but also provides the means of ironic insight. The coup de grace becomes revelatory in the eyes of the witness and through the words of scripture.

John and Peter?

The final section of 19:16b–37 raises some rather interesting questions about the possible relationship between the Gospel of John and the Gospel of Peter. John 19:31–37 is a distinctive section in the Johannine passion narrative. The Judean opposition ask Pilate to perform the *crurifragium*[8] to finish off the condemned victims and remove them before the Sabbath begins. The soldiers proceed to break the legs of the condemned. Coming to Jesus, last of all, they find him already dead. Nevertheless, one soldier pierces his side with a lance. The piercing of the side of Jesus is unique to John. There follow the assertion of eyewitness testimony and two scriptural citations. John 19:38 begins a new section telling of the burial of Jesus' corpse. While some commentators see nothing intrinsically improbable with the scene, others have debated whether there have been redactional insertions (such as vv. 34b–35).

We do not find the matter of the *crurifragium* anywhere but here in John and in the Gospel of Peter. The Gospel of Peter reads like this:

> 4 And they brought two criminals and crucified the lord between them, But he himself remained silent, as if in no pain.
> [2]And when they set up the cross, they put an inscription on it, "This is the king of Israel." [3]And they piled his clothing in front of him; then they divided it among themselves, and gambled for it. 4 But one of those criminals reproached them and said, "We're suffering for the evil that we've done, but this fellow, who has become a savior of humanity, what has he done to you?" [5]And they got angry at him and ordered that his legs not be broken so he would die in agony.

Despite the dismissal of the Gospel of Peter from serious consideration as a source of the Johannine passage,[9] the opposite conclusion—that this section of Peter knows John, even in a "confused" state—has its problems. No residue of distinctive

Johannine language remains in the Petrine text. Nor is there any editorial indication, such as a scene shifting away from the crucifixion site. Rather, the reverse argument is more probable, namely, that John has revised Peter (actually Peter1).[10] Notice how the focus shifts from one of the defenders of Jesus in Peter1 to Jesus himself in the Johannine passage—a typical Johannine editorial move that throws the emphasis solely on Jesus. If John knew Peter1, he follows the order found in Peter1 except for the crurifragium. In Peter1 the order moves as follows:

Jesus' crucifixion between two criminals
inscription
division and gambling for clothing
criminal's defense of Jesus
non-breaking of legs
giving a drink to Jesus
Jesus' death

John follows this order exactly except for the bone-breaking scene which the Fourth Gospel puts after the death of Jesus. The Fourth gospel delivers a revelatory intensity and focus.

Peter/John Comparison

Peter1	John
4 [1]And they brought two criminals and crucified the lord between them. But he himself remained silent, as if in no pain.	19 [16]... So they took Jesus, [17]who carried the cross by himself, out to the place called Skull (known in Hebrew as *Golgotha*). [18]There they crucified him, and with him two others— one on each side, with Jesus in the middle.
[2]And when they set up the cross, they put an inscription on it, "This is the king of Israel."	[19]Pilate also had a notice written and posted it on the cross; it read: "Jesus the Nazorean, the King of the Judeans." [20]Many of the Judeans read the notice, since Jesus was crucified near the city and it was written in Hebrew, Latin, and Greek. [21]The chief Judean priests tried protesting to Pilate: "Don't write, 'The King of the Judeans,' but instead, 'This man said, "I am King of the Judeans."'" [22]Pilate answered them, "What I have written stays written."

Peter1

[3]And they piled his clothing in front of him; then they divided it among themselves, and gambled for it.

[4]But one of those criminals reproached them and said, "We're suffering for the evil that we've done, but this fellow, who has become a savior of humanity, what wrong as he done to you?" [5]And they got angry at him and ordered that his legs not be broken so he would die in agony.
5 It was midday and darkness covered the whole of Judea. They were confused

5 [2]And one of them said, "Give him vinegar mixed with something bitter to drink." And they mixed it and gave it to him to drink. [3]And they fulfilled all things and brought to completion the sins on their head. [4]Now many went about with lamps,

John

[23]When the soldiers had crucified Jesus, they took his clothes and divided them into four shares, one share for each soldier. But his shirt was woven continuously without seam. [24]So they said to each other, "Let's not tear it, but toss to see who gets it."

This happened so that the scripture would be fulfilled that says,

They divided my garments among them, and for my clothes they cast lots.

So that is what the soldiers did.

See John 19:31–37 below.

[25]Meanwhile, Jesus' mother, his mother's sister, Mary the wife of Klopas, and Mary of Magdala were standing near his cross. [26]When Jesus saw his mother, and the disciple he loved standing nearby, he says to his mother, "Lady, here is your son." [27]Then he says to the disciple, "Here is your mother." And from that moment the disciple made her part of his family.
[8]Then, since Jesus knew that everything was now completed, he says (in order to fulfill the scripture), "I'm thirsty."
[29]A bowl of sour wine was sitting there, and so they filled a sponge with wine, stuck it on some hyssop, and held it to his mouth.

and, thinking that it was night, they laid down.

⁵And the lord cried out, saying, "My power, (my) power you have abandoned me." When he said this, he was taken up.
⁶And at that moment, the veil of the Jerusalem temple was torn in two.
6 And then they pulled the nails from the Lord's hands and set him on the ground. And the whole earth shook and there was great fear.
8 ¹ᵇEverybody was moaning and beating their breasts, and saying "If his death has produced these overwhelming signs, he must have been entirely innocent."

See Pet 4:5 above

³⁰When Jesus had taken some wine, he said, "Now it's complete."

Lowering his head, he handed over the spirit.

³¹Since it was the day of preparation, the Judeans asked Pilate to have the legs of the three broken and the bodies taken away. Otherwise their bodies would remain on the cross during the Sabbath. (You see, that Sabbath was a high holy day.)
³²So the soldiers came and broke the legs of the first man, and then of the other who had been crucified with him. ³³But when they came to Jesus, they could see that he was already dead, so they didn't break his legs. ³⁴Instead, one of the soldiers jabbed him in the side with his spear, and right away blood and water came pouring out. (³⁵The one who observed this has given this testimony and his testimony is true. He knows he is telling the truth, so you too will believe.) ³⁶This happened so the scripture that says,

No bone of his shall be broken,

would be fulfilled, ³⁷as well as another scripture that says,

They shall look at the one they have pierced.

We have already noted that this Christological focus fits well the editorial tendency of the Gospel of John. It should also be seen that John follows Peter in not having any mockery of Jesus during the crucifixion, in contrast to Mark 15:27–32, Matthew 27:38–44, and Luke 23:35–39. John does have the Judeans react to the scene by going to Pilate to protest and request. If John knew this portion of Peter1 then we are forced to rethink the "eyewitness"[11] value of 19:32–37.

If the historicizing of prophecy was the earliest layer of the tradition concerning the death of Jesus and, if this prophetic tradition was formatted into an extended narrative through the genre of the Tale of the Suffering Innocent One, then what we find in John 19:31–37 is a further layer of this compositional work. The use of scripture is now enfolded into the developing narrative tradition, thereby augmenting it and causing further interpretive growth. Contrary to Brown's suggestion that the scriptural citation[12] did not give rise to this episode but has been added to bring out theological depth, John 19:35

> The one who observed this has given this testimony and his testimony is true. He knows he is telling the truth, so you too will believe.

may be a later parenthetical insertion into a scene that had been generated precisely from the scriptural quotation in good midrashic fashion. The bone-breaking scene in Peter1 has been re-centered on Jesus as is typical in the Gospel of John. The water and blood, moreover, may be John's midrashic creation, perhaps reflecting the community's prior reflection on the paschal lamb and Zech 12:10:

> And I will pour out a spirit of compassion and supplication on the house of David and the inhabitants of Jerusalem, so that, *when they look on the one whom they have pierced*, they shall mourn for him, as one mourns for an only child, and weeps bitterly over him, as one weeps over a firstborn.

In sum, we may see in this particular section many of the issues of this book's investigation. The writer of John takes over the memory structure of the Tale of the Suffering Innocent One, revises it according to the needs of his community and his literary capacities. He used portions of Peter1 that were not picked up in Mark. Additionally, he has rewritten the tradition of the death of Jesus in his own terms, thereby presenting a sharpened and enduring Christological focus. The death of Jesus in the Gospel of John is neither a hero's death, nor that of a martyr, but the focal point of revelation. As intimated in the Johannine "anticipations" (not predictions as in Mark), the death of Jesus reveals the divine communication of self-giving. What is revealed in the final scenario is self-giving of the life of divine intimacy. Everything, even his mother, is given into the arms of the Johannine community. Everything is poured out, not as redemption, but as life itself.

Coda
The Strange Figure
on Papa Francesco's Cross

The papal election of Jorge Mario Bergoglio brought with it a number of surprises. Perhaps one of the least noticed was the pectoral cross Papa Francesco chose to wear. Remarkably there is no corpus on it, no crucified Jesus. Instead the cross features a depiction of the parable of the shepherd, who carries the lost sheep on his shoulders. Behind the shepherd the ninety-nine other sheep crowd in along the horizontal arms of the cross. At the top of the cross a pigeon or dove swoops down.

In some ways, this cross reflects the artistic tradition found in Latin American crosses, where scenes of life and celebration either surround the crucified Jesus or displace him altogether. However, the papal cross distinctly draws on biblical material. It is important to note that this depiction is not that found in the Gospel of John; it is not that of the "good shepherd" whose sheep know his voice (John 10:11, 14). Rather, the scene portrays the final portion of the parable of the shepherd who suddenly leaves the rest of his entire flock to recover one lost sheep (Matt 18:12b–14; Luke 15:4–7; Thom 107:1–3). While Matthew, Luke, and Thomas try each in their own way to make the shepherd's action somewhat reasonable (Matt 18:14; Luke 15:7; Thom 107:3), astute readers will note that the shepherd leaves ninety-nine sheep on their own. In effect, the shepherd panics in attempting to gather the lost one. Instead of the calm and assuring voice of the good shepherd in John, we hear a rhetorical question actually focusing upon a prodigal act and inviting listeners to identify with that very human moment. It concludes with a brief image of the shepherd carrying back the one that was lost.

The shepherd on Papa Francesco's cross has displaced the usual tortured figure. Of course, the artistic tendency for many centuries has airbrushed away much of the agony of that executed one. In fact, many crosses have been so sanitized, theologically and artistically, that no victim remains (except, perhaps, emblematic indications of the five wounds). Does Papa Francesco's cross follow in that cultural retreat from the tortured scene?

Roman crucifixion meant the *damnatio memoriae*, the liquidation of the victim, the reduction to nothing. The Tale of the Suffering the Innocent One was told in the face of that attempt of extermination. Jesus dies as one with countless innocent victims. Now doesn't the papal cross unwittingly achieve the opposite? Does it not remove the agony of that haunting story? It would if the figure were the Johannine voice, brimming with confidence. But it is quite the contrary. The multitude of sheep milling behind the shepherd points toward the parable. The words of the historical Jesus are rendered in the figure of a shepherd who has risked all to save a lost one.

If the question originally asked ("Who of you wouldn't do this?") still hits home, then the agony of choice comes down to us. The challenge is not to play the sheep, but to extend ourselves, risking all for the sake of a careless one. The Tale of the Suffering Innocent One has not been short circuited but transfigured into another key inviting us to take the mad risk of solidarity with the lost.

13

Remembering the Unspeakable

How do we remember the unimaginable, the unspeakable? How do we make sense of the traumas that undercut our very existence? How do we find words for the violence that changes everything? This investigation into the layers of the earliest social memories of the Jesus tradition has documented the ways in which a number of Jesus communities responded to the devastating shock of Jesus' death.

Jesus' death was tragic—an unmitigated catastrophe for his followers. The heroic figure forcefully predicting his fate had yet to be invented by Mark. Rome had spoken, liquidating another peasant, condemned to shame and oblivion.

The responses by the followers of Jesus were varied and sometimes non-existent, a fact that surprises many today since the death of Jesus is of paramount importance to them. Yet we noted the curious dearth of any iconic evidence of the death of Jesus for the first four centuries. Among the images of Jesus as shepherd, healer, and teacher, the crucified figure cannot be found. A mocking graffito and a tiny magical amulet are the only indications of Jesus' death.

In regard to the literary evidence, the death of Jesus receives passing mention in Josephus and Tacitus. In what may well have been the sayings of the historical Jesus we do not find a proclivity to talk about death, particularly his own death. What many consider to be his predictions of his own death are later constructions. When we do look at the sayings of the historical Jesus we see instead a basic sense of trust in the way in which the God of Israel is present.

Moving from the historical Jesus to the earliest gospel material, a particular reticence about the death of Jesus persists. The Q Gospel briefly hints at Jesus' death as that of a prophet, while the Gospel of Thomas has nothing to say. The Eucharist of the Didache never mentions Jesus' death.

Only in the pre-Pauline traditions do we see indications of attempts to make sense of this violence. The citations tradition ties the death of Jesus to lines from the Jewish Scriptures. The selection of particular verses was not an unusual way in which Jews attempted to find meaning in life. But even here no one extended narrative emerges. We also found that the Syrian Jesus followers probably were the ones who made sense of the death of Jesus through memorial meals. Taking on a format found throughout the Hellenistic world, the Syrian followers began to celebrate the death of Jesus. Paul's letters provide the meager evidence of this tradition. On the other hand, the authentic letters of Paul do not give us much more in regard to the recollection of the death of Jesus. For Paul what was important was that Jesus died and was crucified. Paul takes Jesus' death seriously but does not elaborate on it.

The work of memory is never easy, especially in the face of trauma. The lack of any full-blown narrative of the death of Jesus in the initial stages of the Jesus traditions is actually understandable. Scholars who presume that the death story in all of its permutations was there from the beginning do not recognize the effect of trauma upon the psyche, both individual and social. There needs to be some time for recovery, for re-membering, not for fact-finding, but for putting the debris together. Moreover, one must be sensitive to the reality that the ancients' ways of recovery did not run along modern lines. We already get a hint of this in the use of citations by those unknown Jesus followers. They already were ransacking their collective memories to detect meaning in what was a seismic shock to their world. Modern readers have to read self-consciously. We cannot presume that ancient people remembered the past as we do. Certainly they were not remembering in order to deliver us the facts; they were not providing documents, nor video recordings of what happened.

The reason why the research of Carruthers is so important is this: to understand how the Jesus followers came to grips with trauma, we have to become aware of how the ancients went about remembering. Carruthers has shown how the ancients went about the process of remembering, what it entailed, and what it provided for those remembering. Such an understanding of ancient memory coincides with the Jewish tradition of midrash. We see that the ancient imagination seeks first to construct a memory place wherein all are stored for recall. The citation tradition was literally one step removed from the construction of a story from a verse or two.

Only with the passion narrative of the Gospels of Peter and Mark can we begin to detect an extended storyline. Nickelsburg's work makes it clear that the writers of both Mark and the earliest layer of Peter were aware of this memory structure and literary pattern. In fact, we have argued that the adoption of this very pattern spawned the passion tradition of the Jesus movement. The Tale of the Suffering Innocent One provided the locus, the memory space, the commonplace, to remember the death of Jesus. Here the various citations could be embedded. Here the midrashic story telling capacity has an overarching structure. Moreover, it is out of this memory space that the death story of Jesus can be retold in a variety of ways to meet the needs and concerns of the developing communities.

The transition from the citation tradition to the extended passion narrative allowed, for the first time, a community to take the trauma of Jesus' execution and respond in a creative and meaningful way. *The horror of Jesus death was finally put into words.* This was done not simply to make sense of Jesus' death but to create a space of social meaning for a struggling community. The earliest level of Peter (Peter1) attempted to bring Jew and Gentile together in the story of the Innocent One. The Markan community discerned in the death of Jesus a fundamental solidarity with the suffering Innocent One. The imaginative commonplace that was the Tale of the Suffering Innocent One became a social construct for each community. The story was not told as a recitation of facts but as a heuristic act, an attempt to discover meaning for the particular community.

This search for meaning is present in each of the five gospel variations. Differences in the stories do not mean that one writer is correcting the historical record of an earlier story. Rather, additions and deletions serve to intensify the meaning of the story for that particular community. Never designed to provide objective historical data, the death story of Jesus serves the concerns of the particular community. That is why attempts to search out historical nuggets or facts in order to construct an objective account of Jesus' death are mistaken from the outset. They misconstrue the very nature of the evidence. They take as unvarnished reports what were attempts to construct meaning.

An irony lingers over this investigation. The commonplace of the Tale of the Suffering Innocent One is essentially a *fiction*—a fact that Nickelsburg has shown in his magisterial study. The employment of this story pattern was not done to establish facts but to discover meaning. Originally the stories were designed to give meaning in a time of social vertigo and religious uncertainty. The re-deployment by the writers of Peter1 and Mark resumed the search for meaning for communities undergoing particular stresses. The use of this pattern was not meant to provide the historical facts of Jesus' death but to find in Jesus' death significance for the lives of those communities.

The ongoing history of these stories discloses a darker direction. Once these narratives were read as literal descriptions, they became warrants for prejudice and even murder. The incitement of anti-Jewish and anti-Semitic acts on the grounds that the "Jews" killed Jesus and that they are "cursed" has sadly determined the tragic relationship between Jews and Christians. Readers have missed the dramatic irony intended by Mark, Matthew, and John. Reconciling clues have been stripped from the texts. Sadly, a story format designed to give meaning to the suffering of innocent ones became the tale for further suffering and death.

In a further irony, the original attempt to find meaning in the death of Jesus has caused subsequent generations to forget that Jesus died a Roman death; that he was shamed and his memory damned. Later gospels hid Roman responsibility, aiding and abetting this forgetfulness. Tragically, the fundamental solidarity between the Innocent One and the story's audience was ruptured. Jesus' death became a solitary act upon which later theological scaffoldings were erected. The horror of that death was hardly felt. Nevertheless, it is good to notice that the story of the Innocent One has not stopped being told or sung. The haunting song "Strange Fruit," made famous by Billie Holiday, takes up the tradition. Written by Abel Meeropol, who was haunted by the lynching of Thomas Shipp and Abram Smith in Marion, Indiana, this poem refuses to blunt the trauma of injustice.

Southern trees bear a strange fruit
Blood on the leaves and blood at the root
Black bodies swingin' in the Southern breeze
Strange fruit hangin' from the poplar trees
(Abel Meeropol, 1937)

To hear these simple and sudden words, to recall Billie Holiday's plaintive voice, sends the shiver of the Tale of the Suffering Innocent One echoing through the centuries. Indeed, we see that new voices enable us to hear the ancient story in the way it was intended. We discover that we are not alone in that ever widening commonplace of horror and suffering. We stand in the company of countless witnesses to the shock and awe of injustice.

Appendix A
Jesus Seminar Consensus and Conclusions

The following chart presents the consensus of the Jesus Seminar regarding the passion narratives of the five gospels: Mark, Matthew, Luke, John, Peter. The information in the chart shows how the Seminar voted on the particular sections of the Passion Material. What was agreed upon by all was *that Jesus was crucified and that his death was a Roman execution.* Everything else within the narratives was subject to interpretation and qualification.

The columns are broken down into the following: Text; Source; Vote of the Seminar; Issues; Contrary Vote; Seminar Conclusions and Observations. Notice that the votes of the Seminar are in Red, Pink, Grey and Black:

Red = likely
Pink = somewhat likely
Grey = somewhat unlikely
Black = unlikely

This writer clearly differs from his erstwhile colleagues in some respects. I have argued in a cameo essay (see cameo on "The Temple Incident—Fact or Fiction?" pp. 87–88) that the Temple Incident was quite likely a fiction, at least in the way it is portrayed. I have argued strenuously that a "Markan default" often was presupposed by many of the Fellows (scholars of the Seminar). In other words, instead of recognizing that Mark had opted to use the commonplace of the Tale of the Suffering Innocent One, many of the Fellows appeared to assume that the narrative reflected real events. Moreover, while the Fellows agreed that there is a source in the Gospel of Peter independent of the other gospel accounts, they did not see that it may well have been the source of the passion narrative in Mark. Again, the Markan default held sway.

Other scholars are noted for their difference of judgment on some sections.

Finally, an overview of the conclusions demonstrates that, even with some distinctions, most of the particular material of the passion is fictive.

Consensus of the Jesus Seminar

Source Incidents (Consensus Votes)

- One basic passion narrative underlies all the gospel accounts.
- There is a source in the Gospel of Peter independent of other gospel accounts.
- The underlying structure of the passion narrative was taken from the Septuagint texts.
- The earliest written version of the passion story is found in the Gospel of Mark.
- The Fourth Evangelist knew and used Mark.
- The Fourth Evangelist depended on a pre-Johannine passion source that was independent of and older than Mark.

Seminar Conclusions (Consensus Votes)

- The irreducible minimum (attested by Tacitus & Josephus): there was a Jesus movement; the authorities executed the founder; the movement continued and grew.

Source Incidents	Source	Seminar Vote	Issues	Contra Vote	Seminar Conclusions
Entrance into Jerusalem Mk 11:1–11 Mt 21:1–11 Lk 19:28–40 Jn 12:12–19	Mark Signs (?) John (?)	Black but Grey: Jesus rode into Jerusalem on an ass as a symbolic act.	Editorial hand; Hellenistic tradition of triumphal entrances Mark provocation?	Pink: Paula Fredriksen	• Jesus' riding into Jerusalem on an ass may have been a symbolic act.
Temple incident Mk 11:15–19 Mt 21:12–17 Lk 19:45–48 Jn 2:13–22	Mark Signs (?) John (?)	Pink Mk 11:15a, 17a Grey Mk 11:15b, 17b Jn 2:13–16a Black Mk 11:16, 18–19 Jn 2:16b–22	Relation of words to deeds Thomas 71; how likely in Temple context? How significant a gesture? Mark provocation?	Red: E. P. Sanders Pink: John Dominic Crossan Grey–Black: Fredriksen Black: Burton Mack	• There may be some historical basis for the Temple Incident involving Jesus. • That Jesus is reported to have engaged in an anti-temple act of some kind and that he was accused of intending to destroy the temple in Jerusalem are generally coherent with the evidence of his willingness to identify himself, in some respects, with the message and baptismal activity of John the Baptist. • The Temple Incident, the handing over of Jesus, and Jesus' arrest must have been linked, but our only linkage is a Markan creation and therefore a fiction.

The Sequence of events—all five versions exhibit a single relatively coherent narrative—one source?

Source Incidents	Source	Seminar Vote	Issues	Contra Vote	Seminar Conclusions
The conspiracy against Jesus Mk 14:1–2 Mt 26:3–5 Lk 22:1–2 Jn 11:45–53	Mark	Black	Mark's invention or real person? Time?		• Conspiracy theory = Mark • Role and person of Judas fictive • Dating is inconclusive
The anointing Mk 14:3–9 Mt 26:6–13 Lk 7:36–50 Jn 12:1–8	Mark Luke John	Black except Grey Mk 14:3–5 Jn 12:1–6	Variations, an unrecoverable incident?		
Judas' betrayal Mk 14:10–11 Mt 26:14–16 Lk 22:3–6	Mark	Black	Mark's invention or real person?	Pink: Crossan	• Role and person of Judas are fictive
The last supper Mk 14:12–25 Mt 26:17–29 Lk 22:7–30 Jn 13:1–35; 14:1–17:26	Mark	Black except Grey Mk 14:22–25	Markan redaction		• As depicted the last supper is not historical event. Much Markan overlay. • This reflects Jesus' well-known meal practice.

Source Incidents	Source	Seminar Vote	Issues	Contra Vote	Seminar Conclusions
Peter's denial Mk 14:26–31, 66–72 Mt 26:30–35, 69–75 Lk 22:31–34, 56–62 Jn 13:36–38; 18:15–18, 25–27	Mark John	Black	Markan redaction	Pink: Raymond Brown— kernel	• Resumption of Markan theme • Zech 13:7; 2 Sam 15:21 may factor in here.
Gethsemane Mk 14:32–42 Mt 26:36–46 Lk 22:39–46 Jn 18:1; 12:27	Mark	Black	Later community concerns		• The scene on the Mt. of Olives and across the Kidron is derived from 2 Samuel 15–17.
The arrest Mk 14:43–52 Mt 26:47–56 Lk 22:47–54 Jn 18:2–12	Mark John	Pink Mk 14:46, 50 Jn 18:12b Grey Mk 14:43a Black Mk 14:43b–45, 47–49, 51–52	Location? Any connection with the Temple Incident?		• Jesus was the only one arrested. • The handing over of Jesus to the temple authorities by those who knew him is historical. • Servants of the high priest or temple police were in the arresting body.
Trial before the Council Mk 14:53–65 Mt 26:57–68	Mark John	Black except Red Jn 18:13b	Legality dubious	Pink: Brown	• The trial narrative was created on the basis of Psalm 2. • The assumption that inappropriate speech would automatically result in execution is implausible.

Source Incidents	Source	Seminar Vote	Issues	Contra Vote	Seminar Conclusions
Lk 22:54–55, 63–71 Jn 18:13–14, 19–24		Pink Mk 14:53a Grey Mk 14:58			• The assertion of Roman innocence and Jewish responsibility is Christian propaganda • There was no Jewish trial, no Jewish crowd involved. • It is not just the content of the trial but the fact of a trial that lacks historical foundation.
Trial before Pilate Mk 15:1–15 Mt 27:1–26 Lk 23:1–25 Jn 18:28–19:16 Pet 1:1–2:3	Mark John Peter	Black except Red Mk 15:15b Jn 19:16 Pink Mk 15:1b,d Jn 18:28a; 19:1 Grey Mk 15:1a, 2	Legal basis? Editorial bias		• The trial narrative was created on the basis of Psalm 2. • Caiaphas wished to denounce Jesus to Pilate as a threat to public order. • Jesus was crucified with the participation of the highest Jewish authorities. • Jesus was crucified under Pontius Pilate (26–36 ce) • It is not just the content of the trial but the fact of a trial that lacks historical foundation. • Matt 27:25 is an invention of Matthew. • John 19:15b is an invention of John.
Mocking and crucifixion Mk 15:16–41 Mt 27:27–56 Lk 23:11, 26–49 Jn 19:2–3, 17–37	Mark Peter John	Black except Red Mk 15:24a Jn 19:16; 19:18a Pink	Scriptural memory vs. memory of fact. Composition of scriptural citations in literary format? Source issue—	Pink: Brown	• Jesus may have been flogged as part of the brutality connected with crucifixion • Spitting and nudging are derived from the popular scapegoat ritual. • Scourging, buffeting, and spitting come from Isa 50:6.

Source Incidents	Source	Seminar Vote	Issues	Contra Vote	Seminar Conclusions

Pet 3:1–5:6		Mk 15:40–41
		Jn 19:1
		Grey
		Mk 15:26
		Jn 19:19; 19:25
			Is P the basis for Mark and John (Signs)?		• Disrobing, re-robing, or crowning come from Zech 3:1–5.
					• In sum, the abused scapegoat ritual and the mocked king theater created the mockery of Jesus.
					• Jesus was crucified at Jerusalem.
					• Jesus of Nazareth died.
					• His death was a Roman crucifixion.
					• Detailed information about the crucifixion of Jesus is derived from prophecy historicized.
					  • The two thieves came originally from Ps 21:17 (LXX) supported by Isa 53:12.
					  • The non-breaking of Jesus' legs derives from Exod 12:46, Num 9:12, Ps 34:20 — the unbroken bones of the paschal lamb.
					  • The pierced side, John 19:34, comes from Zech 12:10.
					  • Casting lots for clothes is based on Ps 22:18.
					  • Gall and vinegar to drink derives from Ps 69:21.)
					• Mark's account of the crucifixion was the earliest.
					• It is likely that some women disciples of Jesus, especially Mary of Magdala, watched and lamented the death of Jesus.

Source Incidents	Source	Seminar Vote	Issues	Contra Vote	Seminar Conclusions
					• We can assume that the women, and even some of the men, would have tried to watch the crucifixion, and would have tried to find Jesus' body after he died in spite of the risks that would entail.
					• The flight of Jesus' companions is historical.
Burial Mk 15:42–47 Mt 27:57–61 Lk 23:50–56 Jn 19:38–42 Pet 6:1–4	Mark John Peter	Black	Common source? P? Signs? X? Burial customs?	Pink: Brown	• Joseph of Arimathea is a total Markan creation. • The Johannine Nicodemus as a burial assistant is a creation of the Fourth Evangelist.

Appendix B
Gospel of Peter

1 ... but of the Judeans no one washed his hands, neither Herod nor any one of his judges. Since they were [un]willing to wash, Pilate stood up. [2]Then Herod the king orders the lord to be [taken away], saying to them "Do to him what I commanded you."

2 Joseph, the friend of Pilate and the lord, stood there. When he realized that they were about to crucify him, he went to Pilate and asked for the lord's body for burial. [2]And Pilate sent to Herod and asked for his body. [3]And Herod replied, "Brother Pilate, even if no one had asked for him, we would have buried him, since the Sabbath is drawing near. [4]For it is written in the Law, 'The sun must not set upon one who has been executed.'"

[5]And he turned him over to the people on the day before their festival, known as Unleavened Bread, began.

3 They took the lord and kept pushing him along as they ran; and they were saying, "Let's drag the son of God along, since we have him in our power." [2]And they threw a purple robe around him and sat him upon the judgment seat and said, "Judge justly, king of Israel." [3]And one of them brought a crown of thorns and set it on the head of the lord. [4]And others standing about would spit in his eyes, and others slapped his face, while others poked him with a rod. Some kept flogging him as they said, "Let's pay proper respect to the son of God."

4 And they brought two criminals and crucified the lord between them. But he himself remained silent, as if in no pain.

[2]And when they set up the cross, they put an inscription on it, "This is the king of Israel." [3]And they piled his clothes in front of him; then they divided them among themselves and gambled for them.

[4]But one of those criminals reproached them and said, "We're suffering for the evil that we've done, but this man, who has become a savior of humanity, what wrong has he done to you?"

[5]And they got angry at him and ordered that his legs not be broken so he would die in agony.

5 It was midday and darkness covered the whole of Judea. They were confused and anxious for fear that the sun had set while he was still alive. <For> it is written,

The sun must not set upon one who has been executed.

²And one of them said, "Give him vinegar mixed with something bitter to drink." And they mixed it and gave it to him to drink.

³And they fulfilled all things and brought to completion the sins on their head. ⁴Now many went around with lamps, and, thinking that it was night, they lay down.

⁵And the lord cried out, saying, "My power, <my> power, you have abandoned me." When he said this, he was taken up. ⁶And at that moment, the curtain of the Jerusalem temple was torn in two.

6 And then they pulled the nails from the lord's hands and set him on the ground. And the whole earth shook and there was great fear. ²Then the sun came out and it turned out to be three o'clock in the afternoon. ³Now the Judeans rejoiced and gave his body to Joseph so that he might bury it, since <Joseph> had observed how much good he had done.

⁴<Joseph> took the lord, washed <his body> and wound a linen <shroud> around him, and brought him to his own tomb, called "Joseph's Garden."

7 Then the Judeans and the elders and the priests perceived what evil they had done to themselves, and began to beat their breasts and cry out, "Our sins have brought disasters down on us! The judgment and the end of Jerusalem are at hand!"

²But I began weeping with my friends. And quivering with fear in our hearts, we hid ourselves. (You see we were being sought by them as criminals and as people who wanted to burn down the temple.) ³As a result of all these things, we fasted and sat mourning and weeping night and day until the Sabbath.

8 When the scholars and the Pharisees and the priests had gathered together, and when they heard that all the people were moaning and beating their breasts, and saying, "If his death has produced these overwhelming signs, he must have been completely innocent!" ²They became frightened and went to Pilate and begged him, ³"Give us soldiers so that <we> can guard his tomb for three [days], in case his disciples come and steal his body and the people assume that he is risen from the dead and do us harm."

⁴So Pilate gave them the officer Petronius with soldiers to guard the tomb. And elders and scholars went with them to the tomb. ⁵And all who were there <with> the officer and the soldiers helped roll a large stone against the entrance to the tomb. ⁶And they put seven seals on it. Then they pitched a tent there and kept watch.

9 Early, at first light on the Sabbath, a crowd came from Jerusalem and the surrounding countryside to see the sealed tomb. ²But during the night before the Lord's day dawned, while the soldiers were on guard, in pairs during each watch, a loud noise came from the sky, ³and they saw the skies open up and two men come down from there in a burst of light and approach the tomb. ⁴The stone that had been pushed against the entrance began to roll by itself and moved away to one side; then the tomb opened up and both young men went inside.

10 Now when these soldiers saw this, they roused the officer from his sleep, along with the elders. (Remember, they were also there keeping watch.) ²While they were explaining what they had seen, again they see three men leaving the tomb, two supporting the third. And a cross was following them.

³The heads of the two men reached up to the sky, while the head of the third, whom they led by the hand, reached beyond the skies. ⁴And they heard a voice from the skies that said, "Have you preached to those who sleep?"

⁵And an answer was heard from the cross: "Yes!"

11 These men then consulted with one another about going and reporting these things to Pilate. ²While they were still thinking about it, again the skies appeared to open and some sort of human being came down and entered the tomb. ³When those in the officer's unit saw this, they rushed out into the night to Pilate, leaving the tomb that they were supposed to be guarding. And as they were recounting everything they had seen, they became deeply disturbed and cried, "He really was God's son!"

⁴Pilate responded by saying, "I am clean of the blood of the son of God; this was all your doing."

⁵Then they all crowded around <Pilate> and began to beg and urge him to order the officer and his soldiers to tell no one

what they had seen. ⁶"You see," they said, "it's better for us to be guilty of the greatest sin before God than to fall into the hands of the Judean people and be stoned."

⁷Pilate then ordered the officer and the soldiers to say nothing.

12 Early on the Lord's day, Mary of Magdala, a disciple of the lord, was fearful on account of the Judeans and, since they were inflamed with rage, she did not do at the lord's tomb what women usually do for their loved ones who die. ²Nevertheless, she took her friends with her and went to the tomb where he had been laid. ³And they were afraid that the Judeans might see them and were saying, "Although on the day he was crucified we could not weep and beat our breasts, we should now perform these rites at his tomb. ⁴But who will roll away the stone for us, the one placed at the entrance of the tomb, so that we can enter and sit beside him and do what ought to be done?" ⁵(Remember, it was a huge stone.) "We fear that someone might see us. And if we are unable <to roll the stone away> we should, at least, place at the entrance the memorial we brought for him, and we should weep and beat our breasts until we go home."

13 And they went and found the tomb open. They went up to it, stooped down, and saw a young man sitting there <in> the middle of the tomb; he was handsome and wore a splendid robe. He said to them, ²"Why have you come? Who are you looking for? Surely not the one who was crucified? He is risen and gone. If you don't believe it, stoop down and take a look at the place where he lay—he's not there. You see, he is risen and has gone back to the place he was sent from."

³Then the women fled in fear.

14 Now it was the last day of Unleavened Bread, and many began to return to their homes because the festival was over. ²But we, the twelve disciples of the lord, continued to weep and mourn, and each one, still grieving because of what had happened, left for his own home. ³But I, Simon Peter, and Andrew, my brother, took our fishing nets and went away to the sea. And with us was Levi, the son of Alphaeus, whom the lord …

Appendix C
The Retellings
of the Tale

The Epiphany Material

It is incumbent upon me to fill out the compositional history of Peter so that the argument I advanced above (pp. 100–120) might be seen as fully as possible. The haunting issue of genre is still before us. Is it possible to discern why the rest of the material in Peter has been added and at what level? Does the contention that that the basic story was the Tale of the Suffering Innocent One enable us to see any possibilities?

To some determination of these questions let us return to a critical appraisal of the remaining verses in the Gospel of Peter.[1] First of all, we must agree with Crossan that the pre-narrative scribal activity (such as a midrashic construction from Jewish scriptural verse) is not in evidence once we move away from the passion narrative into the burial account.[2] Second, while 8:1–11:7 might appear to be a self-contained unit, beginning with the various leaders of the Jews going to Pilate and then returning to him (in both cases urging him to issue a command—8:3–4; 11:5, 7), there are significant problems. The unit follows.

> 8 When the scholars and the Pharisees and the priests had gathered together, and when they heard that all the people were moaning and beating their breasts, and saying, "If his death has produced these overwhelming signs, he must have been completely innocent!" [2]They became frightened and went to Pilate and begged him, [3]"Give us soldiers so that <we> can guard his tomb for three [days], in case his disciples come and steal his body and the people assume that he is risen from the dead and do us harm."
>
> [4]So Pilate gave them the officer Petronius with soldiers to guard the tomb. And elders and scholars went with them to the tomb. [5]And all who were there <with> the officer and the soldiers helped roll a large stone against the entrance to the tomb. [6]And they put seven seals on it. Then they pitched a tent there and kept watch.

9 Early, at first light on the Sabbath, a crowd came from Jerusalem and the surrounding countryside to see the sealed tomb. [2]But during the night before the Lord's day dawned, while the soldiers were on guard, in pairs during each watch, a loud noise came from the sky, [3]and they saw the skies open up and two men come down from there in a burst of light and approach the tomb. [4]The stone that had been pushed against the entrance began to roll by itself and moved away to one side; then the tomb opened up and both young men went inside.

10 Now when these soldiers saw this, they roused the officer from his sleep, along with the elders. (Remember, they were also there keeping watch.) [2]While they were explaining what they had seen, again they see three men leaving the tomb, two supporting the third. And a cross was following them.

[3]The heads of the two men reached up to the sky, while the head of the third, whom they led by the hand, reached beyond the skies. [4]And they heard a voice from the skies that said, "Have you preached to those who sleep?"

[5]And an answer was heard from the cross: "Yes!"

11 These men then consulted with one another about going and reporting these things to Pilate. [2]While they were still thinking about it, again the skies appeared to open and some sort of human being came down and entered the tomb. [3]When those in the officer's unit saw this, they rushed out into the night to Pilate, leaving the tomb that they were supposed to be guarding. And as they were recounting everything they had seen, they became deeply disturbed and cried, "He really was God's son!"

[4]Pilate responded by saying, "I am clean of the blood of the son of God; this was all your doing."

[5]Then they all crowded around <Pilate> and began to beg and urge him to order the officer and his soldiers to tell no one what they had seen. [6]"You see," they said, "it's better for us to be guilty of the greatest sin before God than to fall into the hands of the Judean people and be stoned."

[7]Pilate then ordered the officer and the soldiers to say nothing.

It is hard to maintain the compositional unity with the removal of 11:1–2 as a redactional anticipation.

11 These men then consulted with one another about going and reporting these things to Pilate. [2]While they were still thinking about it, again the skies appeared to open and some sort of human being came down and entered the tomb.

I have already argued for the earlier status of 8:1b (p. 107). Then there is 10:4–5 which seems to come literally out of the blue! Moreover, Crossan has rightly argued that 11:2 prepares for 12:1–13:3, with no other reason for its existence at that place in the narrative.[3]

12 Early on the Lord's day, Mary of Magdala, a disciple of the lord, was fearful on account of the Judeans and, since they were inflamed with rage, she did not do at the lord's tomb what women usually do for their loved ones who die. [2]Nevertheless, she took her friends with her and went to the tomb where he had been laid. [3]And they were afraid that the Judeans might see them and were saying, "Although on the day he was crucified we could not weep and beat our breasts, we should now perform these rites at his tomb. [4]But who will roll away the stone for us, the one placed at the entrance of the tomb, so that we can enter and sit beside him and do what ought to be done?" [5](Remember, it was a huge stone.) "We fear that someone might see us. And if we are unable <to roll the stone away> we should, at least, place at the entrance the memorial we brought for him, and we should weep and beat our breasts until we go home."

13 And they went and found the tomb open. They went up to it, stooped down, and saw a young man sitting there <in> the middle of the tomb; he was handsome and wore a splendid robe. He said to them, [2]"Why have you come? Who are you looking for? Surely not the one who was crucified? He is risen and gone. If you don't believe it, stoop down and take a look at the place where he lay—he's not there. You see, he is risen and has gone back to the place he was sent from."

[3]Then the women fled in fear.

Further, 11:4 follows quite unexpectedly from the immediately preceding verse:

11 [3]When those in the officer's unit saw this, they rushed out into the night to Pilate, leaving the tomb that they were

supposed to be guarding. And as they were recounting everything they had seen, they became deeply disturbed and cried,
"He really was God's son!"

⁴Pilate responded by saying, "I am clean of the blood of the
son of God; this was all your doing." ⁵Then they all crowded
around <Pilate> and began to beg and urge him to order the
officer and his soldiers to tell no one what they had seen.

Pilate is not even speaking to those witnesses but is actually
speaking of matters that would make sense to those who will
not have arrived until the next verse!

11 ⁵Then they all crowded around <Pilate> and began to beg
and urge him to order the officer and his soldiers to tell no
one what they had seen.

Pilate's declaration of innocence ties in with 1:1:

but of the Judeans no one washed his hands, neither Herod
nor any one of his judges. Since they were [un]willing to
wash, Pilate stood up.

One could also say that the notion of purity/defilement regis-
tered in 11:4 continues in 11:6 ("it's better for us to be guilty of
the greatest sin before God"). The materials that I have already
removed from the passion narrative that pertain to the sense
of cultic defilement may well be linked with these verses (1:1;
2:3–4; 6:2–3a).

A more significant matter is the very format of this material. Koester has argued that the basis of this section bears the
features of a *miraculous epiphany story*.[4] The above-mentioned
redactional issues I believe become clarified when one discerns
the early epiphany story. Following Koester's proposal, we can
see the following:

Introduction	8:1–9:1
Epiphany	9:2–3
Miracle	9:4
Appearance	10:2–3
Reaction of Witnesses	11:3

I would nuance Koester's suggestion of the Introductory material by noting that 8:2b would be separate and that 8:2a could
have led directly into 8:29b:

> 8 [1a]When the scholars and the Pharisees and the priests had
> gathered together, ... [2b]... went to Pilate and begged him

Verses 8:2a ("they became frightened") and 8:2b ("when they
heard that") I would consider as being included during the
interpolation of 8:2b. The latter nicely serves to include the
earlier material, while the former adds motive and additional
reaction. We should note that Crossan considers 7:1–11:7 to be
two distinct narrative units—minus the particular redactional
material (7:2–3; 9:4; 11:1–2)—that would be on the earliest historical level. The difficulty I have with Crossan's position is that
he does not formally deal with the verses that he describes as
narrative units. If Koester is correct about the epiphany form
and if my earlier formal and redactional observations have any
merit, then one must reevaluate Crossan's primary narrative
units. On the other hand, Koester's redactional points should
not be lost. Indeed, it is precisely the considerations of the form
of the miraculous epiphany story that more cogently push for a
detection of secondary material within 8:1–11:7.

With this in mind one can argue that 10:1 is a secondary
expansion that "tries to involve the centurion and the other
witnesses":[5]

> 10 Now when these soldiers saw this, they roused the officer
> from his sleep, along with the elders. (Remember, they were
> also there keeping watch.)

This passage actually contradicts the later 11:3 (which is part
of the original epiphany story) while it sets up the basis for the
sinfulness of those who would cover up the event (11:6).

> 11 [6]"You see," they said, "it's better for us to be guilty of
> the greatest sin before God than to fall into the hands of the
> Judean people and be stoned."

One can also consider as secondary 10:2a ("while they were
explaining what they had seen") since it follows from 10:1 and
provides a redactional link with the original 10:2b:

> 10 [2b]again they see three men leaving the tomb, two support-
> ing the third. And a cross was following them.

Verses 10:4–5 would also be distinctly secondary as a surprising
intrusion into the material:

10 [4]and they heard a voice from the skies that said, "Have you preached to those who sleep?" [5]And an answer was heard from the cross, "Yes!"

I think that 10:2c ("and a cross was following them") is a redactional insertion preparing for this unusual fragmentary material. Verse 11:1 is a redactional seam both for 10:5 and for what happens in 11:2.

11 [2]These men then consulted with one another about going and reporting these things to Pilate.

I agree with Crossan as to its redactional preparation for 12:1ff. and would therefore place it on the same level as that material. In regard to 11:3, I would agree with Koester in saying that the description of the report to Pilate interrupts the context and seems designed to exonerate Pilate—a secondary motif.[6] We have noted already the problems in 11:4. We should simply point out that this apologetic *pro Pilato* continues in 11:5–6. Verse 11:7 ends this secondary material:

Pilate then ordered the officer and the soldiers to say nothing.

Thus, one can distill the following miraculous epiphany story:

Introduction
8 [1a]When the scholars and the Pharisees and the priests had gathered together, … [2b]they went to Pilate and begged him, [3]"Give us soldiers so that <we> can guard his tomb for three [days], in case his disciples come and steal his body and the people assume that he is risen from the dead and do us harm."[4]So Pilate gave them the officer Petronius with soldiers to guard the tomb. And elders and scholars went with them to the tomb. [5]And all who were there <with> the officer and the soldiers helped roll a large stone against the entrance to the tomb. [6]And they put seven seals on it. Then they pitched a tent there and kept watch. 9 Early, at first light on the Sabbath, a crowd came from Jerusalem and the surrounding countryside to see the sealed tomb.

Epiphany
9 [2]But during the night before the Lord's day dawned, while the soldiers were on guard, in pairs during each watch, a loud noise came from the sky, [3]and they saw the skies open

up and two men come down from there in a burst of light and approach the tomb.

Miracle
9 [4]The stone that had been pushed against the entrance began to roll by itself and moved away to one side; then the tomb opened up and both young men went inside.

Appearance
10 [2b]again they see three men leaving the tomb, two supporting the third. And a cross was following them.

[3]The heads of the two men reached up to the sky, while the head of the third, whom they led by the hand, reached beyond the skies.

Reaction of Witnesses
11 [3]When those in the officer's unit saw this, they rushed out into the night to Pilate, leaving the tomb that they were supposed to be guarding. And as they were recounting everything they had seen, they became deeply disturbed and cried, "He really was God's son!"

Having separated out this probable epiphany story, we must now see how this builds upon the earlier passion narrative. *The original frame or locus of the Suffering Innocent One provides the authorization for further narrative addition and development.* With the simple redactional tie in of 8:1a with 8:1b (and the filling in of 8:2a) we have a major revision of the original story of persecution and vindication. *The epiphany material now functions as an intensification of the vindication side of the story.* Certainly the *reaction* (11:3c) of the guards is an *acclamation.* The elements of persecution still echo throughout this material. A *conspiracy* is present in 8:1–2. Even an *ordeal* could be seen in the setting of the guard, the rolling of the stone, and the sealing of the tomb (8:4b–6). The *rescue* could be viewed in 9:1–4; 10:2b, 3. Significant differences, however, argue for more than a simple repetition of the genre of the Innocent Sufferer. Note, for example, that the *accusation* is now found in the charge that the disciples would steal the body to produce a fraud (8:3b). Here we see a good indication that *the focus upon the figure of the Suffering Innocent One is being displaced by later concerns.* The original narrative provides a basic skeletal frame for a variety of shifts, changes of direction, and significant transformations. In this instance, the addition of the epiphany narrative both expands and reinforces the claims of the original. At the same time, however, there are very important changes. The miraculous apparition outshines the muted exaltation of the crucified just one. Certain historicizing tendencies have markedly entered the picture. This amalgamation of passion narrative and epiphany story may have been intended to provide a more balanced narrative, wherein the downbeat of the persecution is matched by the miraculous note of triumph. What had been an apologetic attempt to make sense of the fate of Jesus becomes a powerful story that could well serve both missionary and defensive purposes. In fact, the introduction of the epiphany material indicates social redefinition. As Mack has cogently argued,[7] such material emerges out of a community's attempt to gain social orientation and identity. Here was an attempt to adjust to a more Gentile audience, while simultaneously maintaining Jewish ties.

Further Redactional Issues

It is now appropriate to consider those verses that have been separated out as secondary, either to the original passion narrative or to the epiphany story. Verses 1:1 and 11:4 would seem to come from the same hand. Verse 1:2 is linked with 1:1, while 11:5–7 follow upon 11:4 (as argued above). The concern for purity/defilement noted in 11:6 seems consistent with the burial taboo noted in 2:3a,b (and hence with 5:1b; 6:2, 3a). But this material seems to have become linked with the Joseph tradition (2:1–2; 6:3–4). Verses 10:1–2a prepare for 11:4–7. Verse 10:2c anticipates the enclosed independent fragment of 10:4–5. Verse 11:1 serves as a redactional seam for the previous interpolation.

When we include this secondary material into the narrative level we see that the story now moves decisively to a focus on individual characters, to a more precise drawing of lines between individuals and groups. One can also still see some telltale indications of building upon the skeletal story frame of the original version. The Joseph narrative fills out the generic lines of *assistance* in the innocent sufferer tradition.[8] Indeed, the figure of Pilate functions within the component of *protest* in that tradition. We now see blame assigned to and discrimination against those who are guilty, especially of covering up the *acclamation* of the son of God. Herod is explicitly named as the one who issues the *condemnation*. This order is juxtaposed with the hypocritical concern for burial observances. This last point would reinforce the focus on the drawing of social lines or boundaries. Even the mysterious 10:2c, 4–5 may well touch upon the *vindication* of the just one, who receives an otherworldly reversal of fate. In other words, we have the early generic lines of the story of the persecuted innocent one now filled in by specific characters in a more historicized and socially defined context. While space does not permit it here, it would be worth investigating whether a structural analysis of this material could flesh out these narrative ramifications.

Furthermore, with more lines of discrimination drawn, the political reality out of which this revision emerged has greatly shifted. Crossan has pointed out that there seems to be a decided shift in what he calls the "original Cross" gospel. A first stage wherein there is no hint of discord between authorities and people gives way to a second where matters are quite changed.[9] His observation, however, rests upon little redactional rigor. The reason for the apparent shift is that there are two distinct layers of composition, wherein the discord between people and the leaders (intimated already in the redactional material of 8:1b, 2a) is explicitly brought out in this secondary material. Quite significant to our discussion is the simple phrase "the Judean people" (11:6); it contrasts with the term "the people" (8:3) found within the addition of the epiphany narrative. The phrase in 11:6 places the leaders over against their own people. The Judean leaders fall in line with the other symbols of political oppression, Herod and Pilate (linked together in this later material). This level of material, which presents the only explicit scriptural citation, along with concerns for purity, reflects further disagreement within the diaspora synagogue. It is crucial to see that the term "the Judeans" dealt with below represents an even further development in terms of social definition and, most likely, alienation. The story, then, recast with the varied secondary additions, focuses more explicitly upon the political dark side. Does this mirror the political upheavals emerging before the siege of Jerusalem?

A Final Layer?

Some verses of Peter are, as yet, still outstanding. We have argued above that 7:1 appears to be linked on the same redactional level as 7:2–3. Accordingly 14:1–3 would be found there also:

7 Then the Judeans and the elders and the priests perceived what evil they had done to themselves, and began to beat their breasts and cry out "Our sins have brought disasters down on us! The judgment and the end of Jerusalem are at hand!"

²But I began weeping with my friends. And quivering with fear in our hearts, we hid ourselves. (You see we were being sought by them as criminals and as people who wanted to burn down the temple.) ³As a result of all these things, we fasted and sat mourning and weeping night and day until the Sabbath.

14 Now it was the last day of Unleavened Bread, and many began to return to their homes because the festival was over. ²But we, the twelve disciples of the lord, continued to weep and mourn, and each one, still grieving because of what had happened, left for his own home. ³But I, Simon Peter, and Andrew, my brother, took our fishing nets and went away to the sea. And with us was Levi, the son of Alphaeus, whom the lord …

We can likewise point out that 12:1b, 3a (and 12:5b?) seem to come from that same redactional level (cf. 7:26–27; 14:58–60):

12 … ¹ᵇfearful on account of the Judeans and, since they were inflamed with rage

³ᵃAnd they were afraid that the Judeans might see them and were saying,

⁵ᵇ"We fear that someone might see us."

The fear of "the Judeans," as well as the "mourning and weeping" of the disciples (male and female), suggests a definite linkage. Of course, the observation of the first person, singular and plural, has been stressed above. Further elements should be indicated. First, we seem to be at a time after the fall of Jerusalem (7:1–2). Second, we now have for the first time a self-conscious indication of a community over against the "Judeans." The "we versus them" mentality, perhaps already gaining impetus in the assignment of guilt to the leaders in the previous version of this tradition, now comes to the fore. Third, the concern for the fate of the Temple (esp. 7:1) enters at this level and may speak to what Nickelsburg has speculated as to a pre-Markan tradition featuring such a component.[10] Fourth, we have an empty tomb story (12:1–13:3), which Crossan argues is dependent upon Mark 16:1–8. His argument basically stands upon the contention that it is the writer of Mark who is responsible for the creation of the empty tomb narrative.[11] While I find his argument fascinating I am not thoroughly convinced. Despite Crossan's argument that Mark 16:7 is so "strange" that it necessitated revision from the slightest (Matt 28:10) to the greatest (John 20:17), I find it difficult to understand why the final redactor of Peter has removed a verse ("He is going ahead of you to Galilee. There you will see him …") which would anticipate 14:3! Furthermore, when one removes what appear to be the final level of redaction from the empty tomb story in Peter (12:1b, 3a, 5b?), one is left with a format strikingly similar to Mark 16:1–8 (minus v. 7). Although Crossan is loathe to multiply solutions, I would suggest that there was a pre-Markan and pre-Petrine tradition, utilized by each independently (perhaps generated from a lament tradition; cf. cameo on "Memorial Meal and Lament," pp. 57–58). The question of the dependency of later portions of Peter upon the canonical gospels is further brought out in regard to 14:1–3, which Crossan argues is dependent upon John 21:7–8. I am not at all convinced about the dependency of 14:1–3 upon John 21. First, only Simon Peter is the same in both accounts; second, we do not have very similar language — no more than found in Luke 5:1–11, where there is a mention of nets, or Mark 1:16–20. The presumption might well be that 14:1–3 matches John 21 since both are post-resurrection stories. But, have not similar arguments been proposed for Luke 5:1–11?[12]

These observations demonstrate that this final layer of material enters into the compositional development of Peter certainly after the group identified with Simon Peter has become alienated from their Jewish matrix. In addition, the brief remarks about the temple suggest the post 70 CE period. We also note echoes — but only distant ones — of the original story format. The addition of the empty tomb story reemphasizes the note of *vindication* somewhat muted by the ending of the third version's negative polemic. The women certainly present still another *reaction*, while the references to "the Judeans" imply the element of *ordeal* or *conspiracy*. However, too great a focus on these weakening reverberations obscures the true direction and function of the revised material. The story now works within a strikingly different social and historical situation. The original story came to grips with the fate of Jesus, which, in turn, felt the explosive force of the addition of the epiphany material, and then received further political and social correction through the addition of fragmentary material. Further redirection occurred through the additions by those who identified around the figure of Simon Peter. Here the lines of inner and outer, of "Judeans" and "us" became keenly drawn. Was the Antiochene connection reasserting itself here? What emerged was a definite alienation from those who identified with the ideology of the Second Temple or its revision in the Pharisaic reinterpretation.

Notes

Introduction

1. Dillenberger, *Religious Art*, 95–97.
2. See Funk, *The Acts of Jesus*, 132–33.
3. For an excellent study of how humans avoid their stance towards death, see Becker, *The Denial of Death*.
4. James Allen's *Without Sanctuary* demonstrates that the transmission of violent death is not a neutral affair. See cameo, pp. 15–16.
5. See Dewey, "Fact of Fiction, Fiction of Fact."

1 How Little There Is

1. Snyder, *Ante Pacem*.
2. See White, *Scripting Jesus*, 133.
3. As we shall see in chapters 4 and 5, pp. 42–43, 62–63, we do not learn much more either from the pre-Pauline fragments or from Paul himself about the death of Jesus, except that he was crucified.

2 Facing Death

1. Matthew and Luke both take over their Markan source in their own fashion. Cf. Matt 17:22–23; Luke 9:43–45; Matt 20:17–19; Luke 18:31–34; Matt 26:2; Luke 17:25. The Gospel of John also carries forward the three passion predictions but they have been revised along Johannine lines. John 3:14; 8:28 and 12:32–34 focus on the "lifting up of the Son of Man" as they anticipate seeing Jesus' death as a revelation of the divine life.
2. See Duling, *The New Testament*, 306, 308–9, 313–16.
3. In fact Luke 13:31–33, where the Lukan Jesus is warned by Pharisees of Herod's murderous intent, can be seen as a Lukan construction. The words of Jesus reflect Luke's conception of the gospel narrative and his fate is cast in the language of the Lukan community. It is certainly possible that the historical Jesus felt pressure from hostile powers. But the question remains: where is the evidence? Many scholars simply assume that Jesus anticipated a tragic end because he lived in uncertain times. But such assumptions run counter to the sayings detected from the historical Jesus. Moreover, by declaring something is plausible, namely, that Jesus plausibly feared for his life or even expected to die, does not make it probable. The shock of his followers following his death speaks volumes about the surprising outcome of Jesus' career.
4. This assertion is contrary to the contention of Resa Aslan, and means that the claim of Albert Schweitzer (and Aslan), namely that Jesus was an apocalyptic visionary determined to use his death as the occasion for the coming of God, cannot be supported by the historical evidence. For a critique of the claim that Jesus was an apocalyptic visionary, see my introduction to *The Gospel of Jesus*, 11, where I argue that the historical Jesus' vision of God's empire strongly countered an apocalyptic view. For an excellent discussion of this question see: Miller, *The Apocalyptic Jesus*; Miller, *The Jesus Seminar and its Critics*; Miller, "Is the Apocalyptic Jesus History?"
5. Crossan, Horsley, Brown, Fredrickson.

6. What happens when peasants conclude that they are "worth more than a flock of sparrows" (Q/Luke 12:6)? Further, Luke 17:21 and Thom 113:4 would argue that Jesus envisioned the reality of God's empire as effectively present (Luke 17:21: "The empire of God is among you." Thom 113:4: "Rather, the Father's empire is spread out upon the earth and people don't see it."). Couple these with "Congratulations, you poor, God's empire belongs to you!" (Luke 6:20) and one can begin to detect a sense that God's empire, although not immediately apparent, was effectively present but listeners had to puzzle through these aphorisms to discover their meaning.

7. The language used in Mark 14:23–24 reflects the liturgical language of a memorial meal, where the death of Jesus has been recalled and understood as a heroic death. See Dennis Smith, *From Symposium to Eucharist*.

8. Ironically this prayer is absent in Mark. This scene in chapter 14 may explain why it is not there.

3 Evidence from the Sayings Gospels

1. The Sayings Gospel (Q) may well have gone through a significant development. Kloppenborg, for example, argues persuasively that there are three distinct layers to the evidence, in light of the Q community's growth and interaction with fellow Jews. See John Kloppenborg, *The Formation of Q* and *Excavating Q*.

2. Brandon Scott has argued that the Sayings Gospel knows of Jesus' death by crucifixion but it has no passion account and does not understand Jesus' death as salvific. It understands the rejection of Jesus in terms of the fate of the prophets of old. The Sayings Gospel as part of the wisdom tradition views Jesus as the just one, who was God's prophet, was rejected and murdered by his enemies and was taken up, assumed, and will then stand in judgment at the end. The pattern is remarkably similar to that of the just one in the Wisdom of Solomon. See Scott, *The Trouble with Resurrection*, 140–41.

3. Evidently a tradition had arisen in Judaism that Lady Wisdom had offspring in every generation. John the Baptizer and Jesus were seen by the Q community as genuine sons of Wisdom. Cf. WisSol 7:27 "In every generation she passes into holy souls, and makes them friends of God and prophets."

4. See chapter 2, pp. 23–26. We have seen how the historical Jesus did not center his focus on the matter of death. Also see Funk, Dewey and the Jesus Seminar, *The Gospel of Jesus*, 11, where I point out that Jesus placed the emphasis on the effective presence of God.

5. In Stoic-cynic sayings the carrying of one's cross was a way of referring to accepting one's fate. Here Q 14:27 emphasizes this sense but it might well echo in retrospect the actual manner of Jesus' death. See Epictetus, *Diatribes* 2.2.20 "For if you wish to be crucified, wait and the cross will come."

6. The dating of Thomas is still highly controversial. The original dating to the second century CE has been challenged by many scholars who see the possibility of a date in the last quarter of the first century CE. See Michael White, *From Jesus to Christianity*, 303.

7. Right from the outset of the gospel there is the provocative saying: "Whoever discovers the interpretation of these sayings will not taste death." Such a saying functions as a wisdom puzzle that provokes an attempt at comprehension. This tantalizing insight recurs throughout (18:3; 19:4; 85:2; 111:2). The person "living from the living one will not see death" (111:2).

8. Milavec, *The Didache*, 884–88. Milavec represents a new assessment of the dating of the Didache. L. Michael White (*From Jesus to Christianity*, 331) would take the majority position of dating the text to the early to middle second cen-

tury CE. Milavec may well be correct that many of the sayings in the Didache can be dated to the middle of the first century.

9. E.g., Did 1:4 If anyone should strike you on the right cheek, turn to him the other, and you will be perfect; if anyone should press you into service for one mile, go with him two; if anyone should take away your cloak, give to him your tunic. Cf. Q 6:29a; QMt 5:41; Q 6:29b.

4 The Re-imagination of a Death

1. As noted, the Sayings Gospel gives us an allusion to the death of Jesus.

2. Traditionally Bible readers have gone to Acts to determine Paul's earlier life and behavior. We cannot use Acts 9:1–9 as a basis for judgment since the text may well reflect a second-century hand. In addition, the story format in Acts 9 is a literary commonplace of the scene of someone who opposes a god (cf. The Bacchae). Recent research has shown that Acts is not a reliable witness to Paul's early life. Rather, it conveys a second century revision of the figure of Paul and the Pauline tradition. In sum, we are forced to go back to the primary source, namely, Paul himself—in all his limitations. See Smith, Tyson and the Acts Seminar, *Acts and Christian Beginnings*. Also, Scott, *The Real Paul*, 9–15.

3. It should be pointed out that Paul does use the term *apocalypsis* (insight, breakthrough) elsewhere in Galatians and there it probably means a communal experience (Gal 2:2). Some scholars have linked the heavenly vision in 2 Cor 12:1–10, but that position has not found much acceptance. Moreover, Paul uses that scene in a comic way as a parody of an apocalyptic vision. Another possibility is that Paul's harassment of early Jesus communities (perhaps in Syria) may well have given him the occasion to observe their communal experience. Did what he saw stop him from his intended action? Was he surprised by what he did find? An indirect witness of Paul's experience might be found in 1 Cor 14:23–25 where Paul speaks of the experience of an outsider who discovers that the deepest dreams of his heart are revealed in the activity of communal prophesying. Could the experience of Paul have been the discovery that "God really was present" among those he zealously wanted to wipe out? This removes Paul's experience from being an individual affair to one embedded in social interaction.

> If then the whole congregation has come together in one place and everyone is speaking in ecstatic languages and outsiders or unbelievers come in, will they not say that you are mad? But if everyone is prophesying and some unbelievers or uninitiated persons come in, they will be convicted by all, called to account by all, the secrets of their hearts are exposed; and so they will fall on their faces and worship God and declare that "God really is present among you." (1 Cor 14:23–25 SV)

4. 1 Thessalonians 4 vv. out of 85 vv. (4.7 percent) 1:10; 2:15; 4:14; 5:10. Galatians 7 vv. out of 149 vv. (4.6 percent) 1:4; 2:19; 2:21; 3:1; 3:13; 6:12; 6:14. 1 Corinthians 11 vv. out of 434 vv. (2.5 percent) 1:13; 1:17; 1:18; 1:23; 2:2; 2:8; 5:8; 8:11; 11:23; 11:26; 15:3. Philippians 3 vv. out of 104 vv. (2.8 percent) 2:8; 3:10; 3:18. 2 Corinthians 4 vv. out of 250 vv. (1.6 percent) 4:10; 5:14; 5:15; 13:4. Philemon 0 v. out of 25 vv. (0 percent). Romans 17 vv. out of 428 vv. (3.9 percent) 3:14; 3:25; 5:6–8; 5:10; 6:3; 6:5; 6:6–8; 6:10; 8:32; 8:34; 10:7; 14:9; 15:3.

5. Many scholars are divided over viewing this passage as a later insertion. However, the fact that this material interrupts the tone and logic of what precedes and what follows, and that the situation alluded to probably reflected the fate of Jerusalem in 70 CE, may well argue for it being a later insertion.

6. This turning of the tables can be dramatically understood in Romans 7–8, where Paul presents the figure of someone who succeeds in embodying the best of Roman and Jewish Law/Culture (Rom 7:6ff.). All this does is to bring out the self-contradiction within such a competitive personality. Only life in solidarity with the beloved community (ch. 8) leads to a meaningful present and hopeful future.

7. For more on the utopian drive of Paul's vision see Dewey, "EIS TEN SPANIAN."

5 Pre-Pauline Traditions

1. Rudolf Bultmann led the twenty-century's attempt to bring the Christian tradition into modernity through what he called demythologization. He already found in the New Testament evidence that the early Jesus communities had interpreted the meaning of what God had done to Jesus and expressed this meaning in their understanding as they proclaimed God's action. The task of the modern believer is to continue to re-interpret this surprising action of God in new terms.

2. In the translation of *The Authentic Letters of Paul*, the translators were aware of the penchant of North Americans for the short sentence and have broken the single sentence into appropriate phrases.

3. Williams, " Righteousness of God in Romans."

4. Seeley, "Concept of the Noble Death in Paul."

5. Mack, *Myth of Innocence*, 109–10.

6. Notice that this death is not the substitutory death found in the later theological writings of Anselm.

7. Smith, *From Symposium to Eucharist*, 188.

8. Romans 8:32 presents the view that God "handed over" Jesus to be killed.

9. Taussig, *In the Beginning Was the Meal*, 131.

10. See Reumann, *Philippians*. Reumann argues that the poem was composed by the community in Philippi (363–64) and that Paul shows his approval by inserting it into his letter. He further sees this passage as exhibiting the characteristics of the rhetorical form of praise—an encomium (333, 339).

11. The meaning of this passage has long been debated in relation to its possible structure. Lohmeyer's influential analysis of the structure of the "hymn," (*Kyrios Jesus*, 1928), saw the material organized into six strophes of three lines each. The one line of the "hymn" that did not fit in this structure, "even death by crucifixion," was thought to be a Pauline addition to a pre-Pauline composition. This structural analysis assumes that underneath the basic pattern of the "hymn" is schema of the descent and ascent of the figure it celebrates. The first three strophes recount the descent, the last three the ascent. On the other hand, Talbert's structural analysis sees the "hymn" as organized in four strophes. This analysis is based on close attention to the parallelism within the passage and offers an arrangement in which each strophe expresses a complete thought that is reinforced by repetition of important terms (Talbert, "The Problem of Pre-Existence"). This analysis of the "hymn's" structure is consistent with the view that the "hymn" intends to contrast the First and Second Adams. The First Adam, as all who have heard the story of his creation and fall in Genesis know, mishandled his status as a creature and blundered into self-exaltation that resulted in his self-destruction. The Second Adam rightly handled his status as a creature and was approved by God as a model of how a human being should conduct himself, and was exalted as the prototype and lord of a recreated human race. James Dunn, Roy Hoover, and Jerome Murphy-O'Connor have argued in terms of this second option. Hellerman has demonstrated that the piece demonstrates an anti-imperial pattern, with

the emperor providing the antitype. Whether it is a hymn or a poem is still problematic. It is at least a poetic encomium (see previous note). Some years ago at a graduate New Testament Seminar at Harvard, Archbishop Demetrios Trakatellis, visiting his alma mater, provided some balance to the knotty problem. He was amused at the intricate attempts to parse various verses as hymns. He observed, "Hymn? Hymn? We do not sing just a few verses, we sing the entire book!"

12. The redeemer myth found throughout the ancient world (where a divine being descends to deliver benefits and then returns to the heavenly realm) has also been offered as a candidate for providing the imaginative matrix for this piece. This option actually affirms the traditional interpretation of the poem.

13. A contrasting example of the grandiose vision of the Emperor can be found in Virgil's famous image of Augustus inaugurating the golden age. Anchises, Aeneas' father, foresees the great glory of the Roman people:

> Turn your two eyes
> This way and see this people, your own Romans.
> Here is Caesar, and all the line of Iulus
> All who shall one day pass under the dome
> Of the great sky: this is the man, this one
> of whom so often you have heard the promise,
> Caesar Augustus, son of the deified,
> Who shall bring once again an Age of Gold
> To Latium, to the land where Saturn reigned
> In early times. He will extend his power
> Beyond the Garamants and Indians
> Over far territories north and south
> Of the zodiacal stars, the solar way,
> Where Atlas, heaven-bearing, on his shoulder
> Turns the night-sphere, studded with burning stars.
> At that man's coming even now the realms
> Of Caspia and Maeotia tremble, warned
> By oracles, and the seven mouths of Nile
> Go dark with fear.
>
> (Aeneid, 6:789–800; Fitzgerald, 187–88)

14. Mack, *Myth of Innocence*, 104.
15. Mack, *Myth of Innocence*, 257.

6 Memory and Midrash

1. Lee and Scott, *Sound Mapping the New Testament*. The literacy percentage hovers around 2 percent for the non-urban world.
2. Carruthers, *The Book of Memory; The Craft of Thought*. My citations all come from the latter volume.
3. Yates, *The Art of Memory*.
4. Carruthers, *The Craft of Thought*, 11.
5. Carruthers, *The Craft of Thought*, 21.
6. Carruthers, *The Craft of Thought*, 57.
7. The World Trade Center has effectively become another "space" for memory. The continued debate over the site was actually a struggle to determine how the event was to be remembered.
8. See Dewey, "The Gospel of Trajan."
9. See chapters 8–9.
10. *Jewish Encyclopedia*.

11. A further distinction of midrash would be Pesiqta which is a whole sermon or exhortation constructed to bring themes of past into the present.
12. Nickelsburg, *Resurrection, Immortality and Eternal Life*, 56–57.
13. Nickelsburg points out that the story pattern can be used in a variety of contexts. Thus, the stories of Shadrach, Meshach and Abednego (Dan 3), of Daniel in the lions' den (Dan 6), of Susanna, and of the "son of God" in Wisdom of Solomon (WisSol 2, 4–5), all work from the same pattern, yet with different intentions. The over-arching story pattern or "locus" permits numerous retellings. The Story locus functions as a basic DNA for subsequent recombinations.

7 The Markan Passion Narrative

1. Funk and the Jesus Seminar, *The Acts of Jesus*, 132, 246.
2. Dibelius, *From Tradition to Gospel*, 178–217. Kahler provides the most famous version of this statement.
3. The model was this: The initial proclamation of the death and resurrection of Jesus was followed by an early historical account that was followed by what appears in Mark. For more on this see Mack, *A Myth of Innocence*, 251ff.
4. See chapter 2 on the Passion Predictions. Here we argued that what looks like predictions from the historical Jesus are actually reflections of the later Markan community.
5. See Michael White, *From Jesus to Christianity*, 231ff. For an excellent introduction: Schmidt, *The Gospel of Mark*.
6. The key to this is found in Mark 13, the apocalyptic chapter, which alerts the community to its response in the end of days.
7. See White, *From Jesus to Christianity*, 231–32.
8. Mark 8:22–10:52 has been called the "heart of the gospel of Mark" (Duling, *The New Testament*), with healing stories providing the structural columns to include a repetitive pattern:

> Geographical Reference: 8:27; 9:30; 10:32
> Prediction: 8:31; 9:31; 10:33–34
> Misunderstanding: 8:32–33; 9:32,33–34; 10:35–41
> Teaching: 8:34–9:1; 9:35–37; 10:42–45

The occasion for the passion predictions becomes also the place where the misunderstanding of the disciples is corrected three times by the Markan Jesus. In other words, this critical section becomes a teaching session for the listening Markan community about the entailments of discipleship as they face the final days.

9. See Mack, *A Myth of Innocence*, 267, where Mack fills out the Markan material with a more detailed usage of Nickelsburg's categories. As such he deepens Nickelsburg's findings.
10. The components listed rely on the findings of Nickelsburg, the additional suggestions of Mack, and my own considerations of the appropriate text. Mack sees Mark 1–10 as an introduction to the passion material.
11. This is the excellent point of Mack, who demonstrates this throughout *A Myth of Innocence.*
12. The attempt to view the death of Jesus as unique follows from later theological convictions, such as the theory of atonement.

8 The Problem of Peter

1. In a conversation with Burton Mack and John Kloppenborg in a deli in Salem, Oregon in 1987, I asked Burton Mack why he didn't consider the Gospel of Peter in his treatment of Mark. Did he not wonder if portions of Peter might

have come before Mark and may have been used by the author? His response was telling. "I did not think of it." This honest remark is not an unusual position for most New Testament scholars.

2. For those scholars who do consider Peter at all, the gospel is seen as something derived from earlier gospels (perhaps a hodgepodge of oral snippets; see Brown, *Death of the Messiah*, 1317–49). Precisely because it is seen as derivative, the Gospel of Peter is relegated to the obscurity of footnotes and not taken seriously as a major clue in the search for the passion narrative of the early communities.

3. See Crossan, *The Cross That Spoke*; "The Gospel of Peter and the Canonical Gospels," and Dewey, "And an Answer was Heard from the Cross"; "Time to Murder and Create"; "The Passion Narrative of the Gospel of Peter."

4. While the Oxyrhynchus fragment alerts us to the possibility of an earlier dating of Peter, we shall actually argue that this Joseph material may come not from the earliest layer of Peter but may well be a secondary redaction to the original layer.

5. Crossan, *Four Other Gospels*, 133.

6. Or, from one championship team to the new one: from Russell to Baez to Rizzo.

7. Crossan has hit upon what may well be the solution to the emphasis upon the figure of Herod in Peter. In responding to the problems listed by Brown, Crossan has argued that the trial material may come from a time soon after the reign of Herod Agrippa (41–44 CE). Crossan has rightly noted that this would not be bad history but excellent popularization, making the "past and present coalesce for popular consumption" (Crossan, *Who Killed Jesus?*, 95). What appears at first blush to be historically or factually implausible becomes the basis for examining a pre-70 CE insertion. This would agree with my layering of the Peter material (Dewey, "Time to Murder and Create," 124).

8. Browne, *The Oxyrhynchus Papyri*, 15–16.

9. Lührmann, "Pox 2949: EvPt 3–5 in einer Handschrift des 2/3 Jahrhunderts."

10. Browne, *The Oxyrhynchus Papyri*, 16.

11. Denker, *Die theologiegeschichtliche Stellung des Petrusevangeliums*, 70.

12. We seem to be at a time after the fall of Jerusalem (7.1–2). Now for the first time do we find a self-conscious indication of a community over against the "Judeans." The "we versus them" mentality, perhaps already gaining impetus in the assignment of guilt to the leaders in the previous version of this tradition, now comes to the fore. The concern for the fate of the Temple (see 7.2) enters at this level and speaks to what Nickelsburg has speculated as to a pre-Markan tradition featuring such a component ("The Genre and Function of the Markan Passion Narrative," 183).

9 The Earliest Layer of Peter

1. Crossan, *The Cross That Spoke*, 12.

2. In brief, the layers of Peter I have detected (1989, 1990) are:

   A. 2:3c–5:1a; 5:2–6:1; 8:1b

   B. 8:1a; 8:1c–9:4; 10:2b–3; 11:3

   C. 2:1–2; 6:3b–4; 10:4–5; 1:1–2; 2:3a,b; 5:1b; 6:2–3a; 8:2a; 10:1–2a,c; 11:1; 11:4–7

   D. 7:1–3; 11:2; 12:1–13:3; 14:1–3

On the other hand, Crossan (1988) has argued for:

   1:1–2; 2:3b–6:2; 7:1; 8:1–9:1; 9:2–10:5; 11:3–7
   6:3–4; 12:1–13:3; 14:3
   2:1–3a; 7:2–3; 14:1–2; 11:1–2

3. Nickelsburg, "The Genre and Function of the Markan Passion Narrative," 153–84.

4. Denker, *Die theologiegeschichtliche Stellung des Petrusevangeliums.*

5. Koester, *Ancient Christian Gospels*, 228.

6. Crossan, *The Cross That Spoke.*

7. Crossan, *Who Killed Jesus?*, 4.

8. This entitlement of "savior" would indicate the non-Jewish member of the community.

10 The Death Story of Jesus in Matthew

1. In the Q Gospel we find that Wisdom speaks of sending prophets and apostles:

> Luke 11 [49]That's why the Wisdom of God has said, "I will send them prophets and apostles, and some of them they are always going to kill and persecute."

Matthew has also appropriated the Q text but now the Matthaean Jesus delivers Wisdom's words:

> Matt 23 [34]Look, that is why I send you prophets and sages and scholars. Some you're going to kill and crucify, and some you're going to flog in your synagogues and hound from town to town.

The Matthaean Jesus is not a new Moses but one greater, that is, the embodiment of Wisdom herself. His pronouncements in the Sermon on the Mount provide a key to interpreting both the oral and written Torah.

2. E.g. White, *From Jesus to Christianity*, 238ff.

3. The material found in a later layer of Peter may also reflect this developing concern.

> 8 [1]When the scholars and the Pharisees and the priests had gathered together, and when they heard that all the people were moaning and beating their breasts, and saying, "If his death has produced these overwhelming signs, he must have been completely innocent!" [2]They became frightened and went to Pilate and begged him, [3]"Give us soldiers so that <we> can guard his tomb for three [days], in case his disciples come and steal his body and the people assume that he is risen from the dead and do us harm."
> [4]So Pilate gave them the officer Petronius with soldiers to guard the tomb. And elders and scholars went with them to the tomb. [5]And all who were there <with> the officer and the soldiers helped roll a large stone against the entrance to the tomb. [6]And they put seven seals on it.

4. A number of notes are sounded to emphasize the innocence of Jesus. Jesus remains non-violent. Judas dies regretting his action towards the innocent one. The request of Pilate's wife further underscores his innocence. The blood curse scene is laced with multiple levels of irony in regard to Jesus' innocence. Even the explicit use of "son of God" evokes the tradition of the innocent ones hard pressed by their enemies (e.g., Wisdom of Solomon 1–5).

11 The Lukan Retelling

1. The prevailing scholarship now argues that Acts was written around the first quarter of the second century. The gospel of Luke may well have been written around 100–110 CE. See Pervo, *Dating Acts.*

2. The writer is quite adept in the style of the Septuagint, the Greek version of the Hebrew Scriptures.

3. On this see White, *From Jesus to Christianity*, 248.

4. In Luke 21:24 ("They will fall by the edge of the sword, and be hauled off as prisoners to all the foreign countries, and Jerusalem will be overrun by pagans, until the period allotted to the pagans has run its course") we can see an allusion not simply to the fall of Jerusalem but the subsequent Roman actions. Jewish prisoners were enslaved and some brought in triumph to Rome. The city of Jerusalem was primarily occupied by its conquerors. It appears that the second Jewish Revolt has not come about.

5. In Luke 9:51 ("It came to pass, as the deadline for him to be taken up [*analepsis*]) was fast approaching, that he set his sights on Jerusalem.") The word "to be taken up" is also found in Pet 5:5b.

6. This echoes the final line in the earliest level of Pet 8:1b.

7. It should be pointed out that Luke slightly modifies the Markan "blood poured out for many" to "blood poured out for you" (22:20). This continues to underscore the understanding that this gospel was written for the audience to apply to their lives. Also novel is the declaration not to eat of the fruit of the vine until the establishment of God's empire (22:17).

8. This addition is most likely not part of the original text but may represent a later scribe carrying forward the logic of the narrative structure.

12 The Gospel of John

1. Brown, *The Gospel of John*, passim. Brown adeptly shows again and again this revision of earlier traditions.

2. Brown's *The Community of the Beloved Disciple* is still an excellent analysis of the Johannine community's rather tragic and meteoric development.

3. The "Advocate" is mentioned five times: 14:16–17 (general setting, colleague of Jesus); 14:26, 16:12–15 (activity of Advocate in the community); 15:26–27, 16:7–11 (activity of Advocate through disciples against world).

4. Robert Fortna has done the foundational work (*Gospel of Signs*) in establishing a Signs Gospel which the writer of John revised.

5. Another example of this re-visioning can be found in the entire farewell discourse (13:31–17:26). It can be read on two levels. There is the ongoing narrative level, where Jesus delivers an address in the style of a great man gathering his followers together on the eve of his death to impart some instruction to help them in his absence. The words of Jesus take on an added dimension when the reader sees that they are actually spoken from the perspective of the Risen One. Again the ultimate identity of the Johannine Jesus is stressed.

6. George MacRae, *Invitation to John, A Commentary on the Gospel of John*, 208. The use of chiasm indicates a conscious rhetorical choice by the writer. It facilitates memorization as well as enabling the listener's focus on the central point.

7. This dramatic construction can be seen earlier in the story of "the man born blind" (9:1–41). We see what was once a simple healing story transformed by the gospel writer into an explosive drama. The midmost section (vv. 18–23) of the seven-scene episode (vv. 1–7 [a], 8–12 [b], 13–17 [c], 18–23 [d], 24–34 [c'], 35–38 [b'], 39–41 [a']) provides the key to the passage. We can also see the law of stage duality where only two figures speak at one time. The scene then reflects a debate over the messianic identity of Jesus that probably resulted in the separation of the Johannine believers from their synagogue. In this story the Johannine community's defends their position against those in the synagogue who disagreed.

8. Crucifixion was actually a slow suffocation process. As long as the victim was able to move their chests, they could continue to exist, albeit in agony.

Crurifragium, or breaking the legs, meant that the victims could no longer push up in order to keep the diaphragm working. Once the legs were broken the victim quickly expired.

9. Brown, *The Death of the Messiah*, 1317–49.
10. Here Crossan and I are on the same page. See Crossan, *Who Killed Jesus?*, 141; Dewey, "The Passion Narrative of the Gospel of Peter," 62.
11. It is commonly held that the figure of the beloved disciple (hereafter BD) in 19:26 is the one referred to in 19:35, thereby establishing the identification of the eyewitness in v. 35. Brown dismissed other possibilities which could make clear who the one referred to as "that one" (*ekeinos*) might be. Brown has concluded that attempts at identifying "that one" as the gospel writer, or as Jesus Christ, or as God, fail to make much sense. He found that the best explanation is that *ekeinos* (that one) refers to the eyewitness who must be the Beloved Disciple, since no other disciple is mentioned at the foot of the cross (Brown, *The Community of the Beloved Disciple*, 936–37). Brown considers that any attempt to explain this as a dramatization more suited to the Fourth Gospel's theological purpose is "implausible." He adds that such interpretations are "highly speculative" and more the result of the "interpreter's ingenuity than of the evangelist's plan" (Brown, 1970, 944–45). While Brown can declare that 19:25–27 represents the symbolic relationship of men and women within the Johannine community, he nevertheless insists that the BD was a real person (since there are clues of a vague involvement of males in the Passion Narrative which may hint at Mark 14:50!) and, thus, present at the crucifixion. This is a desperate attempt by Brown to retain the historicity of the scene. For the eyewitness presumably remembers what happened. Yet, there is no confirmation from any of the other gospels. Nor can we forget that the Johannine community believes that the "advocate" activates the community's memory as they recall the words and deeds of Jesus in light of the Jewish scriptures. Because of that point many scholars find 19:25–27 to be a Johannine creation.
12. Brown, *The Death of the Messiah*, 1179.

Appendix C The Retellings of the Tale

1. The entire Gospel of Peter is found in Appendix B.
2. Crossan, *Four Other Gospels*, 180–81.
3. Crossan, *Four Other Gospels,* 134.
4. Koester, "Apocryphal and Canonical Gospels," 126–30.
5. Koester, "Apocryphal and Canonical Gospels," 128n72.
6. Koester, "Apocryphal and Canonical Gospels," 129n74.
7. Mack, *A Myth of Innocence*, 223.
8. Nickelsburg, "The Genre and Function of the Markan Passion Narrative," 160.
9. Crossan, *The Cross That Spoke*, 10.
10. Nickelsburg, "The Genre and Function of the Markan Passion Narrative," 183.
11. Crossan, *Four Other Gospels*, 157–64.
12. Fuller, *The Formation of Resurrection Narratives*, 160–61.

Bibliography

Adler, William. *The Man Who Never Died: The Life, Times and Legacy of Joe Hill, American Labor Icon.* New York: Bloomsbury, 2012.

Aitken, Ellen B. "Remembering and Remembered Women in Greco-Roman Meals." Pp. 109–22 in *Meals in the Early Christian World: Social Formation, Experimentation, and Conflict at the Table.* Eds. Dennis Smith and Tal Haussig. New York: Palgrave, 2012.

_____. *Jesus' Death in Early Christian Memory. The Poetics of the Passion.* Novum Testamentum et Orbis Antiquus Studien zur Umwelt des Neuen Testaments 53. Göttingen: Vandenhoeck & Ruprecht, 2004.

_____. "τὰ δρώμενα καὶ τὰ λεγόμενα. The Eucharistic Memory of Jesus Words in First Corinthians." *Harvard Theological Review* 90 (1997) 359–70.

Alexiou, Margaret. *The Ritual Lament in Greek Tradition.* Revised by Dimitrios Yatromanolakis and Panagiotis Roilos. Rowan & Littlefield, 2002.

Allen, James. *Without Sanctuary: Lynching Photography in America.* Santa Fe, NM: Twin Palm Publishers, 2000.

Aslan, Reza. *Zealot: The Life and Times of Jesus of Nazareth.* New York: Random House, 2013.

Becker, Ernest. *The Denial of Death.* New York: Free Press, 1973.

Brown, Raymond E. *The Death of the Messiah.* 2 vols. The Anchor Bible Reference Library. Garden City, NY: Doubleday, 1994.

_____. *The Community of the Beloved Disciple.* Mahwah, NJ: Paulist Press, 1979.

_____. *The Gospel According to John.* 2nd ed. 2 vols. Anchor Bible Commentary 29. Garden City, NY: Doubleday, 1979.

Browne, G. M. et al. *The Oxyrhynchus Papyri.* Vol. 41. London: Egypt Exploration Society, 1972.

Carroll, James. *Constantine's Sword: The Church and the Jews.* Boston: Houghton Mifflin, 2001.

Carruthers, Mary. *The Craft of Thought.* Cambridge: University Press, 1998.

_____. *The Book of Memory.* Cambridge: University Press, 1990.

Chagall, Marc. *Exodus (1952).* "Chagall and the Cross," Richard McBee, http://richardmcbee.com/writings/contemporary-jewish-art/item/chagall-and-the-cross.

Cicero. *Pro Lege Manilia. Pro Caecina. Pro Cluentio. Pro Rabirio Perduellionis Reo.* Trans. H. Grose Hodge. Loeb Classical Library 198. Cambridge, MA: Harvard University Press, 1927.

Cone, James H. *The Cross and the Lynching Tree*. Maryknoll, New York: Orbis Books, 2011.

Corley, Kathleen E. *Maranatha. Women's Funerary Rituals and Christian Origins*. Minneapolis: Fortress Press, 2010.

_____. "Women and the Crucifixion and Burial of Jesus." *Forum* 1,1 (1998) 81–225.

Crossan, John Dominic. "The Gospel of Peter and the Canonical Gospels." *Forum* New Series 1,1 (1998) 7–51.

_____. *The Birth of Christianity*. San Francisco: HarperOne, 1998.

_____. *Who Killed Jesus? Exposing the Roots of Anti-Semitism in the Gospel Story of the Death of Jesus*. San Francisco: HarperOne, 1995.

_____. *The Cross That Spoke: The Origin of the Passion and Resurrection Narratives*. San Francisco: HarperCollins, 1988.

_____. *Four Other Gospels: Shadows on the Contours of the Canon*. Minneapolis: Winston Press, 1985.

_____. "Empty Tomb and Absent Lord." Pp. 135–52 in *The Passion in Mark*. Ed. Werner H. Kelber. Philadelphia: Fortress Press 1976.

Denker, Jurgen. *Die theologiegeschichtliche Stellung des Petrusevangeliums: Ein Beitrag zur fruhgeschichte des Doketismus*. Europaische Hochschulshriften 23/36. Bern/Frankfurt: Lang, 1975.

Dewey, Arthur J. "The Memorable Invention of the Death of Jesus." *HTS Teologiese Studies/Theological Studies* 72, no. 4 (2016) 8 pp. University of Pretoria. http://dx.doi.org/10.4102/hts.v72i4.3222

_____. "The Gospel of Trajan." Pp 181–96 in *Jesus, the Voice, and the Text: Beyond the Oral and Written Gospel*. Ed. Tom Thatcher. Waco, TX: Baylor University Press, 2008.

_____. "The Locus for Death: Social Memory and the Passion Narrative." Pp. 119–28 in *Memory, Tradition and Text*. Ed. Alan Kirk and Tom Thatcher. Atlanta, GA: Society of Biblical Literature, 2005.

_____. "The Eyewitness of History: Visionary Consciousness in the Fourth Gospel." Pp. 59–70 in *Jesus in the Johannine Tradition*. Eds. Robert Fortna and Tom Thatcher. Louisville, KY: Westminster John Knox Press, 2001.

_____. "The Death of Jesus: The Fact of Fiction and the Fiction of Fact." *Forum* New Series 4,2 (2001) 229–45.

_____. "Jesus as ... What, Exactly?" *The Harvard Divinity Bulletin* 29 (2000) 1, 25–27. Review of Bart Ehrman's *Jesus, Apocalyptic Prophet of the New Millennium* and Paula Fredriksen's *Jesus of Nazareth, King of the Jews*.

_____. "Some ragged lines: From Christology to Christopoetics." *Forum* New Series 3 (2002) 307–19.

_____. "The Passion Narrative of the Gospel of Peter." *Forum* New Series 1,1 (1998) 53–69.

_____. *Proclamation 6, Series B, Advent Christmas*. Minneapolis: Fortress Press, 1996.

_____. "EIS TEN SPANIAN: The Future and Paul." Pp. 321–49 in *Religious Propaganda and Missionary Competition in the New Testament World*. Eds. Lukas Bormann, Kelly Del Tredici, and Angela Standhartinger. Leiden: Brill, 1994.

_____. "Time to Murder and Create: Visions and Revisions in the Gospel of Peter," in "The Apocryphal Jesus and Christian Origins," ed. Ron Cameron, *Semeia* 49 (1990) 101–27.

_____. "And an Answer Was Heard from the Cross." *Forum* 5,3 (1989) 103–11.

Dewey, Arthur J. and Robert J. Miller. *The Complete Gospel Parallels*. Salem, OR: Polebridge Press, 2012.

Dewey, Arthur J., Roy W. Hoover, Lane G. McGaughy, and Daryl D. Schmidt. *The Authentic Letters of Paul. A New Reading of Paul's Rhetoric and Meaning*. Salem, OR: Polebridge Press, 2010.

Dibelius, Martin. *From Tradition to Gospel*. Trans. B. L. Woolf. Cambridge: James Clarke & Co., 1971.

Dillenberger, Jane Daggett. *The Religious Art of Andy Warhol*. New York: Continuum, 1998.

Duling, Dennis. *The New Testament. History, Literature, and Social Context*. 4th ed. Belmont, CA: Thomson Wadsworth, 2003.

Easton, B. S., trans. *The Apostolic Tradition of Hippolytus*. Cambridge: University Press. Reprint. Ann Arbor, MI: Cushing-Malloy, 1962.

Eisenbaum, Pamela. *Paul Was Not a Christian: The Original Message of a Misunderstood Apostle*. San Francisco: HarperOne, 2010.

Ellacuria, Ignacio. "The Crucified People." Pp. 580–604 in *Mysterium Liberationis*. Maryknoll, NY: Orbis Books, 1993.

Epictetus. *Diatribes*. Trans. W. A. Oldfather. Loeb Classical Library. Cambridge, MA: Harvard University Press, 1925.

Fortna, Robert T. "A Pre-Johannine Passion Narrative." *Forum* New Series 1,1 (1998) 71–94.

_____. *The Gospel of Signs: A Reconstruction of the Narrative Source Underlying the Fourth Gospel*. Society for New Testament Studies Monograph Series 11. Cambridge: University Press, 1970.

Fuller, Reginald H. *The Formation of the Resurrection Narratives*. Philadelphia: Fortress Press, 1980.

Funk, Robert W., Arthur J. Dewey & the Jesus Seminar. *The Gospel of Jesus*. 2d ed. Salem, OR: Polebridge Press, 2014.

Funk, Robert W., Roy W. Hoover, and the Jesus Seminar. *The Five Gospels*. New York: MacMillan, 1993.

Funk Robert W. and the Jesus Seminar. *The Acts of Jesus: What Did Jesus Really Do?* San Francisco: HarperSanFrancisco, 1998.

Frederickson, Paula. *Jesus of Nazareth, King of the Jews: A Jewish Life and the Emergence of Christianity*. New York: Alfred I. Knopf, 1999.

Georgi, Dieter. *Theocracy in Paul's Praxis and Theology*. Minneapolis: Fortress Press, 1991.

Jewish Encyclopedia. http://www.jewishencyclopedia.com/articles/10805-midrash

Hammarskjold, Dag. *Markings.* New York: Ballantine, 1991.

Hengel, Martin. *Crucifixion.* Philadelphia: Fortress Press, 1977.

Hoover, Roy W. "The *Harpagmos* Enigma: A Philological Solution." *Harvard Theological Review* 64 (1971) 95–119.

Horsley, Richard. *Jesus and the Spiral of Violence.* Minneapolis: Augsburg Fortress Publishers, 1993.

Josephus, *Jewish Antiquities.* Trans. Louis Feldman. Loeb Classical Library. Cambridge, MA: Harvard University Press, 1965.

_____. *Jewish War.* Vol. 3. Trans. H. St. J. Thackeray. Loeb Classical Library, 1928.

Kahl, Brigitte. "Peter's Antiochene Apostasy: Re-Judaizing or Imperial Conformism?" *Forum* Third Series 3,1 (2014) 27–38.

Kahler, Martin. *The So-Called Historical Jesus and the Historic, Biblical Christ.* Trans. & ed. C. E. Braaten. Philadelphia: Fortress Press, 1964.

Kelber, Werner H. "The Works of Memory: Christian Origins as MnemoHistory." Pp. 265–96 in *Imprints, Voiceprints and Footprints of Memory.* Resources for Biblical Study 74. Atlanta: Society of Biblical Literature , 2013.

_____. "The Work of Birger Gerhardsson in Perspective." Pp. 173–206 In *Jesus in Memory.* Ed. Samuel Byrskog. Waco, TX: Baylor University Press, 2009.

_____. "The Works of Memory: Christian Origins as Mnemohistory—A Response." Pp. 221–48 in, *Memory, Tradition, and Text: Uses of the past in early Christianity.* Eds. A. Kirk and T. Thatcher. Semeia Studies vol. 52. Atlanta, GA: Society of Biblical Literature, 2005.

_____. "Apocryphal and Canonical Gospels." *Harvard Theological Review* 73 (1980) 105–30.

Kloppenborg, John. *Excavating Q: The History and Setting of the Sayings Gospel.* Edinburgh: T&T Clark, 2000.

_____. *The Formation of Q. Trajectories in Ancient Wisdom Collections.* Philadelphia: Fortress Press, 1987.

Koester, Helmut. *Ancient Christian Gospels.* Philadelphia: Trinity Press International, 1990.

_____. "Apocryphal and Canonical Gospels." *Harvard Theological Review* 73 (1980) 105–30.

Koyama, Kosoke. "The Crucified Christ Challenges Human Power." Pp. 1149–62 in *Asian Faces of Jesus.* Ed. R. S. Sugirtharajah. Maryknoll, NY: Orbis Books, 1993.

Kyung, Chung Hyun, "Who is Jesus for Asian Women?" Pp. 223–46 in *Asian Faces of Jesus.* Ed. R. S. Sugirtharajah. Maryknoll, NY: Orbis Books, 1993.

Lee, Margaret Ellen and Bernard Brandon Scott. *Sound Mapping the New Testament.* Salem, OR: Polebridge Press, 2009.

Lohmeyer, E. *Kyrios Jesus: Eine Untersuchen zu Phil. 2:5–11.* Sitzungberichte der Heidelberger Akademie der Wissensch. Phil. Kl. Jahr 1927–38, 4, Abh. (Heidelberg, 1928.)

Lührmann, Dieter. "Pox 2949: EvPt 3–5 in einer Handschrift des 2/3 Jahrhunderts." *Zeitschrift für die Neutestamentliche Wissenschaft* 72 (1981) 216–26.

Mack, Burton L. *A Myth of Innocence.* Philadelphia: Fortress Press, 1988.

MacRae, George. *Invitation to John: A Commentary on the Gospel of John.* Garden City, NY: Image Books, 1978.

Meeropol, Abel. "Bitter Fruit," Genius, https://genius.com/Abel-meeropol-bitter-fruit-annotated

Milavec, Aaron. *The Didache: Faith, Hope & Life of the Earliest Christian Communities, 50–70 C.E.* New York: The Newman Press, 2003.

Miller, Robert J., ed. *The Apocalyptic Jesus: A Debate.* Santa Rosa: Polebridge Press, 2001.

———. *The Complete Gospels.* 4th ed. Sonoma, CA: Polebridge Press, 2010.

Miller, Robert J. "Historical Method and the Deeds of Jesus: The Test Case of the Temple Demonstration." *Forum* 8,1–2 (1992) 7–30.

———. "Is the Apocalyptic Jesus History?" Pp. 101–16 in *The Once and Future Faith.* Santa Rosa: Polebridge Press, 2001.

———. *The Jesus Seminar and its Critics.* Santa Rosa, CA: Polebridge Press,1999.

Nickelsburg, George W. E. *Resurrection, Immortality, and Eternal Life in Intertestamental Judaism.* Harvard Theological Studies 56, Cambridge, MA: Harvard University Press, 1972.

———. "The Genre and Function of the Markan Passion Narrative." *Harvard Theological Review* 73 (1980) 153–84.

Patterson, Stephen J. *The God of Jesus. The Historical Jesus and the Search For Meaning.* Harrisburg, PA: Trinity Press International, 1998.

Pervo, Richard. *Dating Acts: Between the Evangelists and the Apologists.* Santa Rosa, CA: Polebridge Press, 2006.

Plutarch. *On the Fortune of Alexander in Plutarch Moralia.* Vol. IV. Loeb Classical Library. Cambridge, MA: Harvard University Press. 1936.

Reumann, John. *Philippians.* Anchor Bible Commentary. New Haven: Yale University Press, 2008.

Rasputin, Valentin. *Farewell to Matyora.* Trans. A. Bouis and K Parthe. Evanston, IL: Northwestern University Press, 1995.

Rousseau, John J. and Rami Arav. *Jesus and His World: An Archeological and Cultural Dictionary.* Minneapolis: Fortress Press, 1995.

Sanders, E. P. *Jesus and Judaism.* Philadelphia: Fortress Press, 1985.

Schmidt, Daryl D. *The Gospel of Mark.* The Scholars Bible. Sonoma, CA: Polebridge Press, 1990.

———. "Septuagintal Influence in the Passion Narratives." *Forum* New Series 1,1 (1998) 95–118.

Scott, Brandon. *The Real Paul*. Salem, OR: Polebridge Press, 2015.

_____. *The Trouble with Resurrection*. Salem, OR: Polebridge Press, 2010.

Seeley, David. "The Concept of the Noble Death in Paul." Ph.D. dissertation, Claremont Graduate School, 1987.

Seneca. *Moral Essays*. Vol 1. Trans. J. W. Basore. Cambridge, MA: Harvard University Press, 1928.

Smith, Dennis. *From Symposium to Eucharist: The Banquet in the Early Christian World*. Minneapolis: Fortress Press, 2003.

Smith, Dennis E. and Joseph B. Tyson, eds. *Acts and Christian Beginnings: The Acts Seminar Report*. Salem, OR: Polebridge Press, 2013.

Snyder, Graydon, *Ante Pacem: Archaeological Evidence of Church Life before Constantine*. Macon, GA: Mercer University Press, 1985.

Standhartinger, Angela. "Bringing Back to Life: Laments and the Origin of the So Called Words of Institution" Pp. 71–101 in *Coming Back to Life: The Permeability of Past and Present, Mortality and Immortality, Death and Life in the Ancient Mediterranean*. Eds. Frederick S. Tappenden and Carly Daniel-Hughes, with the assistance of Bradley N. Rice. Montreal, QC: McGill University Library, 2017. http://coming-backtolife.mcgill.ca

_____. "Words to Remember: Women and the Origin of the 'Words of Institution.'" *lectio difficilior, European Electronic Journal of Feminist Exegeisis*. 2015. http://www.lectio.unibe.ch/15_1/standhartinger_words_to_remember.html

_____. "Women in Early Christian Meal Gatherings: Discourse and Reality." Pp. 87–108 in *Meals in the Early Christian World. Social Formation, Experimentation, and Conflict at the Table*. Eds. Dennis E. Smith and Hal Taussig. New York: Palgrave, 2012.

_____. "'And All Ate and Were Filled' (Mark 6.42 par.): The Feeding Narratives in the Context of Hellenistic-Roman Banquet Culture." Pp 62–82 in *Decisive Meals: Table Politics in Biblical Literature*. Eds. Kathy Ehrensperger, Nathan MacDonald, and Luzia Sutter Rehmann. London: T & T Clark, 2012.

_____. "'Dies ist mein Leib.' Zu Kontext und Entstehung der Einsetzungsworte." Pp 122–57 in *Der eine Gott und das gemeinschaftliche Mahl, Inklusion und Exklusion biblischer Vorstellungen von Mahl und Gemeinschaft im Kontext antiker Festkultur*. Ed. Wolfgang Weiß. Neukirchen-Vluyn: Neukirchener Verlagshaus, 2011.

_____. "'What Women Were Accustomed to Do for the Dead Beloved by Them' (Gospel of Peter 12.50): Traces of Laments and Mourning Rituals in Early Easter, Passion, and Lord's Supper Traditions." *Journal of Biblical Literature* 129,3 (2010) 559–74.

_____. "Die Frauen von Jerusalem und die Entstehung des Abendmahls. Zum religionsgeschichtlichen Hintergrund der Einsetzungsworte im Neuen Testament." Pp. 74–104 in *"Eine gewöhnliche und harmlose*

Speise?" Von den Entwicklungen frühchristlicher Abendmahlstraditionen.
Eds. Judith Hartenstein, Silke Petersen, and Angela Standhartinger.
Gütersloh: Gütersloher Verlagshaus, 2008.

Tacitus. *Annals* 13–15. Vol. 5. Trans. J. Jackson. Loeb Classical Library.
Cambridge, MA: Harvard University Press, 1937.

Talbert, Charles H. "The Problem of Pre-Existence in Philippians 2:6–11."
Journal of Biblical Literature 86 (1967) 141–53.

Taussig, Hal. *In the Beginning Was the Meal.* Minneapolis: Fortress Press,
2009.

Veitch, James. "Patrolling the Right Path." *Forum* New Series. 1,2 (1998)
349–85.

Virgil. *Aeneid.* Trans. Robert Fitzgerald. New York: Vintage, 1990.

Waliggo, John M. "African Christology in a Situation of Suffering." Pp.
164–80 in *Faces of Jesus in Africa.* Ed. Robert Schreiter. Maryknoll, NY:
Orbis Books, 1995.

White, John. *The Apostle of God.* Peabody, MA: Hendrickson Publishers,
1999.

White, L. Michael. *From Jesus to Christianity.* New York: HarperOne, 2004.
_____. *Scripting Jesus. The Gospels in Rewrite.* New York: HarperOne, 2010.

Wiesel, Elie. *Night.* New York: Penguin, 2006.

Williams, Sam K. *Jesus' Death as Saving Event: The Background and Origin
of a Concept.* Missoula, MT: Scholars Press, 1975.

_____. "The Righteousness of God in Romans." *Journal of Biblical
Literature* 99 (1980) 241–90.

Yates, Frances. *The Art of Memory.* London: Routledge & Kegan Paul,
1966.

Joe Hill—You Tube
http://www.youtube.com/watch?v=f_yC4ffyGiw
http://www.youtube.com/watch?v=n8Kxq9uFDes&feature=related
http://www.youtube.com/watch?v=_f2J4ceCikI&feature=related

Biko by Peter Gabriel—You Tube
http://www.youtube.com/watch?v=iLg-8Jxi5aE&feature=related
https://www.youtube.com/watch?v=luVpsM3YAgw

James Allen—Without Sanctuary Website
http://withoutsanctuary.org

Scripture Index

Author Index

Subject Index

About the Author

Arthur J. Dewey (Th.D., Harvard University) is Professor of Theology at Xavier University in Cincinnati and a long-time Fellow of the Jesus Seminar. His recent works include *Wisdom Notes* (2016), *The Gospel of Jesus* (re-edited 2015), *The Complete Gospel Parallels* (with Robert J. Miller, 2011) and *The Authentic Letters of Paul* (with Roy W. Hoover, Lane C. McGaughy, and Daryl D. Schmidt, 2010). He has written numerous articles on Paul, the historical Jesus, the Gospel of Thomas and the passion narrative tradition. For over a dozen years he was a commentator for the NPR station WXVU in Cincinnati. In1987 he co-founded and continues to offer "Healing Deadly Enemies," a program dealing with the virus of anti-Semitism and the NT.

CPSIA information can be obtained
at www.ICGtesting.com
Printed in the USA
FFHW01n0645010918
48049817-51752FF